Christmas is a Season! 2009

Published in the United States of America by
Excalibur Press
3090 Dauphin Square Connector
Mobile, Alabama 36607
excaliburpress@msn.com

Cover Design by Hannah Wilson

Printed in the United States of America

ISBN 978-0-9820629-1-3

Christmas is a Season! 2009 is dedicated to all the writers who wrote these beautiful short stories and personal essays and trusted us with their work. The book is also dedicated to writers I've met as I've traveled to workshops, seminars, book festivals, and university programs. Writing is a tough job, requiring dedication to the craft and persistence in molding the vision in the writer's head into words that create the same vision in the heads of readers. From Girlfriend Weekend in Jefferson, Texas, to Books-Alive in Panama City, Florida, to high schools and middle schools in Spartanburg, South Carolina, to Page & Palette Book Store in Fairhope, Alabama, to the University of South Alabama, and on to The Writers Loft at Middle Tennessee State University—I salute you writers wherever you are!

L.B.P.

Christmas is a Season! 2009

Edited by
Linda Busby Parker

Associate Editor: Mahala Church

Excalibur Press 2009
Mobile, Alabama

Acknowledgements

This book would not have been possible without the assistance and support of four very special people—Mahala Church, Tracy Hurley, Hannah Wilson, and Donald Parker. Associate Editor, Mahala Church, did whatever was necessary to bring *Christmas is a Season! 2009* to fruition. She sorted and filed manuscripts and served as a first reader. She assisted in editing the manuscripts for clarity, and finally, she assisted in line-editing. She communicated with contributors and offered encouragement and support whenever and wherever it was needed. Mahala—many thanks!

Tracy Hurley served as a clear-sighted and pains-taking copy editor. In addition to a warm smile, she always showed up to work with her *Chicago Manual of Style* tucked under her arm. Tracy was essential to producing the final copy. Every contributor—and this editor—owes a giant thank you to both Tracy Hurley and Mahala Church.

Once again, Hannah Wilson served as cover designer. Hannah needs only the barest design ideas and she's off and running, integrating those ideas into a lovely, eye-catching cover. I can't imagine anyone easier to work with than Hannah. For all your talent and hard work—thank you!

To my husband, Donald, I owe another enormous thank you. Don formatted the book and interacted with the printer. Home life got a bit unbalanced during the couple of months I spent editing this book. When the ship listed, Don never mentioned it. Thank you for your hard work on the book, and thank you for your hard work on the home front too—you kept the ship from tipping. And to daughter Kiran who put up with it all.

I am so proud of the short stories and personal essays in *Christmas is a Season! 2009*. Last year's book was enjoyed by book clubs and individual readers. It was also used in several university writing programs. I'm certain this year's book will be greeted with similar success. In short, the writing is outstanding! For that, I say thank you to the writers who took the time to share their personal essays and short stories.

Linda Busby Parker
Editor

Table of Contents

Christmas is a Season! 2009

Theodore Pitsios was born in the village of Tsagarada, Greece. During his lifetime, he has sailed as an engineer for the Merchant Marine and lived in the Bahamas, Florida, and Alabama. Now, semi-retired, he divides his time between Mobile, Alabama and Greece. His avid interests include traveling and writing. He is the author of two novels, *The Bellmaker's House* and *In Search of Ithaka..*

Praying for Marigoula was inspired by the author's mother's visit to America, and especially by a trip to the museum of Northern Arizona in Flagstaff.

Short Story

Praying for Marigoula

Theodore Pitsios

It's probably for different reasons, but my mother and I remember the Christmas of 1997 as special in our collection of family memories—a place visited when the mind seeks a respite from the day-to-day hassle.

I am sure there have been expeditions to the far corners of the earth less prepared for than my mother's two hour trip from Prescott to Phoenix that year. But Mother wanted to spend time in a Greek Church as Christmas approached, and I couldn't take time off from work to drive her.

I provided our friend, Irene, and Mother with our home, car, and office phone numbers. I briefed everybody in my office: "If you answer the telephone, and it's a woman that speaks a strange language, come and get me right away. It's probably my mother." I wrote on a piece of paper in large letters in Greek and in English any conceivable sentence that could be of use to Mother.

"In an emergency," I explained, "show this paper to somebody and point at what you want. You can't get lost. Even Columbus didn't have that much—"

"May he burn in hell," Mother cut in before I finished. She never passed up an opportunity to throw curses at him for discovering a continent that entices young men away from their mothers. She took the note and put it in her purse.

The send-off was carried out by the whole family. Irene, being an expert at this, selected the seats on the bus—left side for the best scenery and away from the sun and close to the front for a smooth ride.

They were an odd pair, sitting side by side: Irene, tall

3

and slender with short brown hair and a white dress with red flowers, and Mother, a miniature woman, barely able to see out the window, dressed as always in a plain black dress with a black kerchief covering her long silver hair. Her shoulders bent slightly from carrying the weight of eighty hard years, but her small girlish face beamed with excitement.

Irene was the wife of George Hudson, the fellow that had the cabinet shop next to my plant. She was born in Montreal sixty years ago to Greek Cypriot parents from whom she learned to speak some Greek, which after years of disuse, was barely understandable. I introduced them to Mother when we ran into them one evening at the grocery store, and since then we'd invited them to the house a few times so Mother would have somebody to talk with in her own language.

Nobody else in my family spoke Greek, and the closest Greek Church in Phoenix was too far to drive to on a weekly basis. Mother slowly withdrew into herself, and her favorite pastime became counting the days till she returned home. It had taken a lot of coaxing to convince her to come and stay with us for a while after my father's death, and she wasn't comfortable in Arizona.

After college and a couple of years with an aerospace engineering company, I had settled in Arizona and opened up a state-of-the-art, precision-component machine shop. During Mother's visit, I hoped to impress her with what I and my new country had to show. Instead, she felt intimidated with all the new technology and fancy gadgetry.

It was Irene's suggestion that resulted in the now famous trip. One evening, while having coffee at our house, Irene said that she was going to visit her daughter for a few days in Phoenix, and she thought that Mother might enjoy coming along. Then I could drive over there and bring her home.

In her unique brand of Greek, Irene briefed Mother, "Phoenix have big, big church, have many people of old country, have big festival at Christmas time. I go every year. Marigoula, you will like."

"Maybe I should go. Might find somebody to talk to

before I end up speaking like Irene," Mother told me later. "Your family turned up its nose on your own language."

I didn't answer.

It was quite a send-off at the bus station: lots of hugging, reminding them every thirty seconds to call as soon as they got there, and waving goodbye over and over.

That evening as I was getting up from the dinner table, I commented, "Grandma must be having a ball in Phoenix. She hasn't called us."

"Oh, I forgot," said Marina, our second daughter, "there was this weird message from Irene on the answering machine."

Upset, I ran to the phone and tried to play back the message. There was nothing there.

"You erased it?" I yelled at Marina. "What did it say?"

"I don't remember. She didn't make any sense. She sounded freaked out. Something about not finding Marigoula."

"You should have told me right away! That was more than two hours ago! Can't you..."

"You don't have to yell at her." My wife, Eloise, defended her. "We can call Irene's daughter in Phoenix and find out what's going on."

"Do you have the number?" I asked.

"I thought you got it when you were talking to Irene," she said.

"Damn it! Do I have to think of everything? Now what am I supposed to do? I don't even know Irene's daughter's last name to call information."

"You get flustered so easy," said Eloise. "Just call George Hudson and get the number."

"Yeah, you drown in a spoonful of water like Grandma says," Marina chimed in.

Glaring at them, I dialed George Hudson's number. The phone just kept ringing. The damn guy was probably out partying.

"I told you we should drive them over, but you didn't want to take the time off," Eloise said. "Now you've lost your mother and at Christmas to boot! We could have done some Christmas shopping while we were there. What would have been wrong with that?"

"So now it's my fault. Right? All you think about is shopping. None of you has any sense of responsibility. I've got all of you spoiled, that's what's wrong."

"Now look here," Eloise's voice was also beginning to rise, "whose idea was it to bring your mother over here in the first place? I told you it was going to be hard. I've tried to make her comfortable, and all I get is yelled at."

The phone rang just as I was about to answer her. Marina made a move towards it. "Leave it!" I shouted, and she froze.

I picked up the receiver, and it was George Hudson. He sounded alarmed. He said he spoke to Irene, and she told him that Mother had gotten off the bus, but she had no idea where she was.

I couldn't believe what I was hearing. Irene had lost my mother! I got his daughter's phone number and called her.

"Oh, I am so sorry," started Irene when she came to the phone. "I just closed my eyes for a minute, and she was gone. I am so sorry, if I hadn't—"

I interrupted her. "How far before the last stop did you notice she was missing?"

"Just a bit before the last stop. I told the driver, and he called his supervisor, and they assured me they will find her."

"It's a good thing I gave her that piece of paper with the instructions this morning. All she has to do is show it to somebody, and they will call us," I said, feeling a surge of optimism.

"She left her purse on the bus next to me on the seat. I've got it with me."

The despair quickly chased my optimism away. My head began to pound.

"How could you—" Eloise grabbed the phone from my hand before I finished my sentence.

"Thank you, Irene, for all your help. Sorry to put you through all this trouble. Yes, we will pray too. Let us know if you hear anything." She put the receiver down.

"You don't yell at people trying to help. She's not one

of your shop workers."

"Damn it!" I cried. "This is normal anger of a normal person whose mother is lost. I am not a cold fish like you."

"Oh, so now I'm frigid. Maybe you should have…" We had both gravitated towards the living room when the telephone rang.

"The Lekas residence," Megan, our six year old, answered with the confidence and seriousness of an executive secretary. "Oh, hi, Aunt Eleni."

Of all the people to call at this hour, it had to be her. I rushed to grab the phone. Eleni is my mother's niece, her sister's daughter—short, fat, jumpy, and an old maid. She tutors English in my mother's village and has an opinion about everything. She thinks the United States is overrun by gangsters whose headquarters are in Las Vegas close to Prescott.

"I'm fine," Megan continued, "the weather is fine too, but Grandma is lost, and Mom and Dad are having a fight about it."

The pounding in my head reached a crescendo. "Give me the phone," I snapped and yanked it from her hand.

"Merry Christmas, Eleni," I said. "How is everything in the village?" I tried to get her off the scent of Mother being lost. There was an uncomfortable pause.

"What's this about Aunt Marigoula getting lost?"

"She's not lost," I said lightly. "She just got off the bus on the way to Phoenix. We'll find her soon."

"You mean she is lost, really? Oh my God! Poor Aunt Marigoula! She is probably wandering in the desert. Maybe captured by wild Indians and got her head cut off, if she wasn't kidnapped and tortured by gangsters first. How could you do this to your own mother? And at Christmas."

"Eleni," I tried to cut in but no luck.

"I am going to get the neighbors and the priest and have prayer service at the church of St. Nickolas. He looks after all the travelers you know."

"Eleni," I tried again.

"Poor Marigoula. Poor Marigoula," came the echo from

7

the other end.

"I'll call you back later," I said. I knew she wasn't listening, so I hung up. I walked slowly over to the couch, sat down, and rested my head in my hands. This seemed absurd, almost funny. I was sure that any minute now somebody would call to say they found a sweet little old lady wandering in the bus station.

My watch was showing ten o'clock. In Greece, it would be eight in the morning. I pictured Eleni, her round, plump face aglow with excitement as she rounded up the village women, all in black dresses and black kerchiefs. On the cobblestone paths, the priest walked before them on their pilgrimage to the whitewashed chapel of St. Nickolas. The old chapel stood like a beacon on top of Look-Out Hill at the outskirts of the village.

They would light the oil lamps in front of the icons in the chapel, praying for poor Marigoula, who survived the German invasion, the famine that followed, and the civil war that followed that, only to be abandoned by her uncaring son in a strange country in the middle of the desert, among the scorpions and the poisonous snakes, left to be scalped by savages and machine-gunned by gangsters.

The farmers would stop their plowing and hoeing, bow their heads, and cross themselves as the procession passed whispering, "poor Marigoula. Poor Marigoula. Lost in this holy season." The morning breeze would carry the echo of their whispers to the mountain top like the chorus in a Greek tragedy.

"Poor Marigoula. Poor Marigoula."

"Nick, will you get the phone?" Eloise's sleepy voice from the top of the stairs woke me. I looked at my watch. Five-thirty in the morning. I had fallen asleep on the couch. Nobody had dared to wake me to go to bed.

"Is this Mr. *Le-y-kis* or *La-kais?*" a woman's voice, heavy with a Southern drawl, asked.

"This is Mr. Nick Lekas," I barked.

"Oh honey, I am so glad I found you. Mr. P called and

left a message on my answering machine, but he didn't have your number, and I had a dickens of a time getting it from information. Why do Greeks have names that are so hard?"

"Who is this?" I asked.

"I'm Lea-Ann Parker. I'm the hostess at the Parthenon Restaurant here in Flagstaff. Mr. P, he's the owner. I've worked for him ever since I moved here from Alabama. His real name is Petros or Pahaka or something like that, but we just call him Mr. P. It's easier. You know what I mean?"

"Lady, what do you want?"

"Well, we were closed yesterday, and Mr. P went fishing up at the lake, and he couldn't get hold of me. That's why he left the message on my machine, but I just got home and heard it a while ago."

"What message lady?" I yelled.

"As far as I can make out, he says that Father Francisco from the Church of the Holy Mother in Leupp asked him to talk to a Greek woman that some Indian found. He was hard to understand. Mr. P always is—no offense honey—and his car phone was breaking up real bad. But I think he said she was in intensive care."

"Who was in intensive care?" I was suddenly wide awake, my heart racing.

"The woman, I guess. He told me to call her son and tell him. He didn't even spell the name for me. I hope I got the right person."

"Where is Mr. P, I mean Petros? I'd like to talk to him."

"He won't be back from the lake till Sunday night."

"How about this Father Francisco? Can I talk to him?"

"He's in Leupp. Don't think he has a phone. He's an old priest and lives next to the church. He eats here sometimes."

I cut her short. "Where is Leupp?"

"Oh, about an hour from here, off Highway 99, in the reservation."

"What reservation?"

"The Navaho Reservation, just east of here."

"Is there a hospital over there?"

"Maybe. Never been that way myself. Mr. P goes there all the time. Best thing would be to talk to the priest or wait till Mr. P gets back on Sunday night."

"Thanks," I mumbled, already halfway out the door. I sprinted to my car, grabbed my map from the glove compartment and located Leupp. I ran back inside and told Eloise about the phone call while I threw on my clothes. Back outside, I sprinted to my car, jumped in, and spun out of our driveway.

As I sped down the highway, my mind was a jumble. If that damn sales meeting hadn't been scheduled for yesterday, I would have driven her to Phoenix, and my mother wouldn't be in intensive care.

Maybe Eleni was right. Maybe I wasn't a very considerate son. I had brought Mother to a place where nothing resembled the things she was used to and expected her to jump right in. She was born and had lived all her life in a small village in Greece, and just like the generations of women before her, she was content to excel in motherhood and housekeeping and taking care of others. She was proud that in her youth she was one of the area's best yarn spinners and weavers, having learned the craft from her grandparents. She knew everybody and everybody knew her. She had grown up in a place where as far as she could see there were chestnut trees, olive groves, and apple orchards, only to end her days wandering in a hot, hostile desert not knowing anybody, not being able to ask anybody for help.

Who knows how much she had suffered before that Indian found her?

All the times she'd asked to go to the Greek church in Phoenix, I'd been too busy. *What was wrong with me? Would she be able to forgive me? What if she hit her head and didn't know who I was?*

I got to Leupp around nine o'clock. The church was on the right side of the road as I entered the town. It was not a very large church, but it was the tallest building in the area and easy to spot. It looked very much like the church of Panagia in the village square with the bell tower on the side and a large cross on top of the dome, only this one had red roof tile instead of slate. A simple sagebrush wreath adorned the old mesquite door.

There was a small courtyard in the front with a traditional nativity and real hay in the manger. On either side of the entrance door there were benches. The door was partially open, so I walked up and looked in. There were very few furnishings. I called out but there was no answer. When I stepped back outside, I saw the priest coming from the direction of a little house by the side of the church, so I introduced myself.

"We have been expecting you, my son," he said.

"How is my mother?"

"Come, my son, I will take you to her," he said and started walking in the direction of a small hill, away from the church. He was a tall man, dressed in black, priestly clothes, and I guessed his age as mid-seventies. As we walked, I began to perspire trying to keep up with his long stride.

"My car is over there," I said.

"It's only a short distance. We can walk."

I had to take two strides for every one of his to keep up with his pace. I looked around for anything that looked like a hospital. All I saw were small concrete houses with tin roofs.

"Is she going to be all right?" I asked again.

"Your mother has been through an enlightening experience, my son."

"Is she hurt badly? Did she get dehydrated?"

"God looks after those who have faith. God and the Holy Mother."

He was beginning to get on my nerves. I was about to explode when the priest pointed to a small house a few yards over the hill.

It looked like all the other houses around—white stucco with a small yard. A tiny vegetable garden in the yard was barely clinging to life. There were a few chickens wandering about, and I could see a goat tied under a tree chewing on

11

cabbage leaves. Not like any hospital I'd ever seen.

We approached the house from the back and followed a path around to the front door. In my panic, I quickened my pace, practically running to get ahead of the priest.

As I rounded the corner, I stopped dead in my tracks to take in the scene. It could have been one of those posters from the tourist bureau. Sitting on a bench by the front door under a thatched canopy were my mother and another woman about the same age, spinning yard. Coils of bright Christmas red and green yarn hung on lines strung between the canopy poles.

Both women seemed absorbed in their task and didn't hear us approach. "Mother, are you all right?" I asked as soon as I got closer.

She looked up, and her face showed some surprise. "Niko, you come," she said. "You didn't have to rush over."

Another woman, about mid-fifties, appeared at the door. She introduced herself as Maria. "I just made some fresh coffee, I'll get some cups," she said.

When she returned, she put the coffee pot and cups on a homemade wooden table under the canopy and introduced me to the woman sitting next to Mother.

"This is my mother, Helen." The older woman smiled and nodded her head. "It looks like our mothers have gotten to be pretty good friends. You have a very sweet mother," she added.

"Thank you," I said, "where did you find her?"

"I was on my way back from the store, and when I passed by the church, I saw her sitting on the bench crying. I couldn't understand what she was saying, but it sounded like the prayers that Father says sometimes, so I went and got him."

"Maria thought your mother spoke Latin," Father Francisco interjected, "but I recognized the language right away. I called my friend Peter, and when he talked to her on the telephone, she relaxed."

"Your mother has been a special Christmas blessing," Maria said. "My mother is really glad to be with somebody her own age. Your mother seems to know all about yarn and weaving and dying. Yesterday she helped us dye all that yarn hanging there."

"Her grandfather was a dyer," I said. "In her village in Greece, almost everybody used to spin their own yarn."

"It used to be like that here too," Maria said.

"Mother gave us quite a scare," I told them.

"Didn't Mr. Peter call you?" Father Francisco asked. "When he was leaving yesterday, he said he was going to call you right away to let you know your mother was safe and in tender care."

For an instant, I replayed in my mind what the priest had just said, and I burst out laughing. It was a spontaneous, uncontrollable laughter that originated deep inside and burst out without any prior warning, making me spray everyone around me with the coffee I had just sipped.

I put my coffee cup down and continued laughing while Maria and the priest and Mother and her new friend stared at me. When I finally stopped, I told them about the call I'd received and how worried I was.

All this time, Mother and the Indian woman kept on spinning. Each had a clump of wool mounted on a distaff which they held under one arm. Then delicately, they stretched the strands of wool in front of them, and with the other hand, they moved the spindle by twisting their thumbs and forefingers. The spindle spun for a few seconds, and then the process was repeated all over. Both women had radiant glows on their faces, and I could swear my mother was humming a tune.

Apparently, the weights for the spindles, the small wooden pieces attached to the bottom to give speed and balance, had been lost because both spindles had small potatoes stuck in their place. My mother being right handed, held the distaff under her left arm and spun with her right. Helen must have been left handed because she was doing it exactly the opposite, which made it easy for both women to occupy the same bench.

Maria refilled the coffee cups, then told me about her family. Her husband had died some years ago, and her only son was working construction in Vegas. They kept a few chickens and a goat and a small garden mainly because her mother wanted it. They bought the wool from somebody on the reservation and processed it into blankets which they sold in Flagstaff.

I declined an invitation to stay for lunch saying I needed to get back early, but Mother made me promise we would come back to stay a weekend after Christmas. Then the mothers said goodbye, each in her own language, and we left.

"It would be nice to get some new weights for the spindles. A good Christmas present," Mother said. "We could take them next time we visit. You think you could make them in your machine shop?"

"Mother, we make parts for NASA, don't you think we can drill a hole in a piece of wood?"

"Don't get so angry," she replied. "I didn't know you could make useful things too."

I had to pry every word out of her in order to learn how she got lost. The way Mother saw it, she hadn't been lost at all. It was God's hand that made her change seats when Irene fell asleep. At the next stop, she got off to go to the bathroom and accidentally boarded the wrong bus on her return. When the bus stopped by a church that looked just like hers in the village of Panagia, and she saw the nativity set up for Christmas, she thought she was at Irene's church, so she got off.

She let out a sigh. "It would have been nice to have a church to go to, such days as these," she murmured.

"On Christmas Eve, we'll go to the Greek church in Phoenix," I said.

"You'd drive all the way over there?"

"It only takes a little over an hour by car," I said. "We'll all go, the whole family."

"*Doxasi Kyrie,*" she whispered and crossed herself.

Mary Anne Wright lives in Cornelia, Georgia, and is a leader of the Clarkesville Writing Society. Holder of bachelor's, master's, and a doctoral degree in Aerospace Engineering from Georgia Tech, she has concentrated on creative writing for the past ten years, trying to prove that engineers *can* write. Her short story, *Personals,* won second prize in the 2002 South Florida Chapter of the National Writers Association contest and was published in *The Sea Oats Review.* She has won numerous writing contests, and two of her short stories—*War Relic* and *Coyote Moon*—were published in *Writers' Journal.* Her first novel, *No Right Way,* won second prize in the Mainstream Category (2005), Maryland Writers Association Novel Contest.

Haley's Gift is fiction inspired by personal experiences when I was in high school a long time ago. While the adolescent's vernacular changes, the quest to find one's place in the world does not. Like Amanda, many of us expend valuable energy on goals of dubious value. Sometimes the simplest event can open our eyes to the influence we have over others. It *is* better to give than to receive.

Short Story

Haley's Gift

Mary Anne Wright

The lunch bell rings, and I bolt from Trig class as fast as I can so I can get to the lunchroom in time to maybe get to sit at Stacy's table. I fish my billfold from my backpack as I hurry along, and by the time I get to the lunchroom I have three or four ones and some coins in my hand. No way I'm going to eat the mystery meat on today's menu. I head to the vending machines to buy a sandwich and a Coke.

I look around to see who's where. There's Stacy, sitting with Trent, of course, and Morgan and Ashleigh. I wave. Stacy waves back, just barely. Suddenly Jonathan is there, sliding into the seat beside Morgan, who smiles so wide I think she's going to split her face in two. I'm two tables away when Taylor cuts in front of me and plops down in the last seat, next to Ashleigh. I look at Stacy. She lifts her shoulders ever so slightly and mouths, "Sorry, Amanda." Taylor glances at me but doesn't even wave. As she turns back to the others, I watch her say something, and they all laugh.

Trying to make it look like that's where I was heading all along, I veer toward the table where Katherine and Sharon are sitting. Katherine scoots her backpack out of the way as I sit with the other nerds. She glances over at Stacy's table, then back at me, and goes, "So glad you could join *us* today—again."

Busted, I choose to ignore it. Then I see David coming this way. Ohmigosh. He's so hot. I smile, but he walks on by like he doesn't even see me.

I'm still smiling when I realize that I'm looking right at Haley, who's wandering around with a cafeteria tray. As usual,

17

her head is down and her shoulders are slumped. She glances at first one table and then another, collecting frowns and head shakes. There are empty seats at our table. She heads our way.

Sharon goes, "Oh no. Here comes half-wit Haley."

Katherine unwraps her sandwich and studies the tuna salad like it's the cure for cancer or something. Then she takes a bite.

I still wear the remains of my David smile as Haley shuffles up to our table.

"Can I sit with you?"

I shift my eyes to Sharon, who turns one corner of her mouth down and shrugs. Katherine stares at the table as she chews. I look at Haley, my smile wavering, and go, "Sure."

Haley puts her tray on the table and goes, "Thanks," as she slides into a chair.

I see that she has the mystery meat and green beans and Jell-O, and my stomach flips. She digs in like it's ambrosia or something. As I unwrap my turkey club, I'm like, "How can you eat that stuff?"

She turns red and keeps chewing. Katherine and Sharon are both looking at her now. She swallows. "It's not so bad," she goes. "Besides Mother didn't give me enough lunch money for the machines today."

I can't believe she just said that. Haley's parents are both well-dressed and drive nice cars. I know. I see them just about every week because they go to the same church as me and my family. They can afford to give her enough money for a better lunch.

Katherine tosses her head and goes, "You'd never catch me eating that garbage. Use your own money and get what you want. That's what I do. Working after school has its advantages."

"Yeah me too," Sharon chimes in.

Haley turns even redder and chews faster.

I'm thinking, *Yeah, right.* Sharon doesn't have any lunch at all today, except a Diet Pepsi. In her case I think it's by choice, though. She wears about a size zero.

I take a bite from my sandwich to avoid having to say

anything.

A bitchy little smile twitches at Sharon's lips. "How're you doing in General Math, Haley? My little brother's in your class you know."

Haley swallows and keeps her eyes on her plate. "Which one's your little brother?"

"Kyle."

Haley nods, right before she puts the last bite of lunch in her mouth. "I didn't know he's your brother."

"Sometimes I wish he wasn't, but there's nothing I can do, you know." Sharon laughs and Katherine joins in.

Haley swallows. She looks up, but not really. Kind of like she's looking at a space between Katherine and Sharon's shoulders. She grabs her tray and she goes, "Thanks for letting me sit with you."

She's gone before I can swallow my bite and go, "Sure."

Sharon stares after her as she puts her tray on the conveyer. "She got a D, you know."

Katherine's like, "So? That's passing."

"Just barely. Nobody gets a D in that course. Kyle got a B, and he never studies. He sure didn't do any of the homework. And he's no Einstein."

I go, "She's in my English class, and she's pretty good at poetry." I didn't tell them she's helped me a couple of times.

Katherine laughs. "She's got to be good at something."

Sharon wrinkles her nose as we gather our lunch trash, dump it in the can, and head for classes. She goes, "Anyway, I think Haley tries. She's just stupid. Really stupid." Sharon sounds disgusted, like she'd just put her foot in dog doo or something.

I laugh and go, "Don't worry. It's not catching."

Katherine giggles. She goes, "Oh, what if it is? Eeww. We're contaminated."

We all laugh and hurry on to our classes. I see Stacy and Trent up ahead, but I'll never be able to catch up to them before they turn into their classroom. I mean, not without being obvious.

A few days later at Sunday school David's sitting two seats in front of me. Haley's there, too. She's sitting across the room kind of by herself. There's an empty chair beside her. Nobody's sitting by me either, but I don't get up and go sit with her. I mean, that would just be the perfect beginning to another crummy week.

Every day this past week someone beat me to Stacy's table at lunch. I've smiled at David till I think my lips are going to split, and he still hasn't noticed me. Not to mention I got a B on a Trig test because I missed an A by one point. Crummy week.

But things are looking up. Christmas is coming, and Mr. and Mrs. Gordon, the Sunday school teachers, are planning a party at their house for next Saturday. It'll be pretty lame, but most of us will go anyway.

Somebody goes, "Hey, let's have a gift exchange."

Mr. Gordon's like, "Okay by me."

Haley looks worried and raises her hand, up close to her head and not very high. Mr. Gordon finally calls on her.

Haley frowns. She's like, "Uh, won't that be kind of expensive?"

Mrs. Gordon goes, "Not at all. We'll draw names, and we'll put a limit on the price of the gifts."

Haley's frown eases a little. "Okay. What's the price limit?"

Mr. Gordon goes, "How about five dollars?"

Everybody starts talking at once, and Mr. Gordon has a hard time getting them to be quiet. Some think five dollars is way too little. Others think it's all right. It's sort of a *thought that counts* thing. Anyway, after a while it gets settled at five dollars.

Mr. Gordon writes all our names on slips of paper, folds them, and drops them into a basket. He passes the basket around. Each person draws a slip and opens it right away. A couple of people have to put their slips back in and draw again because they drew their own names. The basket comes to me. I close my eyes and think *David, David, David,* as I draw a slip.

I open it. *Haley*. Wonderful.

So Monday I'm eating lunch with Sharon and Katherine again and I'm like, "What can I get for Haley?"

Sharon goes, "Take her math test for her." She sees my frown and goes, "Just a thought."

Katherine's like, "You could just give her the five dollars. Then she could get a better lunch for a day or two."

I go, "That's totally insulting."

"Whatever."

Sharon sips her Diet Pepsi, frowning slightly, as she stares across the cafeteria. I follow her gaze and see Haley sitting with two girls I don't know. I think they're new here.

Sharon goes, "You ever notice that Haley's hair is a pretty color? And it's got nice texture."

I'm like, "So?"

"So, get her some fancy hair clips."

"Hmm," I go, like I don't think her idea's so hot. Actually, it's pretty good.

Saturday night I go to the Gordon's for the Christmas party. Most of the Sunday school class is there, including David. And Haley.

I put my present for Haley under the tree and go stand with the other girls. The guys have their own clump. The Gordons organize a couple of games to get us to mix—but not *too* much, of course. The games are really dumb, but before we know it, most of us are having fun anyway. After a while we hit the refreshments table, and then it's time for the gift exchange. Mr. Gordon plays Santa, picking up gifts from under the tree, reading the tags, and handing them to us. I wonder who drew my name.

People are opening packages and saying, "Wow," and "Thanks," or they're laughing at the joke of a gift. I see Mr. Gordon pick up my gift for Haley, but somebody says something to me just when he hands it to her, so I don't see her open it.

Then Mr. Gordon's there in front of me, handing me a kind of flat package wrapped in green paper with a white bow.

I read the tag: "To Amanda, From David." I can feel my face turning red, right before I feel like I'm going to pass out.

Ohmigosh. I look across the room at him, and for the first time ever, he's looking at me. Ohmigosh! I smile. He smiles a little and ducks his head. From the corner of my eye I see Haley grin.

I look back at the package. It's hard and doesn't weigh much. I carefully open the wrapping. It's a book of poetry, kind of scuffed on the corners. I don't recognize the poet. I flip it open and read one short poem. It's very good—about the importance of friends, but not sappy. How did he know I would like this?

I see him glance at Haley.

Haley?

He walks across the room and stands in front of me. *Oh-my-gosh!* I go, "Thank you for the present. It's wonderful."

He goes, "Merry Christmas. I'm glad you like it."

And then Haley is there in front of me too, holding the hair clips I gave her. She goes, "Thank you, Amanda. They're so pretty." She blinks a time or two, and I realize that she's crying. She sniffs a little bit and goes, "No one ever gave me such a nice present before. I don't deserve such a pretty gift."

I'm thinking, like, *They're just cheap hair clips. Nobody ever gave her such a nice present? That's really sad.* I hug her and go, "I'm glad you like them."

I find I really mean it. I add, "Merry Christmas, Haley."

She hugs me back, hard. She sniffles, fishes a tissue from her pocket, and dabs her eyes and then her nose. "Merry Christmas, Amanda"

I hug her again.

I don't care what Katherine and Sharon say, Haley will be eating lunch at my table now. They can join us if they wish. I just hope Haley gives up the cafeteria mystery meat.

Terry Wright is a consulting engineer and writer living in the mountains of northeast Georgia. He earned his Ph.D. in Aerospace Engineering and has published extensively in that area. In addition to his technical and professional writing, he has turned his attention to creative writing. He has published in a variety of literary magazines and anthologies including *Seven Hills Review* and *Sea Oats Review*.

Christmas at the Burger-Box draws on my own experiences as a young enlistee in the U.S. Air Force. My boyhood memories of a warm and cozy family Christmas were rudely displaced by the realities of a holiday spent in harsher surroundings. Through this experience, I was led to a deeper understanding of the holiday spirit.

Short Story

Christmas at the Burger-Box

Terry Wright

Christmas loomed ahead, like dark clouds on the horizon, bringing a cold sense of dread instead of the joy and warmth I'd expected. What to do? Where to go? My parents had moved to Europe and my closest brother's Army unit was deployed. My sisters were immersed in the creation of a perfect holiday for their small children, and my youngest brother, Fred, had moved to Baton Rouge to live with our oldest brother, James. I faced spending Christmas in the barracks on the Air Force base.

I called James in Baton Rouge, angling for an invitation to his house for Christmas. After a short silence he finally said, "Sure. You're welcome to come here." As I breathed a silent sigh of relief, he added, "But I won't be here. We're all set to pack up the kids and drive up to Indiana to spend the holidays with Melissa's family."

I didn't hear any hint of an invitation to go with him, so I asked, "What about Fred? Is he going to Indiana with you?"

After a long pause, he said, "Why don't you ask him?" He gave me Fred's work number and then said, "Merry Christmas, man—and Happy New Year!" And he hung up.

I held the phone to my ear a long moment trying to figure out what had happened. I finally switched off my cell, walked across the squadron dayroom and flopped down on an old, worn, vinyl sofa. I sat there a while, trying to make my new set of facts fit my old expectations about a family Christmas. The facts pointed in a direction I didn't want to go. Checking the time, I figured Fred would be at work for another hour or so, and I thought about calling the work number James

25

had given me.

I debated with myself, but went ahead and punched in the call. A voice with a foreign sounding, guttural accent said, "Shoe King! May I help you?"

Great. I'd gotten the owner. I decided to go ahead with the call. "Can I speak to Fred, please?"

"Fred iss working. He hass a customer." Like that ended the conversation.

I bit my tongue. "Sir, can you ask Fred to call me back? It's important."

"You waste my time. What am I, a secretary? So, name and number?

I gave him the information. What a jerk!

I figured it might be a while till Fred called back, so I drew a mug of coffee from the urn in the dayroom and sat down to wait, looking around in vain for a reasonably up-to-date magazine. With nothing on the TV, I ended up watching a couple of the guys play ping pong.

About thirty minutes later, Fred returned my call. "Ted, listen man, try not to call me here. My boss is always looking for an excuse to bust me, and getting personal calls is a big damn red flag for him."

"Yeah, Fred, I hear you, but this is kind of important."

"Look, can it wait another hour? I'll be home at James' place by six. Call me there. I got to go."

I stared at the Verizon logo for a moment thinking this must be my day for people hanging up on me. I tried to relax. No point in overreacting. It would keep that long.

The hour finally passed. I called James' number and Fred answered. "This has got to be about Christmas, right?"

"Well yeah—"

"Listen. Things aren't working out too well. James and Melissa are hauling the kids up to Indiana for Christmas, and there's no room in the car for me, much less you. So it looks like I'll spend Christmas in Baton Rouge. What about you?"

I sighed. "I don't know. I sure dread spending Christmas in the barracks. I'll be the only one here."

After a short silence Fred said, "Well, you can come

26

here if you want to. There's plenty of room with everybody gone. Only thing is, I'll be working part of Christmas Eve and then the days after. Big sale time, you know."

I shook my head. "I don't know, man. It's a long bus ride for just one day. But I'll think about it. I really can't see spending the holiday alone."

"Yeah, I hear you. I'm trying to get a girl I know to invite me over for Christmas dinner with her family. I could bring you along, I guess. Listen, come to Baton Rouge. We'll think of something."

"Well, okay, Fred. I'll see you on Christmas Eve. I'll be at James' house around four. All right?"

"That'll work. I should be out of the old Shoe King by five at the latest. I'll leave a key under the mat. But just one thing—this year's a bummer, so try not to wish me a Merry Christmas. Okay?"

When Christmas Eve arrived, I had to hunt for a spot on the bus to Baton Rouge. Nearly everybody on the bus had big wrapped boxes full of presents, so I couldn't find a spot in the overhead rack for my AWOL bag. I held it on my lap for three hundred miles, trying not to cramp the fat lady sitting next to me, and trying to look interested in her endless tales about her grandchildren.

The ride took forever.

When I got off the bus in Baton Rouge, I started to head for the Shoe King, which was nearby, but I decided against it. I remembered Fred's boss' friendly attitude, and I knew he wouldn't want me in the store. There were the usual grubby panhandlers hanging around the bus station, and one of them stepped aggressively in front of me. The guy had a three-day beard and a couple of nasty looking cuts crusted up on his nose and forehead.

"You got some change, man?" he demanded.

I tried to sidestep him. He blocked my path again.

"I need yore change!"

I started to explain how broke I was, and then I got lucky. A police cruiser turned the corner rolling nice and slow.

It stopped alongside the curb only a few feet from me, and suddenly the panhandler discovered he had business to conduct down the street. *Damn bum! They ought to round those guys up and put them in jail.*

The policeman shook a finger at me. "You'd better move along, son. This here's a rough area, but you can catch a cab around the corner."

I walked around the corner close to a couple of hotels where I saw several cabs. I asked the first guy in line how much a ride to James' house would be.

"That's over by the city park. Let's see…" He came up with a number about equal to what I had left after the round-trip bus ticket.

"That's too much money," I said. "I don't have it."

The cabby shook his head and cursed under his breath. Then he flipped the passenger door open. "Get in, kid. It's a slow night. I'll do it for half the fare."

I threw my bag in and followed it. "Thanks, man. I appreciate it."

When we got to James' house I climbed out, handed the cabby a bill and held my hand out for the change. He floored the gas and nearly knocked me down in his rush to cheat me out of the last of my cash. What a rotten trick. Here I stood in Baton Rouge, broke—down to my pocket change. On Christmas Eve. *Ho. Ho. Ho.*

I stood there for a minute cursing him and finally ran out of steam. I looked under the door mat, found a couple of dead leaves and a roach, but no key. Somehow I wasn't surprised. I dug my windbreaker out of my bag, sat down on the rusty old porch glider, and listened to the wind. It blew hard, and the rain slapped on the porch steps and roof. I tried to stay warm.

I felt a hand shaking my shoulder and looked up to see Fred standing over me. I felt stiff from the cold, but glad to see him, looking spiffy in his blazer, white shirt, and tie. He rubbed his hand over his spiky crew-cut. "Sorry I'm late, Ted. My boss kept me past closing time. We still had a few customers trying on shoes. No sales, but he wouldn't let any of us leave."

28

I sighed and told Fred about my evening with the panhandler, the cop, and the cabbie. "It really sucked, man. The worst."

Fred shook his head. "Well anyway, here we are. Sorry about the key. Let's get inside and warm up."

I scooped up my bag and followed him inside. Fred bustled around in the kitchen. "Melissa left some stuff in the fridge. A meatloaf and a sack of salad greens, so I guess we won't starve. Let me heat up the coffee and we'll eat."

I didn't have much appetite. It had been a long, crappy day, and the prospect of cold, greasy leftovers and stale coffee made my stomach squirm. I thought about tomorrow and Christmas dinner.

"What about your girlfriend? Did you get the invitation to dinner? Am I invited, too?"

Fred set out some plates, the cold meatloaf, the ketchup, and A1 Steak Sauce. He finally quit stalling. "Uh. Well. That didn't work out. Her mother told her that Christmas is for family. And we aren't family. To hell with her and her mother. Know what I mean?"

Yeah, I knew what he meant. Like, we were on our own for Christmas dinner.

The next morning I tried to sleep late, but I struggled with it. Out of practice, I guess. Anyway, Fred had gotten up and he was banging around in the kitchen. When I smelled fresh coffee, I gave it up and stumbled out to join him. I started to say good morning, but Fred put his hand up and scowled. "Remember, no Merry Christmas crap, okay?"

I blinked. "Okay. Okay. I remember. So good morning. Anything for breakfast?"

"Yeah. Cold meatloaf. Cereal, but no milk."

"Great." I sat down and stared at the table. "Maybe I'll just have some coffee."

He poured me a cup, and it wasn't bad. "So what's the plan for today, man?" I asked. "Where can we get dinner—or at least a decent lunch?"

"Well, there's a few places open, but most of them are pretty steep—like the high class buffets and family restaurants.

You got any money, Ted? Cause I'm about broke."

"Your boss didn't pay you on Christmas Eve?" I asked.

"No, man. It's not the end of the month."

"You work for good ole Uncle Sam. He's got deep pockets," Fred said.

"He didn't dole out Christmas bonuses this year." I laughed.

We laid our money out on the table, and it looked pitiful—a few bills and some change. Fred stared at the little heap and slowly shook his head. "You know, I hate to even say this, but about all we can afford is a couple of burgers at the Burger-Box. It's a local joint. The burgers are pretty good."

I wanted to laugh, but I couldn't bring it off. I sat there staring at my coffee. "Fred, that's gotta be the saddest thing I ever heard. Christmas dinner at the Burger-Box. Damn!"

Fred stood up and clenched his fists. "Well, Ted, it sure as hell beats Melissa's cold meatloaf."

I thought about it and nodded. "Yeah, Fred. You're right. I'd feel like old Melissa won if we did that. It's what she had in mind, I guess. Burger-Box it is. Let's do it."

The Burger-Box was only a few blocks away, but it started to rain while we were walking, a cold, and miserable, steady rain. We picked up our pace and rushed through the front door. The place looked deserted until we spotted the bored looking cook leaning against his sink. He looked about as thrilled to be there as we were.

We grabbed a booth, and Fred stared at the menu for a minute. "What, Fred?" I asked. "Looking for a miracle? Order your burger and coffee and quit torturing yourself."

He looked up with a rueful grin. "Just habit, man. Just habit. Let's order."

We finally got the cook's attention. He came over with his pad. He took our orders, went back to the griddle, and started in on our food. The place seemed dead except for the hiss of the little burgers on the griddle. Fred looked up and grinned. "Isn't this great!" He burst into song—"It's the most won-der-ful time of the year!"

"Shut up, Fred. If I can't say Merry Christmas, you

can't sing Christmas carols, okay?" Just then the street door opened, and a guy came shuffling in, hunched over and shivering, dripping water.

"Fred! It's him. That's the guy who hounded me for change last night."

Fred gaped. "You're right. He is rough looking."

The cook scowled at the guy and came out from behind his counter. "All right, man. Out. No free coffee and no handouts. This ain't no charity shelter for guys like you. Out!"

The panhandler stood there shaking from the cold with a stricken, hopeless expression on his dirty face.

The cook's attitude struck me as harsh—too harsh, and my panhandler looked so miserable. I felt sorry for him. I raised my hand to the cook. "Give the man a cup of coffee, on me. And a refill if he wants it."

I hesitated. "Give him that burger I ordered too."

"What's going on, man?" Fred asked.

"It's Christmas! Right? I can force down Melissa's cold meatloaf one more time."

The cook stopped dead still and stared at me, then pulled a cup and saucer off his rack and set it on the counter. He poured the coffee and gestured to the panhandler. "Sit down, man," he muttered. "I guess you're a customer now." He wiped his spotless counter before turning toward the stove.

The panhandler sat down and turned toward me and Fred. He studied us with reddened eyes. "Thanks. And Merry Christmas." He hunched over his cup and slurped at his coffee while I tried to avoid Fred's widening smirk.

"Well damn, Ted, You're a real Father Christmas, aren't you?"

"Yeah. That's me, I guess."

"I'll get my burger to go," Fred said. "We'll split it with the meatloaf."

I sat there thinking about my family and Christmas. Things had changed since the time when we were all kids, and we got up early, giggling and opening presents. But today, my miserable panhandler had shown me things could be a lot worse than Christmas at the Burger-Box.

31

Joan Stidham Nist has lived forty-three years in Alabama and was on the faculty of Auburn University for half that time. Before finishing her doctoral degree, she raised four sons and taught briefly at Indiana University, Eastern Michigan University, and Austin College (Texas). She has lived in Sao Paulo, Rio, and Rome. Awards have enabled her to spend academic summers in Munich (International Youth Library), the USSR, China, and the University of Connecticut. She has also had an opportunity to return to her "Paradise of the Pacific."

In *A Depression Christmas In Paradise*, I wanted to show that even in the poverty of the 1930s, most people scraped along, and a few who were able, like my generous lady, embodied the spirit of Christmas giving. Also, of course, I hoped to describe the paradise which rural Hawaii became for a lonely eleven-year-old.

Personal Essay

A Depression Christmas in Paradise

Joan Stidham Nist

I grew up in paradise, which is what the Hawaii Tourist Bureau still calls the Islands: *the Paradise of the Pacific*. It wasn't touristy in the 1930s, though. There were only two hotels along Waikiki Beach, the Moana and the Royal Hawaiian. The Royal had been built in the late 1920s just before the Great Depression, but even then, hotels were for people much richer than we were.

Hawaii might have been paradise, but I was unhappy going there. My parents had divorced when I was five. Later, Mother inherited a little money when her mother, Grandma Irene, who had raised me, died. It was just enough to fulfill Mother's dream of going from Chicago, where I had been born, to the most tropical and exotic part of the United States—the Territory of Hawaii.

For me at first, it was a nightmare. I'd be four-and-a-half thousand miles away from my father and my stepmother, Mimi, whom I liked, and from my other grandparents, aunts, uncles, and cousins. This was a time just before commercial air travel and even before airmail, so letters from home would take two to three weeks by ship. Phone calls cost too much.

Mother had met a couple from Hawaii—Muriel and Johnny—who were returning home, driving across the country, and then taking one of the ocean liners which stopped at Honolulu. They were happy to have Mother share expenses of the drive during this time of national financial hardship. So, off we went despite my misgivings.

That was also before there were roadside motels. Most people couldn't afford the luxury of travel, and many didn't have a car. So on our way west, we stayed in homes, a kind of early bed and breakfast without the breakfast. People would put a sign in the yard, *Room for Rent*, and we'd stop to ask the price. Generally, a couple of dollars.

We drove to San Francisco—the major California city then—where we stayed for a while before boarding our ship. Clipper planes were soon to begin service, but they were very expensive. So was first-class on the ocean liner. But second-class was fine, just not fancy. For instance, second-class had a swimming pool too, but smaller and plainer than the first-class pool.

We sailed for four-and-a-half days before arriving in Honolulu, which was bright with sun and color, and cool from the lovely trade winds. The air was fragrant with flower scents.

Muriel and Johnny had set sail from California some days before Mother and I left, so when we arrived in Honolulu, they met us at the dock. Along with them, we stayed with Mrs. M., Muriel's generous half-Hawaiian mother in a community called Kalihi, a part of Honolulu some distance from Waikiki. The people in Kalihi were *kamaainas,* Island residents, rather than *malihinis,* newcomers or tourists. Most Hawaiian homes were small and simple. We spent most of our time in the cool open-air room of the ground floor.

Our stay with Mrs. M. eased my homesickness and, for a time, she became a substitute grandmother for me, but our stay with her soon ended when Mother received an appointment as a teacher at a school on another island. I was about to learn that rural Hawaii could indeed be paradise.

Pahala was a small sugar-mill town on Hawaii, the southern Big Island which gives its name to all the eight islands. The wooden one-story school served ten grades. Most of the students would not graduate from high school, but after tenth grade would begin work in the cane fields or the mill. Sugar was then the Island's main business.

Mother later observed that I was one of only two *haoles,* Anglos or white people, in Pahala School. As a child, this didn't bother me at all. My best friends had varied backgrounds: Betty was *hapa-haole,* Hawaiian mother, *haole* father; Margie was Portuguese, *Portagees* were separate from *haoles,* perhaps because of suspected Moorish ancestry; and Jean was Chinese American. We were all friends and none of us thought of the other's race or background.

In the classroom, we studied math, English, science, and history, but on the playground, I quickly learned an important skill—pidgin English. It was the ordinary speech of the kids and their parents. Mother never really picked it up. Those early days, when a pupil raised a hand in class, she later confessed that she said yes to whatever the student might want because she wasn't sure whether or not the student was asking for bathroom permission. She didn't want to risk a mishap.

Mother bought a small coupe with a rumble seat. Where modern autos have trunks, some cars then had a rumble seat on the outside, which was like a pull-down drawer. Of course, Mother almost never let me ride outside in the rumble seat. Too dangerous since she roared down the roads—most paved, but sometimes one-laned—at the racing speed of 35 mph.

On weekends we often drove to visit my mother's friend Mary and her family. They lived on a ranch nearby in Wood Valley. While I was beginning to actually like paradise, the Big Island's isolation must have been lonely for my pretty and still young, mid-thirties, mother.

When she wasn't looking, I'd shuck off my shoes, since many of my schoolmates attended school barefoot. A few times I snuck off with some of them to the flumes, large troughs or chutes of water which carried the sugar cane swiftly down from the upland fields to the mill. We'd swipe one or two stalks of cane, peel off the husk, and suck the sweet juice from the fibers. Of course as we balanced over the flumes, we never considered that we might fall in and end up at the mill in molasses.

Mother found a Hawaiian lady, Mrs K., who not only wove *lauhala* (leaf) mats for us, but who also taught genuine *hula,* not the wiggles used in some tourist programs, but the dance which was so important a part of the old Hawaiian religious ceremonies. She gave Jean and me, her only pupils,

35

lessons in seated *hula* too, using feathered gourds or split bamboo sticks. And the tales she told! Though most Hawaiians are Christians, they have maintained their history and myths in storytelling. We wanted to hear about Pele, the powerful and tricky goddess of volcanoes.

"Up there," Mrs. K, pointed to great Mauna Loa, stretching skyward two and a half miles. "There is a way between it and Mauna Kea, the other great mountain beyond— a Saddle Road. At dusk sometimes," she lowered her voice, "you can see a reddish glow along the roadside. A reddish glow like flowing lava."

She paused, smiled slightly at our widening eyes and whispered, "it is Pele. She wants to lure travelers into the black lava wasteland. Especially handsome young men."

Romance and danger! We giggled nervously.

Then, Mrs. K. teased us. She smiled and said, "Lesson time is over." And she left us without the story's end until our next lesson. As she told the stories of Pele, she often advised, "Don't go on the Saddle Road after sunset." Years later, Mother and I did drive across the island on that high mountain road between two 13,000 foot peaks. In daytime—of course!

Pahala, where we lived, is some miles inland. To go swimming, we drove a short distance on the round-the-island highway—still only two lanes today. We took the short turnoff southward to Punaluu. It wasn't the prettiest of the black beaches, their sparkling sand made of lava ground up by waves. The prettiest was Kalapana on the other side of the volcano. But it wasn't safe to swim at Kalapana because of rip currents. Now that beach and nearby town are gone, covered by recent lava flow.

At Punaluu, waves were strong enough to roll us over, but not sweep us out to sea. Boys especially loved to get wet and roll in the sand until they were coated with shiny black crystals up to their faces, and then they would jump in the natural pools to rinse off.

Mother and I agreed that our favorite weekend destination was the volcano Kilauea. Like Punaluu, it was a few miles drive. The Big Island had everything: tropical rain forests, the largest private ranch in the United States, black and green sand beaches, lava deserts, two 13,000 foot mountains—snow on top sometimes—and a Chain of Craters, which are still active volcanoes.

That first year we lived in Puhala, though, was quiet. The volcanoes weren't erupting, and the frequent earthquakes were too mild to be noticed except by the observatory machines and occasional crooked pictures on our walls.

Grace, a friendly fellow teacher from Mother's school, took us on our first visit to explore Kilauea and its national park. Grace drove us to the edge of a huge flat, black hole, hundreds of feet deep and miles around: Kilauea caldera. While the volcano wasn't erupting, it was steaming a bit. Here and there white mist came up from cracks in the uneven surface. We'd passed one place where the steam smelled of rotten eggs and glittered with yellowish sulfur crystals.

Then we took the road leading off the rim right down into the great caldera. We left the car in a parking area, walked to the railed edge of the crater, and looked down hundreds of feet into *Halemaumau*, the pit. Despite its name, which means House of Everlasting Fire, it was quiet—no fountains of fire or molten lava flows. Only wisps of steam rising here and there from the hard surface showed that the giant volcano was only sleeping. One day it would wake with a roar.

As we walked back to the car, Grace said, "We're following in Mark Twain's footsteps. He came here before the safe paths were marked. His friend fell into a crack."

Worried, since I felt the heat of the steam from some of the large cracks, which were fenced around for safety, I asked, "What happened?"

"Twain pulled his friend out, and they got safely back up the rim." She smiled. "Good thing, or I wouldn't be teaching *Tom Sawyer* and *Huck Finn.*"

Another place we discovered that first year was the western part of the Big Island—Kona. There, in Kailua, we walked in the garden of the King's Summer Palace. The Palace itself was disappointing—just a light, airy, two-story frame house. But next to it was the large grass house of Princess

Ruth. The Princess had ordered the native building because she refused to walk up and down the stairs of the Palace. She was over six feet tall and weighed almost three hundred pounds.

Best of all was the City of Refuge, farther down the coast. Several times my friend, Margie, came along, and the two of us pretended that we were girls of long ago. "We have to get into the City," we'd call to Mother.

"What have you done?" Mother replied in mock worry, going along with our game.

"Bumped into a *kahuna*." A *kahuna* was a priest in the old Hawaiian religion. The punishment for bumping into a priest could have been death.

"Didn't mean to," Margie explained.

"Just don't fall and skin your knees." Mother was back to giving parental advice.

So we scrambled up the tall, wide, lava-rock wall at a spot where it had crumbled somewhat. Now the City of Refuge, known by its Hawaiian name of Puuhonua o Honaunau, is a protected national park, but back then it was open to anyone and mostly deserted. All these special places were part of the wonder of Hawaii in the 1930s.

By Thanksgiving of my first year in Hawaii, my homesickness was mostly gone, though I continued to miss my family. After Thanksgiving, as the Christmas season drew near, not even the troubles of the Depression and its poverty could dim my joy.

Mother taught music as well as English and social studies, so she was asked to direct a Christmas pageant. No one could afford costumes, so she decided to have a shadow-play. Students grouped in scenes from the Bible gathered behind backlighted curtains made of sheets. Cutout cardboard was used for most of the props, but Mother had a fine idea when she decided to use leaves from the large elephant-ear plant for angels' wings.

Years later, I realized that a number of my schoolmates, like their parents, were Buddhists, but they participated fully in the Christmas pageant. They were ready to be part of a big celebration.

While Christmas vacation brought a respite from school, it also introduced some worries. Mother was to go to the hospital for needed surgery. I was to stay with kind friends. In those days before Christmas, Mother mentioned to a volunteer lady at the hospital how worried she was that she couldn't get me roller skates, which she could barely afford. My friends and I sometimes went to an outdoor roller rink, and I very much wanted my own skates. Mother especially wanted me to have a pair for Christmas.

Skates then were metal and not in-line or part of a one-piece boot. They had clamps which tightened to the soles of shoes with a metal skate key. Likely as not, too, your shoes and those of all your friends were re-soled to save the cost of a new pair during those Depression days.

That volunteer lady, who I never met, brought skates for me to our friends' home. All these years later, I'm still grateful to that generous lady. She was the spirit of Christmas for me that year. Her kindness matched everything else I discovered in Hawaii of the 1930s—a foreboding, yet gorgeous natural environment with kind and generous people. Mother and I celebrated Christmas with our new friends, and we looked forward to all the future Christmases we would celebrate in this exotic place we now called home.

Mary Popham is a freelance writer and a seventh generation Kentuckian who lives with her husband in Louisville. The oldest of seven children, she was born and reared in Nelson County. After thirty years, she retired from the corporate world and began a writing career. In 2003, she graduated with the inaugural class of Spalding University's MFA in Writing program. She currently writes book reviews for: Louisville's *Courier-Journal; ForeWord* magazine; and *New Southerner*. She has published a collection of poetry, and her fiction, nonfiction, and book reviews have appeared in: *The Louisville Review*; BookClub KET; *Arts Across Kentucky;* and *Wind,* among other publications. Last year, one of her stories appeared in *Christmas is a Season! 2008.*

Home For Christmas—Bardstown, Kentucky, 1910, is based on a final chapter in my novel-in-progress, *Landing Run.* With three sisters who live out of state, I attempt to show their feelings of loss at not being *home* at Christmas. Growing older, I have the bittersweet realization that our memories of the holidays can never be exactly recaptured. Like a child that matures, or a flower that blooms and fades, we can carry our traditions into each holiday season, but times are not meant to stay the same. Most of my fiction is set in 1910, in rural South Central Kentucky. It is a time and place that my father knew and taught me to love through his stories.

Short Story

Home for Christmas – Bardstown, Kentucky, 1910

Mary Popham

Nothing seemed like Christmas Eve to me. When I stepped off the train in Bardstown, I shook one leg then the other to unkink the cramps from sitting in the railcar all day and the night before. My throat burned from smoking so much.

I pulled my hat down over my eyebrows and stole a look at the freight handlers. They were strangers to me.

There wasn't any moon, and the falling snow dimmed the lamp beams around the station house. I watched the handlers rolling barrels and packing off cardboard boxes from the train into the stone section of the depot.

I would give a lot to already be home where I didn't have to slink around, shielding my face from the law.

I walked, trying not to hurry, into the shadows of the station. I kept my head down and slowly looked around from under the bill of my hat, feeling like a scoundrel and afraid some fat-ass deputy would spot me and yell, "Les Richman! You're under arrest!" Then I'd spend Christmas Eve in a dark, stinking jail cell. And who knows how long I'd be there after that?

All the familiar shapes of home were hidden by black night or white snow. For a minute, I wished it was daylight so I could see the rocky hillsides and feel more at home. But I quickly changed my mind, because soon I'd either get caught or have to hide out again on the farm in Illinois.

I drew a long breath and held it, taking stock of what lay around me. The reflecting snow disappeared against the rise of the dark knobs and hills I knew were in the distance.

41

I felt somebody staring at me, and I looked over at a man in a black, knee-length overcoat. I hated the cold fear racketing around my rib cage. Was it a sheriff new to Nelson County since I left? How long had I been gone? *Five months,* I recollected.

My throat tightened as I recognized the man in the dandy clothes. Judge McPherson's son! If I knew him, he'd know me, and my goose was cooked!

He looked past me and strode over to reach out his gloved hand to a woman passenger, late departing the train steps. He pulled her close, and she giggled while they hugged tight; then he led her to his shiny, black buggy.

A depot worker followed them, holding an armload of packages wrapped in silver paper and red ribbons. He put the parcels in the buggy and then tipped his hat to the judge's son.

I stood by, not yet moving, and watched the woman gather up her layers of skirts and purple coat. She pulled a fur collar up close to her throat, and the feathers on her hat waved back and forth at each turn of her head.

Why does ever woman I set eyes on have dark hair and a fine figure? I fretted as the man helped her up the step to the front seat. His horse seemed happy, also, to see the lady, for he wagged his head and snorted damp clouds and jerked at the reins that hitched him to the railing.

Hidden in the shadows, I scanned around the depot from its pitched roof with pennants flying in the cold wind to the outer edge of the rail yard as far as I could see. I focused in to make out a lettered sign on the small building's platform: FAST DAILY TRAINS.

Most of the passengers had left, their voices smothered in the snow cover. Only two figures straggled back onto the train bound for the south.

"Bo'oard!" the conductor's voice sang out. The train picked up speed and steamed away, and everything settled quiet.

I began to see Christmas candles burning in windows of the closest buildings. This Christmas Eve sure was different from any other I'd spent in all my twenty-eight years. Here I was coming home in the dark of night hoping old Santy Claus was making his rounds, keeping the likes of Judge McPherson or the local deputy off the streets. Although I knew it wasn't likely that the law would just forget what had happened and let me come home and go my way.

I pulled the collar of my sheepskin coat up to cover the earflaps of my hat and turned west. I kicked my boots through the snow as I came into the heart of downtown Bardstown. While looking up into the elms and oaks that stood heavy with snow, a sheet of white powder blew into my face. I smiled to think how much the folks at Landing Run treasured a white Christmas—a big snow didn't come but ever eight or ten years or so. I thought about the women making snow cream, about hearing bells ring on the horse and sleigh, and the kids playing outdoors, building snowmen and having snowball fights, and the little girls taking big steps in the older ones' footprints.

Emmalene. Never far from my day and night dreams. And why hadn't I been able to tell her my heart? If I could have let her know something after her husband died, she might have returned my feelings.

I got to loving her while she was still married and taking care of Dolin's burns. But I couldn't say anything about it—couldn't betray her husband, Old Man Hershall, who had kindly given me a job working his moonshine. I just sat there at her kitchen table drinking coffee while pretending I came to see Dolin.

I threw my canvas sack over my shoulder and stepped onto the concrete sidewalk on the east side of the main street. The place was empty, no one spilling out the doors of the saloons and pool hall. No music, no laughing, no cussing. Tavern-keepers have wives that make them take off work on Christmas.

A picture of what my family'd be doing at home came to me as clear as the night air, and it twisted inside me in a sweet, hurtful way.

Daddy would be scratching out *Silent Night* on his fiddle, and my half-sisters, Beulina and Nan Mary, would be stringing popcorn to trim a fine cedar tree in the corner. I could see Ma Richman, sweet as a real mother to me. She'd have tears in her eyes because she'd be so happy, and Daddy'd be a-teasing her about it. I reckoned they'd soon be getting ready for midnight Mass.

The snow-packed streets slowed me down, and I stamped my boots to kick off snow on the stone walkways at each corner. I searched the tall windows above and the awnings over the store doorways. My heart pounded when, on the roof of a low building, I saw what looked like a man holding a rifle with a bead on me.

I shook off the fear when I saw that it was a narrow chimney with a piece of metal leaning against it.

From the light of a kerosene streetlamp, I read the letters on a familiar sign: Spalding's Dry Goods Store. Cedar boughs lined the windowsills, and a great wreath with pinecones and gold paper stars hung on the door. A placard in the largest window said: *Merry Christmas to our Patrons.*

I wished the store was open so I could buy a little something to take home to Ma. Probably she'd say not to spend my money on foolishness for her, but how I'd love to see her face if I handed her a parcel of tissue paper that hid a brooch for her coat lapel or a sweet-smelling sachet for her letterbox.

Dolin's last letter popped into my mind, and I moaned out loud. It was the reason I'd risked getting locked up to come home. I can't forget the lines he scribbled in such a hurry:

I guess you know most people here are crazy over Emmalene. Especially what all she did for me when I was burned at the sawmill. It's about time for old Santy Claus and I sure wish you could come home for all the Christmas doings. I have to sign off or will miss getting this to the mailbox out to the store. I wish you could see me get married before Midnight Mass the 24th. But you and me know how things is.

Your friend, Dolin.

Well, no, I didn't know how things is, no matter how

many times I read his letter.

I turned toward the livery stable to rent a saddle horse, as I couldn't walk eight miles to Our Lady of Hope Church before midnight. And it was surely too late to catch a ride toward Landing Run this time of night—at Christmas.

You know how things is. Dolin's words tore at me. Yes, I knew Dolin was struck on Emmalene the first time he laid eyes on those black curls and white arms of hers, whether she was married or not. Dolin and I were both happy the old man slept at the moonshine still and not in her bedroom. Everbody in Landing Run knew about that.

I got mad at myself, but truth was, Dolin wasn't the only one struck on Emmalene. Her blazing blue eyes. But sometimes they weren't blue. Seems they changed color depending on the time of day. But her hair was always dark. I knew how it looked when some of the curls strayed out of her dust cap while she was running around the Hershall farmhouse, putting medicine on Dolin's burns, changing his bandages, laughing at my jokes while making us a pot of coffee.

My fancy of Emmalene gave me pause to wonder what I ever saw in Maribelle Meadors. How was I taken in with seeing her silk-stockinged ankle when she stepped into her daddy's buggy at church last spring? And after that I sat with her outside on a Sunday evening—her being just seventeen, a fraction older than Beulina. I might have been thinking more serious about her if I hadn't been around Emmalene and found out the difference in feeling for a grown woman instead of a kid.

I stomped in front of the double doors to the livery stable and yelled a little too loud for the livery keeper. The man opened the window up above, and his pipe smoke floated out from his warm rooms. Candles lit up the night. Laughter and sounds of a piano drifted down to me, and couples in bright clothes danced in front of a Christmas tree. I felt like crying seeing all the young people at ease and wearing big smiles.

"This is Christmas Eve, fella!"

"I'll pay extra," I said. "For I'm in a real hurry."

The man grumbled and seemed like he took his sweet

time searching out a blanket and a saddle.

He was still frowning when I handed him the money, but it was a good little horse he rented me, and she plopped sure-footed through the snow.

By the time I pulled the reins to go left at the curve headed south out Jackson Highway, I rested more easy about any sheriff watching me. The heavy chimes on St. Joseph's Cathedral rang ten times. If my horse kept up its good ambling gait, I would be there in time. I would see Emmalene get married, see her eyes sparkle with how happy she was. I'd see her black hair covered in lace.

I cringed as I pictured her pressing close to Dolin and old Father Donnelly saying, "I pronounce you man and wife."

But I have to do it. I have to see that she is lost to me, that all the doors are closed. I have to let it go, for Dolin loves her too, and he's a good man. And if it kills me, I'll witness it. I can't be sinking to the floor any more with my knees drawn up grieving.

My horse could see better than I could in the dark, and she followed the buggy ruts cut into the snow-packed road. Up ahead I spotted a lantern beam, and I hoped it was a friend from out Landing Run way. My mouth went dry, and my hands felt weak holding the reins. If it was a neighbor, I needn't worry. Nobody I knew felt that moonshining was anything wrong—just not legal. In fact, it was the revenuers doing harm, trying to keep poor people from making a living in one of the few ways they could. My neighbors would be happy to shield me.

I drew closer. John L. Meadors stood beside his horse and buggy.

"John L., is that you?" I shouted.

"Les? Name of God! It's good to see you! I think the axle is about to break."

Relieved as I was to find it was not the law, I thought about this trouble making me late. But there was nothing to do but help. I got off my horse, and my eye caught a flash of skirts and petticoats jumping down from the buggy steps. Maribelle. I felt blood flush my face, and I hoped she didn't see me frown.

46

"Oh, Les! You've come to save us! We might have frozen to death!" she cried.

What a child she is. Making a big to-do for show.

From the front seat, the girl's mother, Retta, climbed out. "Maribelle, don't walk in that snow! You'll get your feet wet and ruin your new shoes. I told you to wear your rubbers."

"Mama, they're so ugly!"

It surprised me how I wished they'd both shut up. I turned to John L. "Set that lantern close and let's take a look."

John L. lifted the edge of the buggy frame, and I twisted off the wheel. The axle clip had worn clean in two.

"It's a good thing you stopped before it flung the buggy ever which away," I said. "You got anything in that gear kit?"

"I can't find a regular clip, but I got a couple perch pins. You think they'll work?" I took the box and rummaged through the metal washers, lynch pins, and boxings. I found some pieces that would fix the wheel and opened the can of axle grease. I had nothing to dip it with, and my bare hands were already greasy, so I grabbed a handful of gunk and spread it over the axle.

Ain't this the way of it? I hated to go into the church smelling like oil but it didn't matter anyway. I wasn't aiming to get near Emmalene.

My hands grew numb working with the cold parts while Maribelle stood over my shoulder.

"I hope we won't be late for church," she said. "I bought a fringed shawl in Bardstown, and for a while there, I thought I wasn't going to get to show off my Christmas clothes."

I frowned and sniffed but couldn't take time to find my handkerchief.

Maribelle stooped down closer to me, her skirts dragging in the snow.

What now?

"I got something to tell you," she whispered.

I didn't pay much attention to what she was saying. I wasn't going to leave them stranded, but I kept worrying about how late it was getting—surely close to midnight.

"Lift that buggy," I said to John L., and I positioned the wheel back on the axle.

Maribelle said under her breath, "Since I'll be boarding at the college, I wouldn't get to see you anyway."

I tried to remember what she was talking about.

"I really hate to break your heart like this," she said in a little voice.

I searched my memory for how I left things with her after the moonshine raid. *Had I said anything about coming back to her? Did I ever say I cared that much about her?*

As I slid the clip in place on the wheel, I looked up at Maribelle. She shook her curls and had such a sad look, I wanted to laugh.

John L. packed up the box of tools and spare parts, throwing them in the boot of the buggy. "How'd you get the news so quick?" he asked me.

What news? I tried to figure what John L. meant. *Did it have anything to do with Maribelle's whisperings?*

I stared at him, and he clapped his gloved hand on my shoulder. "I wondered how you'd know to come home."

Come home? Did he mean it was okay to come home? My mouth opened, and I couldn't get enough air. I couldn't speak.

"It was just yesterday Judge McPherson cleared his docket for Christmas break." John L. smiled real big. "All charges against you are dismissed!"

Confusion, then relief pounded through my body. I imagined Ma hearing the news and throwing her apron over her eyes, her shoulders heaving. I could smell her baked ham and sweet potatoes and see her best glasses shining with Daddy's elderberry wine. Beulina and Nan Mary would be putting icing on a couple of big cakes, and all the little kids would be yelling and running around the kitchen table excited about the feasting and what Old Santy would bring.

I wasn't sure I could yet talk. Or walk. So I stood there for a minute, wiping my hands on an old work rag. "That's good news," I finally said. I felt a smile spread over my face. I bent down and scooped up a snowball and threw it at the trees lining the right side of the road.

The women waved from the buggy window, and Retta leaned her head out. "Les, thanks ever so much for stopping to give us a hand. I guess we'd all better hurry, now. You sure don't want to miss seeing your sister get married!"

Wait a minute! My sister? What about Emmalene? I wondered if I was still asleep on the train. I couldn't take it all in. *Was it Beulina getting married and not Emmalene?*

Maribelle leaned her head around her mother, saying something about how excited Beulina was to be marrying Dolin.

I didn't want to let on that I had thought Emmalene was the bride. I wanted to read Dolin's letter again. *Was Beulina's name mentioned?*

My horse pawed the crusted snow in the road, eager to be off. I wanted to race ahead of John L.'s buggy to get to the church, but I held myself in check. It wouldn't do to hurt my good little horse just because I was flying high.

I saw the twinkle of lanterns up ahead and heard church bells ringing across the snow. Christmas. I thought of home and all the cookies and mistletoe, and our family sitting around the fireplace singing. I wanted to take it all in, and I hoped for this same joy in Christmases to come, but I wondered if any Christmas would ever again be as sweet as this one.

Terry Rozum is a native Alabamian with a penchant for storytelling. A graduate of both Auburn University and the University of Alabama, she knows the value of a well-told tale. Her short story, *No Man Left Behind*, was published in *Christmas is a Season! 2008* and was well received by the veterans she serves. She is currently the editor for *The Power of Social Work*, the quarterly newsletter for the Social Work Department of the VA Gulf Coast. With regard to her future writing, she is working on a collection of rejection letters as she perfects her voice and point of view.

I would like to dedicate my story to Marge "Oma" Moreau who passed away earlier this year. She leaves a pleasantly dysfunctional but well fed family of which I am proud to be included. ***Christmas Dinner for One*** is ultimately a tale of when life gives you lemons, you make ceviche. It's either that or go home to have dinner with the cat who may or may not share that last can of tuna!

Personal Essay

Christmas Dinner for One

Terry Rozum

Special events are linked with special foods. Would you think of having Valentine's Day without chocolate? How about Thanksgiving without a huge, succulent, perfectly roasted turkey? Or a birthday without cake and ice cream? Special events call for feasts and the gathering of significant friends and family. Although this was never the tradition in my home.

Growing up with my grandparents had its advantages and its drawbacks. One advantage was that my grandmother, my Nona, was a good cook—not a spectacular cook or even a great cook, but a good, basic, queen-of-the-kitchen cook. She knew how to make vegetables taste better than candy, make jams and preserves melt in your mouth, and fry chicken that was so crispy it would hurt your ears when you crunched into it. She baked mouth watering pound cakes, but not everything she cooked was as good. She made the worst soup you ever tasted! She had a cookbook stuffed with family recipes, but she kept a few favorites written down that were missing a key ingredient that only she knew. This was her way to maintain the mystery and keep her recipes a family secret.

I learned to love cooking from my grandmother. I loved the idea of creating something for others, and I liked the power of being the chef. Although truth be told, Nona never taught me to cook. She let me watch. It was strictly look but don't touch in Nona's kitchen. I learned to measure and mix from watching and from being a lick-the-spoon taste tester. I learned how things were supposed to taste when you got it right. Eager for the day to come when I would be turned loose to make my

51

own culinary creations, I knew they would rival my grandmother's time-tested, proven recipes.

Of course, my road to culinary expertise was not without mishap. My first pound cake was not only riddled with eggshell, but I truly added a little of myself when I sliced open a finger on the beater. I attempted to retrieve an eggshell I had dropped in the spinning bowl before it could be incorporated throughout the batter. Not only did I wound myself, I missed the eggshell. My grandfather chuckled with each bite of that moist, dense, but crunchy cake. He even told me how delicious it was after he saw my bloody, bandaged finger.

On another cooking adventure, I found out the hard way that boiling salted water should not be left unattended. It was far too easy for another cook in the kitchen to mistake it for plain boiling water. Nona made iced tea with the salted water I'd intended for rice. That was the strangest tasting tea we ever had. Usually syrupy sweet, this pitcher had an odd, savory quality to it. It took a few sips to realize what had happened and figure out that no amount of sugar would correct it.

As much as I loved my Nona, I recognized she was not the most altruistic person when it came to sharing her talents for many things, but especially her ability to be the chief chef. She loved being the gatekeeper to secrets especially about her recipes and methods of cooking. Since observing was all she would allow in her kitchen, many of her secret dishes died with her. But the spirit of adventure I developed in the kitchen lived on and only grew with time.

In all the years I observed Nona's cooking rituals, we never had a traditional holiday meal. We never had a turkey for Thanksgiving. Nona hated turkey; she preferred ham. We never had a pumpkin pie; Nona liked sweet potato. Unlike others' traditional feasts, we might have Christmas rump roast or birthday gingerbread cake with lemon sauce.

Holidays in our house were usually a small gathering without extended family or friends since we never knew what Nona would prepare or whether she would prepare a feast at all. Some years she would announce at the last minute that the cook was on vacation, and we would be left to our own devices. I remember one Christmas with peanut butter and jelly sandwiches as the main course.

As I grew older, I longed for traditions and the bonding holiday experiences that other families spoke of so fondly. But being from the universe's most tradition-challenged family, I knew that would never happen. So I resolved to learn to cook a traditional holiday meal one day, and I waited for that special day to arrive.

After Nona died, I moved away from my family. I loved my career choice and my job in Washington, DC, but holidays were still tough. Perpetually single, I spent special days, whether birthdays or holidays, either working or in some excruciatingly uncomfortable settings with other peoples' families substituting for the one I imagined. My pastor and his family—the Worthy's—filled the Christmas void as I spent Christmas Day with them for seven years in a row. When their oven died one Christmas Eve, we used my oven and an over-sized toaster oven to cook that day's meal. The Worthy family eventually moved away, and I was on my own once again to find something to do and somewhere to be for the holidays.

Years later, the Moreau's became my second family, and I spent many birthdays and holidays with them in their glorious dysfunctional chaos. Oma, their family matriarch, made special birthday meals for each of her adult children and all the grand and great-grand kids in their expansive family. Celebrations could include a hodge-podge of age groups, belief systems, and sexual orientations. I loved the chaos as much as they loved being with each other.

When I bought my first home, a condo in suburban Maryland, I decided it was time to start my own traditions. I had just refurbished the sixties style kitchen with new appliances including a state-of-the-art double-oven that I was dying to test. I decided to do a trial-run Christmas dinner in preparation for an upcoming solo holiday dining experience. I invited a few friends and told them we would be having an early, traditional holiday meal. I headed to the grocery store and got everything I thought I would need for the run-through.

I intended to serve turkey with home-made cornbread dressing, greens, and a dessert.

The day before the gathering I made the cornbread from scratch and began to realize that watching might not be the same as doing when it came to cooking. I had gotten regular cornmeal as opposed to self-rising so my cornbread was more corn*brick*. No big deal. I decided it would just take a little more chicken stock to moisten it to the consistency of Nona's, and I cooked on.

While Nona cooked delicious, mildly meat-seasoned vegetables like collards or green beans, I decided to go a little healthier and make a softly sautéed Swiss chard. I struggled to figure out what to do with the woody rib in each leaf. Years later I would learn that you sauté them first and then add the chard so you don't wind up with a plate of mush with inedible crunchy stems strewn throughout the dish.

For dessert, I chose a frozen apple pie since I had never had pumpkin, and I wasn't too sure how to make pie crust. A frozen pie seemed easy enough to pop in the oven and cover with ice cream just before serving. Over time, I learned how to wrap the edges of the crust so they don't burn while the center of the pie stays frozen. I found it better to wait until the pie cools to add the ice cream, so I don't end up with a puddle of melted goo around a steaming hot piece of pie.

I selected a turkey breast to roast since I guessed no one liked the dark meat, and the thought of leftover white turkey meat sandwiches in my lunch for the rest of the week thrilled me. I put the frozen breast in the fridge to thaw and read the roasting instructions to make sure I knew how long to cook the main attraction for my dry run. I figured I would treat it like chicken and just add a little salt and pepper. How hard could this be?

On the day of the dinner, I prepared the turkey breast and placed it the oven to start roasting. I knew I had at least a couple of hours according to the instructions on how to cook a bird of this size. Having some last minute loose ends to tie up, I went to take a shower so I could run some errands. I figured I would run out, and then come home to the wonderful smell of

Christmas roasting in my new oven in my newly refurbished condo.

As I stepped out of the shower, I smelled the unmistakable odor of smoke. I opened the bathroom door, and as I approached the kitchen I had to fight my way through a heavy veil of thick, black smoke that permeated the top half of my condo. Smoke was billowing out of the oven and the vent. A greasy film covered the top of my new stove. I frantically turned the oven off, opened the door, and removed a charred semblance of a turkey breast that I had so lovingly placed there no more than twenty minutes earlier.

As I opened the windows and doors and turned on the fans, smoke poured out of my condo. Neighbors began to gather. Luckily none of them called the fire department, and I assured them that my attempt at Cajun blackened food was over.

Still stunned, I grabbed the oven instruction manual and found an 800 number for emergency service with the assumption that the oven had malfunctioned. I discovered I could get an emergency repairman to come out within a couple of hours. Hoping to avoid canceling my dinner party, I called my friends and told them we would be dining a little later than anticipated, and I waited for the repairman to arrive.

Within the hour, the service repairman was at my door with his box of tools and an attitude. I had aired out the condo and cleaned up some of the sooty mess but had left the charred bird out as evidence of whatever had happened. Mr. Know-It-All entered my unit saying that he had read my complaint.

"Are you sure that you removed all of the packing materials from your new stove? This happens all the time. Don't feel bad."

As he rounded the corner into my kitchen, he stared at the sight of the charcoal lump on the stove top.

"Well, maybe you turned the oven up higher to cook in a hurry, or I'll bet you set the oven on self-clean instead of bake. Happens occasionally."

He changed his verbal reassurances to that of blame. He went on to reiterate that this had to be owner error and not a manufacturing issue. After all, in his experience it was usually operator error not appliance error.

I may have been a kitchen novice, but I didn't check my brain at the cook top.

"I turned the oven on, put the turkey in, and went to take a shower. I was only out of the room for twenty or twenty-five minutes," I explained. "How could something like that," I said, pointing at the black coal-like blob, "happen so quickly?" I suggested that maybe the oven temperature was not correct somehow—a thermostat issue perhaps.

He proceeded to turn on the oven to test the temperature settings by placing a probe in the oven and a digital readout device on the counter next to the oven. In an exceedingly condescending voice, he began explaining in great detail how an oven thermostat works.

"The temperature will rise and go slightly higher than the chosen temp. It will then begin to fall, and the oven will cycle the temperature to average the cooking temp you've chosen. It's not a constant temp, you understand, but an average temp. Get it?" He smirked relating this technical information, as if he were delivering some long lost culinary secret.

He then asked me how many times I had ever cooked a turkey, so I had to admit that this was my first. He may as well have had a cartoon bubble above his head. I could clearly see the word *amateur* as it popped into his mind.

I stood in the kitchen and watched the digital readout begin to climb. Mr. Know-It-All took a knife from the drawer and cut into the breast to find it charred on the outside but cool and raw on the inside. He again reiterated that I had just set the oven at too high a temperature for the task at hand. I watched as the temperature gauge registered 350 degrees, then 360 degrees, then 375 degrees. He commented that the cycling process would now start as the chosen oven temp was to be 350 degrees.

I watched as the temperature continued to climb. The gauge read 400 degrees, 450 degrees, 500 degrees. When it reached 625 degrees, I put on my best dumb-blonde face and asked, "So, when did you say that cycling thing is going to start?"

As the oven expert finished installing the new thermostat, he had to admit that given the time I had left it unattended and the fact that the thermostat was never sending the message to the oven to stop heating, my oven most likely heated to over 850 degrees. Maybe the temperature even reached a thousand degrees before I turned it off. A self-cleaning oven with a working thermostat can reach temps close to twelve hundred degrees. That would be great for firing pottery but not for cooking a turkey. Thank God I had not left to run errands without taking a shower as I might have returned to a charred condo.

It was too late now to cook dinner for my friends, and I wasn't all that sure that I trusted the oven even with a new thermostat. So I did what I do best, I called for Chinese take-out. So much for my early, traditional Christmas feast. Who knows, maybe Moo Shoo Pork started out as a roasted suckling pig gone wrong.

Since my early cooking catastrophe, I've had many Christmas dinners alone. I've learned that even if I dine alone on Christmas, a specially prepared feast brightens the day. Remembering that first attempt makes me smile as I now expertly roast my citrus and herb rubbed, sugar brined turkey breast, whip up my special herb and pecan laced cornbread dressing, prepare garlic and parmesan-creamed roasted potatoes, and make garlic, red-pepper-flake sautéed collards. For dessert, I enjoy a little candied-citrus sabayon. I'm still working on making that perfect pitcher of sweet tea though.

Bon appétit!

Tracy Hurley writes between taxiing her son to and from school and an abundance of after-school activities. She's also housetraining a new boxer puppy. She is the Mobile, Alabama contact person for the Society of Children's Book Writers and Illustrators and has a short story published in *Christmas is a Season! 2008*. She is currently working on a mystery novel and a young adult novel. With degrees in Computer Information Studies, English, and Education, as well as countless credits in assorted other areas, she would love to add a certificate from Santa School to her vitae.

Every day for two weeks this past April, I sat in a lawn chair in the backyard with our dog, Riley. He'd been diagnosed with inoperable cancer and wanted to spend his last good days lying under his favorite tree. I spent many bittersweet hours enjoying his company and journaling while he watched the squirrels, listened to the mocking birds, and snuffled the various scents wafting on the spring breezes. The seed of *What You Need Most* was planted then as I contemplated facing the coming seasons and holidays without him.

Short Story

What You Need Most

Tracy Hurley

For Riley

Marshall lowered himself onto the lawn chair, gripping the aluminum arms until he was sure the frayed seat would hold. Replacing the worn webbing had been on his Honey-Do list for months. He'd intended to get it done over the winter, but, as with everything else, he thought he'd have more time.

The chair settled into place, stable for now. Buster, who'd been fervently sniffing underneath the barbeque grill, limped over to Marshall and lay down across his feet. He dropped his red rubber ball between his front paws and panted contentedly.

When Buster looked up at him, his caramel-colored eyes dulled by a milky sheen, Marshall rubbed his head. "When did we get so old, eh, buddy?"

A squirrel dashed past them and skittered up the trunk of the old sugar maple by the tool shed. Buster woofed once, but didn't stir. Last year he would have scampered gleefully after the trespasser, who now teetered on a low branch, chattering at them.

While Marshall wasn't paying attention, the buds on the maple tree had burst into leaf clusters. He remembered he'd had to wipe off a thick, yellow coat of pollen from the small cedar patio table before setting down his glass of Sprite. Spring had snuck up on him. The paper white crocuses in Elaine's flowerbed had come and gone, the bright yellow daffodils too. Already the heads of the late-blooming tulips drooped, red petals littering the flower bed. He'd planted the bulbs last fall while Elaine was getting treatments, savoring the look of surprise that would cross her face when her favorite flowers

59

emerged. He sighed. He was old enough to know that things rarely turned out the way you expected them to.

The old chair lurched sideways. Marshall grabbed the arms and planted his feet, ready to abandon ship if the last of the webbing gave way. But the chair only listed to the left, sinking into the rain-softened sod he'd laid when he wasn't at the hospital. Buster picked up his ball and cocked his head at Marshall, now with a little surge of energy, ready to play.

"Sorry, buddy. False alarm." Marshall bent and scratched Buster's back, and his stubbed tail wagged furiously.

Buster's tail would have been a menace had the breeder not docked it before Elaine picked him from a litter of seven puppies. Elaine had refused to clip his ears, though, saying it was cruel. Besides, she'd told him the long floppy lobes were more expressive. Marshall hadn't cared either way. Twelve years later, he couldn't imagine Buster any other way. Elaine had dubbed him Otto's Maximilian of Ulrich on the AKC forms, but after Marshall kept referring to him as Buster, as in "stop chewing my shoes, buster," or "listen, buster, if you pee on my pant leg one more time…" the name stuck.

A soft breeze scented by cut grass, loamy earth, and sweet lilacs ruffled Marshall's thinning hair. A leaf blower droned in the distance. He should lime the grass, clean the rain gutters, sharpen the lawnmower blades. Instead, he pulled a crumpled piece of paper from the pocket of his flannel shirt and unfolded it. As long as items remained unchecked on Elaine's last Honey-Do list, Marshall could pretend he still had time to take her on a cruise to Alaska, remodel the attic bedroom into a craft room, or go dancing at that fancy hotel at the beach. The should-dos were easy to ignore; it was the should-have-dones that kept him awake at night.

"Come on, Buster." He pushed himself out of the chair. "We shouldn't keep Shannon waiting."

"Dad, I understand you want to hang onto Mom's jewelry," Shannon said. "Maybe even some of her personal things like her apron. But this is, well, just silly." His eldest daughter stood in the bathroom doorway and held up her mother's toothbrush.

"You're right, dear," he said, lifting Elaine's old gardening Crocs out of the waste can and placing them inside his closet.

Shannon dropped the toothbrush into the kitchen trash bag looped over her wrist. The toothbrush fell to the bottom, barely causing a ripple.

"Well, there. We've finally made some progress." Shannon peered into the nearly empty bag, but when she looked up into his face, she dropped the bag and wrapped her arms around him. "I know this is hard, Dad. It's hard for me, too. But it's been five months."

"Five months, one week, and three days." He backed out of Shannon's hug and forced a smile.

Marshall wondered if she had been designated by her two sisters for this duty because she lived the closest or because she was the least sentimental.

Downstairs, a high-pitched whine grew louder and more insistent.

"What's wrong with Buster?" Shannon asked.

"Arthritis. He can't manage the stairs anymore. I got him that orthopedic bed in the living room, but he doesn't like being left alone." Marshall shrugged.

Neither did he.

Shannon nodded. "How about we start small and just tackle Mom's dresser for now?" she said a little too brightly. "We can make two piles. You choose what to keep and what goes to Goodwill. Okay?"

"Okay," Marshall said, though it didn't feel okay at all.

A half hour later, they'd sorted through three drawers in the highboy. Marshall was surprised to see that the Goodwill pile towered over the to-keep pile. Maybe he was beginning to heal.

"Two more to go." Shannon pulled open the next-to-the-bottom drawer. It was crammed full of Christmas presents decorated in brightly colored papers and ribbons, each with an envelope taped beneath the bow. She slammed the drawer shut and glanced at her father. "Sorry, Dad." When she eased the drawer open again, they both peered inside.

Marshall's mouth went dry. "Your mom always bought extra Christmas presents."

"I don't think these are extras. They've got cards on them with names on the cards. She must have sat wrapping these all the while knowing..." Shannon's voice squeaked. Marshall hugged her, and she buried her face against his chest. He rubbed her back until the hiccupping sobs stopped.

Shannon disengaged herself. She swiped her cheeks, then handed him the large package on top.

All day Marshall had mustered a tight command on his emotions, tamping them down whenever they bubbled up too close to the surface. But, one glimpse at his name written in Elaine's familiar loopy handwriting, and a raw ache flooded through him.

"I have to go check on Buster," he croaked and stumbled down to the garage. As he squeezed the large box under his arm, the silver wrapping paper blurred until it looked like he was carrying a ball of light.

Marshall set the package down on his workbench and blinked hard until his vision cleared. Behind him, Buster's toenails clicked across the kitchen tile and through the open door into the garage.

"It'll be okay, buddy." Marshall slid a thick finger under the cellophane tap, and the envelope slid loose. On the cover of the card stood a snowman and snowwoman in matching scarves sharing a milkshake under a starry sky. His hands shook as he took out a folded sheet of paper. He unfolded it, struck again by the familiar handwriting.

My Darling Marshall,

The next time I go to the hospital, I know I will be leaving for the last time. Please don't grieve too hard. I've had a wonderful life with you and the girls. While it saddens me to think I won't see our grandchildren grow up, I know you will tell them how much I loved them.

If I'm not home for Christmas, I suspect it will have long passed before you—or more likely

Shannon—find these gifts.

Once I'm gone, I worry that you will cocoon yourself in this house with no one for company except Buster.

The words blurred, so he set the letter down and ripped the silver paper off the box. He removed the top of the box and pushed aside a layer of green tissue paper revealing a manila file folder on top of something bulky, woolen, and bright red. Elaine knew he never wore red—with his round beer gut he'd feel like an over-ripe tomato. He exhaled, an uneasy disappointment settling over him. He realized he'd been hoping Elaine had left him some magical gift that would ease the pain and loneliness. Instead, she'd given him red pajamas.

He pulled a glossy brochure from the folder. On the front, a man dressed as Santa Claus smiled. He sat on a gold throne and a little girl, her head haloed with ringlets, perched on his lap. SANTA SCHOOL was written in bold letters across the top, followed by: "Santa Claus is coming to town, and that Jolly Old Elf could be you!"

What in the world? Marshall shook out the wooly bundle, and it unfolded into a big red coat cuffed with white fur and matching pants. A stocking cap fell to the floor. Buster sniffed the holly sprig on the fuzzy brim. Marshall picked it up by the pom-pom and tossed it back in the box before pulling out another paper from the folder. He squinted at the small type, a prepaid registration receipt and course syllabus.

"Putting the Ho! into Ho! Ho! Ho!" he read aloud. Then he turned to Buster, "Why would she think I'd want this?"

Buster nuzzled his hand in reply, and Marshall scanned further down the page. The course started in November, ending with a practical final exam during Thanksgiving weekend at the Remington Plaza Mall. Two weeks before the anniversary of Elaine's...

He slammed everything back into the box and mentally noted the deadline for a full refund. October first.

When Sophie found them, Marshall was raking leaves in the backyard while Buster lay on the grass bathing in the late morning sun. She carried two mugs, steam swirling around her gloved hands.

"Coffee, black," she said and handed one of the mugs to her father.

Marshall leaned the rake against the trunk of a maple tree. "There's a nip in the air."

Sophie sipped from her mug. "Dad, can I help you sort Mom's stuff while I'm here?"

"Naw. I'm getting to it. Besides, you're a worse packrat than I am."

Sophie laughed. "Come on, birthday boy. I've got a surprise for you." She took his hand and led him to the driveway. Buster padded behind. With a push of a button and a squeal of metal, the garage door rose revealing two patio chairs in the empty car bay next to his Ford Explorer. Buster trotted over and sniffed them.

"So what are these?" Marshall asked.

Sophie beamed. "Shannon, Sarah, and I chipped in together."

"Thanks," Marshall said, putting his arm around Sophie.

No webbing, he noticed. A single sheet of canvas-like material was tied to an aluminum frame that was bent into a sitting position. "Are they rockers?"

"They're zero-gravity chairs." Sophie nudged him. "Try one."

"I don't have anything against a little gravity. Keeps you grounded," Marshall said. "Does it recline?" He plopped down in the seat, then gasped as his feet swung out from under him, and he fell backwards. Buster started barking frantically as the chair swung to and fro.

"Sorry, Daddy!" Sophie grabbed his arms, slowing the swaying chair until it came to a stop. "I forgot to set the lock."

Marshall lay panting, still reclined with his feet higher than his head, the chair rocking slightly. He startled when something warm and wet squished in his ear. "I'm okay,

Buster." The dog lay down next to him but continued a low growl at the chair.

Sophie dropped into the other chair, and it oscillated gently until she too rested in a semi-reclined position. "See, it automatically finds the perfect position based on your body frame. Good for your back and your heart. It helps relieve tension."

Marshall laughed and patted his chest. "I'm going to need it." He couldn't shake the feeling that the chair was about to pitch him on his head.

Sophie smiled at him. "You'll get used to it. Now you can get rid of that ratty old one."

"But I just put new webbing on it. It's like new."

"I can take the chairs back—"

"No. Like you said. It'll just take a little getting used to." He couldn't tell her that sitting in the zero-gravity chair gave him the same sense of imbalance that he'd felt after Elaine died.

After serving his favorite dinner—lasagna and garlic bread—Sophie brought out a cake aglow with dozens of candles.

"Careful. You'll set the house on fire," he warned. He'd told her not to make a fuss—he was too old for such nonsense—but he had to laugh when she serenaded him with *Happy Birthday*. What she lacked in pitch, she made up for in sheer volume. Buster huddled under the table between Marshall's legs until she was done.

They carried their cake into the living room. Sophie sipped wine while her father nursed a bourbon and water. Buster sprawled so close to the fire that Marshall worried his fur might get singed, but he figured the heat must feel good to the dog's aching joints.

"So are you really going to Santa School?"

Marshall polished off his drink. "I'm considering it." The cancellation deadline had slipped by a week earlier.

"So, do I get to see you in that outfit?"

"In what?"

"The Santa suit. Come on, model it for me." The reflection of the fire danced in her hazel eyes that looked so much like Elaine's.

"Sure," he said, "but promise you won't laugh."

He climbed the stairs slowly. He didn't know when he'd decided to go through with this Santa School thing. But Elaine was right. He was becoming a hermit. He rarely left the house except to go to the store or to take Buster to the vet. He missed being around people. Throughout their marriage, Elaine was the one who'd nurtured friendships and networked, as they called it these days. He'd simply been happy to tag along with her. Once she was gone, some of their friends called with invitations, but Marshall wasn't ready then. After he'd said "no" enough times, the invites dried up.

He sat on the bed and pulled out the worn Honey-Do list and a pencil stub from the pocket of his flannel shirt. He added "Santa School" in his own cramped writing to the bottom.

After he donned the red pants, white ruffled shirt, red and white striped vest, and red coat, he checked himself in the mirror. Not too bad, he thought, twisting right and left like Elaine used to do. He'd better watch the French fries and ice cream, though, or he wouldn't need any stuffing. He tried out a quiet, "Ho! Ho! Ho!" and patted the sides of his belly. Something bulged in the coat pocket. He pulled out wire spectacles, a set of red suspenders, and a pair of white gloves—all the extras he needed to complete the outfit.

"Are you okay, Daddy?"

"Yes, honey." He slipped on the spectacles and said, "I'm coming."

When Marshall entered the living room still struggling with the tight gloves, Sophie leapt off the couch. "Daddy, you look great!"

Buster barked and tried to push himself up. After a few false starts, he got to his feet and staggered over to sniff Marshall.

"It's only me. Guess the old eyes are going, eh, Buster?"

"And his legs, too. Poor baby." Sophie scratched his ears, and he licked her hand.

"He still thinks he's a puppy. We both do." Marshall helped the dog back onto his bed. When he straightened, Sophie was studying him. "You've got a good head start on the beard too," she said.

"I keep forgetting to buy shaving cream."

Elaine had always taken care of those things. Truth was, shaving seemed unnecessary now.

Sophie caressed the white scruff on her father's face. "All you need now is a sleigh and eight tiny reindeer."

"And a pair of boots." Marshall pulled up his pant legs and displayed a pair of hole-riddled socks.

"And new socks," Sophie added. "I should have gotten you some for your birthday."

He hadn't bought socks for himself since he got married. "Yup, there's nothing a man looks forward to more on his birthday than new socks."

The morning after Sophie left, Marshall discovered his top dresser drawer crammed full of new t-shirts, socks, and briefs. While he was deciding which color Fruit of the Loom he wanted to wear, he heard a low moan from the living room. Marshall raced down the stairs to find Buster laying half in and half out of his bed. He lifted his grizzled muzzle off the carpet and moved one paw as if trying to get up, then slumped back down.

Oh, no. No. Marshall lifted Buster to his feet, but the dog crumpled as soon as Marshall tried to let go. Marshall gently laid him back on the bed. He bundled Buster in an afghan he'd pulled from the couch and carried him to the car, all the while cooing into his floppy ear, "It's going to be all right." *It had to be all right.* Buster lay across the back seat, panting shallowly, as Marshall raced to the vet's office.

An hour later Marshall walked out, carrying only a leash and dog collar. He sat in his car for a long time, unable to drive.

Santa School was out of the question now. He had no

interest in going there—or anywhere else for that matter. *What was the point?*

Marshall stared at his reflection in the bathroom mirror. *So what was he doing here at the Econo Lodge?* He scratched his chin. The last time he'd grown a beard, it was as black as his boots. Now his whiskers were almost completely white, with only a few streaks of gray matching what was left of his hair. The beard looked Santa-like, but the dark circles under his eyes gave him away. He turned on the tap and splashed cold water on his face, dried it with a thin paper towel, and headed for Conference Room B.

Marshall expected the class to be made up of old fogies like him, and there were a few including a couple of older women. He was surprised, however, that most of the people sitting in folding chairs around the stuffy room were young or middle-aged.

He was more surprised when one of the old fogies stood up and introduced himself as their instructor, Ralph Salisbury. "Tonight's meeting is an opportunity for us to get to know each other. I spend most of the year in Reno performing in a ventriloquism act, but starting tomorrow, I will be Santa Ralph. My number one rule is that once you put on The Suit, you never break character. *Ever.* Kids can sniff out a fake a mile away, and once that magical illusion is broken, there's no fixing it."

He paused to scan the room. "How many of you remember the moment you realized that Santa isn't real?"

Marshall raised his hand. So did most of the others.

"And how many of you wished almost immediately that you could go back to believing?"

Everybody's hands shot into the air.

Ralph Salisbury nodded his head. "What's done can't be undone. It's up to you to keep the magic alive."

The next morning they arrived at the Econo Lodge to find Santa Ralph in full costume standing at the front of the room. For the entire day and the next two weekends he showed them how to become the world's most beloved character. Santa

Ralph taught them everything from using their diaphragms to produce the deepest "Ho! Ho! Ho's," to obtaining liability insurance. They learned all the reindeer names (it's Donder not Donner), Santa's favorite cookies (whatever the child likes), balancing a child on your lap (use your whole arm to cradle them), and how the magical sleigh works (they were sworn to secrecy).

Before Marshall knew it, it was the last day of class before the practicum, and Santa Ralph sat on the edge of a table and reviewed the guidelines for Mall Santa behavior.

"No drinking or drugs before shifts. Come clean and tidy—trim those nose hairs and buff those boots. And for Santa's sake, brush your teeth and stay away from the garlic. Accepting gratuities is not allowed. Show up on time. Stay in character. No grousing to the Santa's helpers or mall staff. Oh, and I gotta say this one nowadays. For your own protection, keep your hands visible at all times. Most important of all, never promise the kids that they will get what they ask for. Now repeat the Santa Pledge with me."

They all said in unison, "I will keep the magic alive!"

"You have your schedules," said Santa Ralph. "See you this weekend."

For his first official Santa shift, Marshall pulled Sunday at eleven o'clock.

When Marshall got home from class that afternoon, he was met by the delicious and unaccustomed aroma of dinner cooking. Sarah, his youngest, had drawn the "Thanksgiving with Dad" straw.

"You didn't have to cook," he said, tousling his grandsons' white-blond hair. "I was going to take you out."

Both boys chimed, "McDonalds! McDonalds!"

Sarah rolled her eyes. "Clearly, it's been a while since you've dined out with four- and six-year-old wigglybutts."

"Wigglybutts?" Preston asked, wiggling in his chair.

Jayden, thumb stuck firmly in his mouth, wiggled his bottom too.

"You're all wigglybutts," Marshall said, winking at the boys. "And when is Daddy Wigglybutts going to arrive?"

The boys giggled, but Sarah frowned. "He called. He can't get away. Something about a difficult client. He's going to the office on Friday."

"Then don't bother cooking Thanksgiving dinner," Marshall said, taking a slice of meatloaf. "While everyone else is dining at home, the Wigglybutt family will have the whole restaurant to ourselves."

"Da-ad," Sarah moaned. "The turkey's already defrosting, and I have pies in the oven. Besides I like to cook, and you'll have lots of leftovers after we're gone."

Marshall had taken a bite of mashed potatoes when Preston said, "Where's Buster, Grampa? I wanna play with him."

Marshall choked, but managed to sputter, "Sorry," through a coughing spasm. He pushed away from the table and headed for the kitchen, his eyes tearing up and still hacking into his napkin. He stood at the sink and sipped water while he caught his breath.

Although she spoke softly, he heard Sarah say, "Remember, I told you that Buster is up in heaven playing ball with Gramma. Talking about both of them makes Grampa sad, so let's not say anything else."

"Why does it make him sad?" Preston asked.

"Because Grampa misses them."

"Can we come to live with Grampa? He wouldn't be sad then."

"No, but Daddy would be sad if we left him alone."

"Maybe Grampa can come live with us."

"Preston," Sarah said, "that's not a bad idea."

Marshall set his glass in the sink. He could sell the house and move closer to Sarah and the kids. He tapped the dog tags he'd hung from the hook that used to hold Elaine's spider plant. They spun, glistening in the fading November twilight. He'd spread Buster's ashes in Elaine's flowerbed just beyond the window. How could he leave Buster? How could he leave Elaine?

Fortunately, no one mentioned him moving again. Sarah cooked up a Thanksgiving dinner that would have made Elaine proud. While the kids were napping, Marshall took a cup of coffee and a slice of pecan pie out back. The barely-used zero gravity chairs were put up for the winter. He sank into his old aluminum chair.

When he'd finished the pie, he pulled the Honey-Do list from his pocket and penciled out the next-to-last item, re-web chair. After his shift at the mall, he could cross out the last item on the list—Santa School.

On Sunday morning Marshall took Sarah and the kids to the airport before heading to the Remington Plaza Mall. He changed in the employee lounge and waited until Santa Carlos finished his shift. Marshall's stomach fluttered as he walked through Santa Land, a large expanse of fake snow with robotic, toy-making elves and animated snowmen singing Christmas songs. He sat in the large gold throne and pasted a smile on his face.

By the time the giant Santa Land clock struck his shift's end at 12:55, Santa Marshall had been smacked, pinched, puked on, sneezed at, peed on, and told he was "a big old doo-doo head." His head pounded and his cheeks hurt from forced smiling. Santa Ralph had told them seventy-five percent of children under the age of ten were terrified of Santa. By Marshall's reckoning it was closer to ninety-eight. And those over ten didn't believe in Santa anymore, so they came for the fun of trying to make him break character. A couple almost succeeded.

When Santa Marshall finally trudged back to the employee lounge, he found Santa Ralph by the employee refrigerator eating from a Tupperware container. He took a big forkful and asked, "How did it go?"

Marshall sighed. "It wasn't what I expected." He pulled off the heavy black boots.

"It never is."

"Christmas isn't what it used to be. If the kids weren't asking for Xboxes or iPhones, they wanted hang gliders and

ATVs and Jet Skis. What happened to baseball gloves and bicycles and pogo sticks?" Marshall slipped on his boat shoes.

"Mall duty is the toughest. In this economy you're lucky the kids weren't asking for jobs for their daddies, winter boots for their sister or brother, or a sack of groceries. Playing a mall Santa isn't for everyone. My advice: find yourself a nice department store gig. Maybe a holiday parade. Office parties— now those are fun!"

"Thanks for the tip." Marshall was too tired to change into his street clothes, so he gathered up his coat and hat and headed for the door.

"Don't forget your diploma." Santa Ralph handed him a red and green certificate. "I have to go cover Santa Brad's shift."

On the way home, Marshall pulled into the strip mall near his house to exchange the black boots for more practical Timberlands. He had a lot of yard work to do if he was going to sell the house. The mall was busy, so he had to park several stores down from the shoe store. Before he got out of the car, he pulled out the Honey-Do list again and scratched off the last item. He crumpled it up and tossed it in the console, then grabbed the boots.

When he stepped onto the sidewalk, he activated a set of automatic doors. When they slid open, his heart clenched. He'd parked right in front of Pet Station. The last time he'd shopped there, he'd bought Buster's red rubber ball. He tucked his head and hurried up the sidewalk.

Behind him, he heard, "Santa! Santa, wait!"

Marshall remembered he was still dressed in the baggy red pants, holly covered suspenders, white shirt, and candy cane striped vest. He should have changed. He picked up his pace, sure he'd lose control if some nutcase asked to sit on his lap.

Too late. The nutcase tugged on his shirt sleeve. Marshall whirled, his fist clenched, ready to pummel the guy.

"Santa?" The young man wore a green Pet Station polo

shirt. "I'm sorry, but when I saw you walk by, I had to ask you."

"Listen, buddy. I can't promise you'll get that tricycle you want. Or anything else."

The man laughed. "No, nothing like that. I'm Jason, the pet store manager. We're in a pickle, and you could really help us out." He steered Marshall back toward the pet store entrance. The door slid open again revealing the worst looking Santa that Marshall had ever seen. Painfully thin and no older than twenty, his cheap Santa costume hung lifelessly from bony shoulders. His cotton-ball beard drooped below his own dark stubble.

"Darryl stepped in when the real Santa cancelled," Jason said. "He's a great kid, but we're doing our Pet Pictures with Santa. It starts in twenty minutes, and the animal shelter people are already here for their annual adoption drive."

He glanced around, and his voice became a pleading whisper. "Kids come to this."

A tow-headed boy, holding a turtle, stopped and stared at the awful Santa. A puzzled line deepened between his hazel eyes.

"I'll do it," Marshall said. *I will keep the magic alive.*

"Great! I'll show you where you can finish dressing. You've saved our event, Mr. ..."

"Santa Marshall."

"Name your price, Santa Marshall," Jason said, racing toward a woman holding a camera.

Most of the animals were well-behaved. Marshall still got smacked, pinched, spit-up on, sneezed on, and peed on. And he was pretty sure that cranky bulldog thought he was "a big old doo-doo head," but he was okay with that. Marshall smiled through dozens of photos with cats and dogs. He mugged with parakeets, turtles, ferrets, guinea pigs, a snake, and a goldfish in a plastic baggie. He beamed when a kid brought four boxers, one kissing his cheek just as the flash went off. He was still smiling when he climbed into his car and headed for home. For payment, he'd picked out a puppy for adoption, a mutt with eyes the color of caramel.

After a quick turkey and stuffing sandwich, he climbed the stairs to his bedroom. He had some packing to do. He took Elaine's gardening Crocs out of his closet and set them in the Goodwill box Shannon had left. By the time the news came on, the box was full. *That's a start*, he thought. Maybe more tomorrow. There was no rush.

When he folded his clean Santa pants over a hanger, ready for next weekend, a piece of paper fluttered from one of the pockets onto his bed. He had to hold it at arm's length to read the loopy writing.

> *Dearest Marshall, I know this gift isn't the one you most desired, but I knew it would be the one you needed most.*
> *All my love forever, Elaine.*

Marshall kissed the paper lightly and slipped it into his shirt pocket.

Liz McCormick has lived in Alabama all her life. She retired from the federal government with thirty-one years of service during which time she received more than fifty work performance awards, including being selected as "One of the Ten Most Outstanding Employees in the Department of Health and Human Services." After retiring, she started a second career as a volunteer advocate for abused kids, later becoming Executive Director of Alabama CASA Network (Court Appointed Special Advocates). In 2002, she was named Volunteer of the Year by Child Protect Alabama. She was also awarded a grant from the Alabama Bar Foundation to write *A Guide to Abuse and Neglect Cases in Juvenile and Family Court*. Other than a poem for which she received a blue ribbon, this is her first attempt at writing anything other than training materials and court reports.

The Christmas Camera is a true story from my childhood which brings memories of fun and laughter even when times were hard. I was prompted to write the story after spending several days taking applications for Christmas Wish Lists for kids with two different social agencies where I volunteer. I am amazed by how families have changed since I was a kid. Even more amazing is the expectations that kids have. Times are tough once again, and I wonder how many kids will be upset when they don't get that Wii or PlayStation III they asked for. When one gets to be my age, we do tend to look at the world from an entirely different perspective. But fortunately we still have those memories to fall back on.

Personal Essay

The Christmas Camera

Liz McCormick

This morning while packing for a short trip, I discovered I had misplaced my new digital camera. I couldn't leave home without it. My search for the digital camera led my mind back to a Christmas over fifty-five years ago. I had just turned twelve, too old for Santa and yet too young not to want to believe.

Christmas was always the highlight of the year for my three sisters and me. Times were not so good financially that year, so our parents had prepared us three older girls for not getting what they referred to as frivolous things. We were told to expect only the necessities such as new shoes, clothes, and books. Only our youngest sister, who was six and still believed in Santa, would be getting a doll and a tea set. They justified their decision by saying we were too old for dolls, tea sets, paper dolls, and such. Needless to say their decision was a huge disappointment for us. Don't get me wrong, we loved getting new clothes and heaven knows we needed them. Nevertheless, all kids want Santa to bring more than just clothes for Christmas, and we were no exception.

All I wanted for Christmas that year was a camera. Not just any camera would do. I wanted the one on display at the Texaco gas station where my Daddy bought gas every week. It was a simple Ansco flash camera in a bright yellow box with one roll of film and six flashbulbs. Can you believe it cost less than ten dollars? Every Saturday morning for months I drooled over the camera while Daddy filled his 1949 Chevy with gas. Every night I dreamed about that little camera and how much fun it would be to make pictures of my family and Jip, our big collie.

On Christmas morning we gathered around the Christmas tree to open presents before breakfast. I have to admit that I went to the living room with a heavy heart because I knew I would not be getting the special gift I wished for—the camera. The gifts were always wrapped and tagged with our names. As tradition would have it, Daddy made a big production of playing Santa by sitting under the tree and calling out the names on the packages as he passed them out.

My name was the first he called. My heart pounded when he handed me the gift-wrapped box. I was certain it had not been under the tree when we went to bed the night before. I knew it was too small for the clothes we were told to expect. My hands shook as I ripped off the paper. A huge lump caught in my throat and tears ran down my cheeks when I saw the bright yellow box as I tore the paper away.

Could this be for real? Did I actually get that little Ansco flash camera I had coveted all those months? Daddy had tears in his eyes as I ran to give him a great big hug. I knew that somehow Daddy had convinced Mama it was a good thing to splurge just this once. Daddy was the tender-hearted parent, while Mama was the more stern and practical one. I can only imagine how difficult his task of convincing her had been.

Daddy waited to give out the other gifts while I took the camera out of the box and read the instructions. I was even allowed to ready the camera with film and flashbulbs without assistance from either parent. What a grown up feeling! I took the entire roll of pictures that morning.

Although the camera was my gift, it turned out to be a gift for the entire family. No one in our family had ever owned a camera, and I felt rich for being so blessed. My sisters were as excited as I was. They loved clowning and posing for pictures. We couldn't wait for Daddy to take the film to the local drugstore for developing. Waiting on that first roll to be developed was the longest week in our young lives. When Daddy came home with the finished product, we spent hours looking at the pictures and laughing about the fun we had that Christmas morning.

Over the years I've had many cameras, with the newest being a rather complicated digital camera I am struggling to master. I have even won a few ribbons for some of my amateur photography. But I rarely take my camera out that I don't recall that Christmas morning and the little Ansco flash camera that brought so many happy memories to all my family.

I have no idea what happened to that little camera. But tucked away in a big box with other family pictures are those that I so excitedly took that Christmas morning so many years ago.

Kathleen Thompson holds a B.S. degree from The University of Alabama and an MFA in Fiction and Poetry from Spalding University. A former teacher of high school English, she operates an on-line editing and writing business with her son, Stephen. She also conducts writing workshops as a "Road Scholar" for the Alabama Humanities Foundation. Her poems, short stories, and essays have been published in various literary magazines. *Searching for Ambergris* was her first published chapbook of poetry. She now has two new poetry books: *The Nights, The Days* won the 2008 Negative Capability Press Chapbook Series Award; and her full-length poetry collection, *The Shortest Distance,* was recently published by Coosa River Books. Both of the new books arrived in January within three days of each other.

Finding The Lord is another of the linked stories I'm drafting in my Clyde series. I've discovered a character rife with story. The title is not meant to imply irreverence or humor, although the characters may embody those traits. On the contrary, the story is undergirded by the theological issue of free will which is often pondered by scholars. Do we have free will? Just *how* free is our free will? Paul Zahl (*Grace in Practice*) suggests that addiction, as well as depression, worry, and mourning, can strip us of our free will. My story explores an ancillary question: how can coincidence, or a single happenstance, shape or change a life?

Short Story

Finding The Lord

Kathleen Thompson

Clyde's mind was like a sharpened axe blade, filed fine enough to chop firewood. After being hopped up on coke last night, he was looking for revenge with a capital R. He slammed the front door. Whenever he caught up with his thieving ex-wife, Sybil, and her lying husband, he'd split them both in two and stack them up to burn like pine knots.

He pulled his jacket on and zipped it to his chin before going out the door. He stopped in mid-step. *Good grief.* He must be slipping. Snoopy, riding in the sleigh, and Pooh Bear, holding an armload of gifts, had been left on all night. He opened the door and reached back inside to unplug the extension cord that ran through the window to the six-foot-tall lighted figures. He always cut off his Christmas lights at night, unlike the other idiots on his street.

It was just getting daylight, and the sky was streaked rosy behind the old pecan tree. He had to locate his weapons. The houses on his street were outlined with lights, some colored and some white, enough to light up a third world country. The icicles next door hung limply off the roofline all year long. And they stayed lit twenty-four-seven during the Christmas season. Made no sense to Clyde. That man was not just lazy, but crazy. He worked at the rubber plant and had no worry about power bills, even after the artificial trees had been boxed up and every crumb of the Lane Cake devoured.

Clyde caught himself. Wouldn't be any Lane Cake this year at his house. From now on the chance of having a Lane Cake was about as good as having snow on Christmas morning. He was usually the one to pick up the pecans for

Mama. Without her to remind him, he had forgotten all about pecans this year. No Lane Cake and, now, with only two weeks left, maybe no grave marker before Christmas either.

He had sworn to his sisters on Decoration Day in May that Mama and Daddy would have one of the best looking pieces of granite in Possum Ridge before Christmas. And he had put his sisters on notice: he was going to throw away all of those plastic flowers and wire stands when they got faded and rusted, and he intended to do it too. He knew the plush bears and rabbits they'd put out would get soppy-wet and mildewed within a week. He would get rid of them. He envisioned covering both graves with fine white marble chips. After he put the chips out, he was giving the sisters fair warning, they'd better not go setting one Godblessed thing down on top of either one of those graves. He would add a little something new for Christmas, but he couldn't trust what his sisters might pick. His throat lumped up. It would be hard for him to throw away all his sisters' gewgaws.

Clyde had been searching all morning like some maniac. He'd looked everywhere for his missing funds. He needed to clear his head. It was pounding. How stupid he'd been to even let those two through the door last night. This search shouldn't take a Sherlock Holmes. The last thing he remembered was stretching out on the bed for a little shuteye. Sybil was in the altogether on the sofa already loop-legged, and her no-good husband, who bragged he didn't need to smoke or toot, was at the stove, looking around Clyde's kitchen, about to cook up a fresh batch.

Clyde had two hiding places in the pantry—the most likely was the mushroom cookie jar with a chip in its orange lid. He jangled the lid back onto the empty jar. He was so frustrated he felt like just slinging something across the room, but not this. His mama had packed too many peanut butter cookies in it over the years for him just to bust it up into smithereens. He jerked the lid off the sugar canister, Tupperware yellowed with age. Not there. He turned his pants pockets inside out, jerked the covers off the bed, and actually flipped the mattress off to the floor. Sybil and her old man had his nest egg. There was no other answer.

He could have freely snapped a piece of barbed wire in two with his bare teeth. While he slept, those two thieves left last night twelve hundred dollars richer. By now he would bet his eyeteeth they would be on their way to the riverboats in Mississippi to blow all twelve hundred. He went out back to the storage shed. He would get his money back if it was the last thing he ever did. He jerked his shovel from a tangled mass of rakes, hoes, and broomsticks nested together in the back corner.

Standing under the pecan tree, Clyde, as straight backed as his rooster weathervane, began stepping off ten yards due east toward the Rebel Rose which was just a mass of tall sticks in this season. Then he turned right and counted off ten more paces. He was standing in the middle of an overgrown empty lot. He used the shovel to scrape away the leaves. Tifton Bermuda was worming itself over the topsoil he'd added. He might have to change his hiding place if that Bermuda grass got started. When it got a toehold, it was the greenest, hardiest, fastest-growing grass you could get. And he might need his guns in a hurry. Like now. Clyde placed the shovel into the grass, put his right foot on top, and shoved it into the soft topsoil.

He was about to become a murderer. It hit him hard. But he was not one to change his mind once his mind was set on something. If his mind was set on it, he could sell a funeral plot to a guy who'd always figured he was going to live forever, and who had planned to be cremated if he did happen to die. Even Mama gave him credit for that.

But—killing two people was another ball of wax. Mama's *thou shalt nots* echoed in his head. But Clyde knew himself well enough to know that anything short of a lightning bolt was not about to stop him. So, here he was, digging up his two nine millimeters for the first time since he had wrapped them in plastic and buried them here. An acid taste ran up into his throat as he continued to dig. He wished he had a pack of Tums.

The very thought of the word murderer made his hands

shake. He grunted as he pried the lid of the metal box up with his thumbs. Trying to untwist the ties around the plastic bag that kept his guns dry was too tedious. He finally just ripped into the plastic. He rubbed the cool metal. He had done a lot of things in his life: he'd busted a few lips, slapped a few people around, and he beat up eight men at once in a fair-and-square rumble. But most of that was all necessary—at least by his reasoning. If he ever had to get a little rough, he'd give the man fair warning, "Ain't never done no killing before. Don't make me start now."

And he hadn't done jail time either. That thought weakened his knees, too. A picture of his poor mama, lying in the hospital bed, came to him—a woman waiting until her son got there before she died, telling him the secret she should have carried to the grave. She'd spilled her guts about another man being his daddy, not the man he'd always thought was his daddy.

As the cold wind blew through his hair under the pecan tree, he remembered too the promise he had made to her. "Will you just start talking to the Lord again?" she had whispered that day in the hospital after she'd made her confession. "He's not hiding from you. You can't hide from Him. Promise me, Clyde?"

He had seen no reason to honor that promise before now. But there it was—his mama's voice, the outline of her face in a dark puffy cloud on the horizon. Suddenly, nothing mattered except his mama and that promise. He fell forward and stretched out fully in the dirt.

"Lord," he shouted out loud, the dead grass brushing against his lips. "If you're going to stop me from being a murderer, you'd better do it right now. This is your last chance."

He waited, not wiggling a finger, like he'd seen Muslims do, praying on TV, their bodies flattened to the east. But—no answer. He remained perfectly still for several long minutes.

Nothing.

Well, he'd done his part. He got up and rested on his

knees. He brushed the dirt off the front of his shirt. Not only had Mama kept a regular praying time every night where she made everybody in the house stop what they were doing while she got down on her knees and "took them to the Lord," but she regularly whispered prayers as she pulled weeds from a bed or deadheaded hydrangeas.

Clyde had very little of his mama's patience. He tilted his chin to the sky and shook his fist. "I didn't mean tomorrow or the next day, Lord. I meant now, or I'm gone."

The faint notes of "Dixie" startled Clyde. He struggled to stand and inch the phone from his deep jeans pocket as the tune got progressively louder.

"Yeah?" he barked.

"Yeah! Hello yourself, and hallelujah."

"Who the hell is this?" Clyde had jumped up too fast and felt a little dizzy. He lay the gun down and sat on the damp grass cross-legged.

"The mouthpiece of God, I reckon."

"You reckon? Well, maybe your mouth can tell me who run off with my money, huh?"

"Hold on just a minute."

"Mister, I'm warning you. You've got just two more seconds to waste my time, else I'm gonna come looking for you. Whoever you are. I've got my finger on the trigger of a nine millimeter here."

"Wait a minute now. Could be I've dialed the wrong number. No cause to get riled up." He paused. "Seems, though, I may be getting a word from the Lord for you."

"A word? Just one word? I'm gonna need more than a word to change my mind."

"Hey, man. What's your ten-forty?"

Clyde softened a little. He hadn't heard anybody talking CB talk for a long time. He still drove his rig when he could get a haul, but most of the younger drivers hadn't even heard of a CB. But he would not be taken for a fool twice in twenty-four hours.

"I'm at the North Pole. What's your ten-forty?"

"Oh, I'm a long way from the North Pole. Matter of

fact, I see you got a Tuscaloosa number, too."

"No shit." Clyde moaned quietly, as the man told him he was calling from Lakeview Baptist on Hargrove Road. Wouldn't you know this would be some jackleg from his mama's very own church? And the wrong number at that.

"Well, what I want to know is how'd you come by my phone number and what do you want?"

"My bad, man. Ain't you ever dialed a wrong number? Although I do believe, yissirree, that every blessed thing in life happens for a reason."

"You'd better have a hell of a good reason for bothering me."

"Man, be cool. I'm not selling anything. Matter of fact, I'm giving away. I guess the Lord knew you was thirsty."

"Ain't it a little early in the day for grape juice?" Clyde quipped.

"Sounds like you need a drink to me."

"Looks like you ain't got nothing right this morning, man. First you get the wrong number and now you got the wrong drug of choice. You got me *all* wrong, mister."

"And you got me all wrong, buddy. I'm offering you the Lord's living water." His voice was low and convincing. It was the same tone Clyde knew well, one he used when he was trying to convince somebody to see things his way, or when he was trying to seal a deal.

Clyde heard pages swishing on the other end of the phone. He thought about this: he called on God for the first time in years, and the result was some cornpone preacher calling, telling him he was offering up the Lord's water. Clyde's head was pounding and he tasted bile. The idea of a drink of water didn't sound bad right now, but he needed to get rid of this guy.

"Now I know you didn't call me about no water. No way, no how. Let me remind you that one teeny tiny squeeze of the trigger and this piece I'm holding could blow somebody off the planet."

Clyde held the nine millimeter up to the light and the early morning sun glinted from its barrel. "If you try to mess with me about what I'm planning to do, you'll be just another notch on this barrel."

"Hold on now, good buddy. I just need to read you something. Just one little verse. Listen here, and then my job is done. I'm going to hang up this phone and just let the Lord take over while I make my other phone calls. Wait just another second."

More pages swished and the man spoke. "He that is without sin among you, let him cast the first stone. John 8:7."

Clyde laughed but it came out like a loud howl. "Tell me, brother, are you about to go casting some stones?" Just his luck to get this Bible thumper. "Man, the only time I've ever been casting is from a fishing boat, and I deal strictly in rocks. Smokin' rocks, not casting 'em."

Clyde thought back to last night. Sybil laid out on the couch buck naked like a cow under a shade tree, her cow eyes oblivious to everything. Her old man hunkered over the stove. Him cooking. Them passing the glass pipe. He was the one Clyde would shoot first. Clyde was sure his twelve hundred bucks was right now resting in that big bull's back pocket. Soon to be on some blackjack table.

"The word I got from the Lord is about adultery."

"Adultery?" Clyde hooted at that one. "Does anybody even know that word anymore?"

The preacher ignored his question. "Her enemies wanted to stone this woman, but the Lord forgave her sins."

"Look here, preacherman. You listen to me." Clyde aimed one of the guns through the top of the pecan tree and fired.

"I wouldn't push the Lord too far if I was you. Keep talking to me, buddy. Lay down your weapon. Put it down. Can you hear me?"

Pushing the Lord too far. That warning echoed what his mama had said so many times. It was halfway funny. Old preacherman thought Clyde was about to use the gun on himself. He could tell by the pleading desperation in his voice.

"Are you for real, preacherman? I want to see you in person and see if you're really a preacher."

"Come on then. I'll be right here waiting."

Was this an answer? Clyde *had* called on the Lord.

If he cut through an alley, it wouldn't take but a few minutes to see if the preacher was at his mama's church. And if he wasn't at his mama's church, Clyde figured it wasn't meant to be.

He left one gun in the metal box and shoveled some leaves and debris back over it. He stood the shovel up against the pecan tree. He began walking fast, hoping not too many people were up this early. He ducked down as he cut across backyards so that he couldn't be spotted.

Clyde was only a block over behind the church. When Mama first moved the family to Tuscaloosa, he had gone to church a few Sundays, but without his daddy around, he soon learned that his mama couldn't force him. He found plenty to keep him busy besides Sunday sermons. Such as a job at the Seven-Eleven as soon as he was old enough to work.

Clyde was limping now. His toes on his right foot were killing him. The same sole he'd used super glue on that week. He'd actually had this same pair of boots for eleven years. Maybe his boots were finally worn out and hurting his feet. But this time something was wrong. Every time he took a step, that pain in his toes reminded him of squeezing every dime he got and just why he was carrying the gun.

His neighbors were all older and so were their homes, but the old homes were surrounded by oaks, camellias, and azaleas. Shrubs covered picture windows of all the ranch-style houses. Nearly every house needed some pruning. Maybe he could pick up a few little jobs here and there after he'd finished the task at hand.

When he reached the back parking lot of his mama's church, there was only one black Camaro there. He stayed close to the unwieldy azaleas as he quietly made his way around to the front door. There sat a boy in an overcoat on the top step. Still wet behind the ears. He had a Bible on his lap and both hands wrapped around a steaming Styrofoam cup. The preacherman.

He went with the preacherman to get himself a cup of that good smelling coffee. That first morning cup of coffee was as precious as his favorite boots, and the little joint where they went had some half and half and some real sugar. You just didn't see that much. Clyde could drink coffee with a sweetener and with almost any kind of milk, but cream and sugar in coffee was the closest thing to a snort of his real nectar. Especially with a Winston on the side. He wasn't so far gone that he didn't appreciate nice things—he was human, flesh and blood, a man who liked a few simple things.

After they'd had coffee, the details got fuzzy. He remembered how the pounding of his head had eased off when they walked into the sanctuary. *O come, O come, Emmanuel* drifted softly from speakers mounted above the doors. The one thing Clyde never would forget was what happened right there on the altar. He took one look at the preacherman kneeling next to him and figured this was a waste of his time. This kid was wearing a red polo shirt and jeans. Looked as green as a gourd. What could he know about preaching? What could anybody that young know about life and death? Clyde looked up at the pulpit. He wondered what had happened to the old preacher with a lisp and a drooping moustache.

On one side of the altar was an artificial tree loaded with white and gold ornaments. Mama had crocheted several of the fish. His younger sisters used to skip up the aisle and sit down for the children's sermons. He could imagine all three of his sisters in their Sunday dresses, sometimes waving to his mama on her pew close to the front. The morning sun lit up the stained glass window of Mary and Jesus behind the choir loft. He suddenly saw his mother sitting right there on her pew, young again, with the colored light dancing in her dark hair. His knees buckled. He had let her down again. He'd lost the money for the tombstone. He fell down at the altar and began to sob.

By then Clyde's whole foot was killing him. He wrenched his boot off. He ran his hand up into the toe. He felt something. A sock? He pulled his hand out and began laughing. He laughed and cried as he counted out the wad of bills. Twelve hundred dollars. Every last bill.

The Lord had spoken. Clyde wouldn't have to murder anybody after all.

The preacherman had waited and watched Clyde straighten out all the bills as he counted them. He asked no questions as Clyde told him what had happened. He offered to drive up to Fayette with Clyde to pick out the tombstone. Better prices there, he told Clyde.

On the way back home from Fayette, Clyde asked the preacherman if it was okay to stop at the cemetery at Possum Ridge. Just for a little while. He had a little Christmas tree for the graves.

"You ever been to Sweden?" Clyde asked as they came to a stop on the hillside.

"Nah. You kidding? Panama City is the only foreign country I've ever been in."

Clyde let out a laugh that reverberated off the graves as he got out of the car. He liked a guy who could laugh at himself.

They got out, and Clyde began walking toward his family's plot. He picked up a rotten limb that had fallen from the water oak and threw it on the side of the road that meandered around the cemetery.

"Have you?" said the preacherman.

"Have I what?"

"Been to Sweden?"

Clyde was kneeling now and shaking the dirt off a large white rabbit propped up with a rough wooden cross at the head of his mama's grave.

"I work for a guy who has. You see this?" He held up the rabbit. "Imagine how white this rabbit was when it was new. There's a place in Sweden this guy's told me about that has little red-topped houses and churches—really old—and when the snow covers it all, when the ice sheets the lakes, and distant hills become blue-white, the man says the world looks purified."

The preacherman took the rabbit.

"Sometimes I think that's what heaven is like," Clyde continued.

"Purified? Sure sounds like the opposite of hell."

"It's just come to me what I might want on a tombstone too."

Picking out the tombstone had been a piece of cake. Clyde knew exactly how much money he had, and he knew he wanted an angel of some kind on the stone as well as some kind of saying. The woman had told him not to worry. He could add the epitaph even after the stone was set in the ground.

Clyde felt exhilarated by the cold wind that had picked up, but he shivered and folded his arms over his chest.

"What's that?" preacherman asked.

"Something that same guy saw on a tombstone in Sweden. He's a real talker. Made it sound like a poem. It stuck with me."

Clyde picked up the small Christmas tree crisscrossed with little strings of silver bells and beads. Tiny red apples were attached with ribbon. He shoved the trunk into the ground at the head of the graves and set the bells jingling.

"Well?"

"Well what?"

"You gonna let me in on it?"

Clyde scratched his head. He wanted to get the words just right. When the words came to him, he spoke quietly— "How sweet to have lived. How beautiful that one can die."

"That's it?" said the preacherman.

"Yeah, you have to think on it a while. Let it take root in your mind."

"How about your sisters? You have to think about your kin when you start writing an epitaph."

Clyde reached for the soiled rabbit. He knew the preacherman was right. His sisters would be hard to convince there was anything beautiful about dying. He'd have to add something good about Mama and Daddy. His daddy's strong hands. His mama who had the strength of a man if she willed it.

Clyde rubbed the rabbit and tried to fluff out the soiled fur. Mama's funeral was a little blurred now except for the white rabbit running down the hillside. He hadn't had a flashback all year. That was good. He also felt proud. That stone would be on his mama and daddy's graves by Christmas just like he'd said. He might not be good at much, but this proved he was a man of his word. Clyde knelt by the grave. He felt the light touch of the preacherman's hand on his shoulder.

He snuggled the rabbit carefully against the Christmas tree. He might buy a new white rabbit before Christmas. Snow was predicted for the weekend, but weathermen were never right on that. If it snowed at all, it wouldn't be more than a sprinkling. The little gold bells and beads on the Christmas tree tinkled in the breeze.

Clyde had promised the preacherman on the spot he'd gladly prune the azaleas around the church. He also promised that every Sunday morning when he was straight, without fail, he'd come and listen to the sermon. And Clyde always kept his promises.

Wanda Wood lives in Pensacola, Florida. She holds a master's degree in Communication Arts and worked for twenty years in business. She has won three prizes for her short fiction, and is currently working on a novel titled *Living in Mercy*. She has written two other books which are, as yet, unpublished. The first is a work of nonfiction titled *Funny Bones*, which explores the different ways men and women communicate with humor. The second is a mystery titled *Love You to Death*. Another short story, "How a Bed Became My Undoing," will be published next year in *Southern Voices*.

Rubicon explores the conflicts people experience as they struggle with the difficult choices they are forced to make throughout their lives. The story highlights the fact that holidays sometimes cause us to reflect on both the joys and disappointments stemming from our major decisions. It also suggests that holiday reflections may serve as impetus for change.

Short Story

Rubicon

Wanda Wood

Silver Bells streams from the speakers on the counter, and holiday fragrances—nutmeg, cinnamon, cranberry, pine, and fresh oranges—waft about me as I finish cleanup. Wiping my hands on a dish towel, I press the OFF button on the CD player to silence the music. With dinner over and the crowd cleared out, the song that sounded so festive and cheerful this morning has taken on a decidedly sad tone—that bittersweet *party is over* sensation that always overtakes me on Christmas evening.

I pick up stacks of Christmas china that I've hand-washed to preserve each shiny gold band and hand-painted holly sprig, and tuck them into the bottom of the hutch. Then I slip the sterling into the chest, gently sliding each piece into its slot. I remember how Will and Amy always debate inheritance rights to the Christmas china and silver during Christmas dinner, and how the whole family cracks jokes and laughs over the same endless dialogue that's transpired between them since they were eight and ten.

Another Christmas celebration is over, gifts exchanged, boxes and paper discarded, feast devoured, cleanup complete—weeks of preparation gone in a few hours. I return the holly and poinsettia centerpiece to the dining table where, only a few hours ago, my family carried on a flurry of conversation as they filled themselves with a repast fit to feed an army—a twenty-pound turkey, mounds of dressing, sweet potato casserole, green beans, hot rolls, and more. Pecan pie, Lane cake, English trifle, bread pudding topped with rum sauce and fluffy pillows of whipped cream. Enough sweets for an

95

emergency insulin injection.

Last week my husband had asked, "Why don't we mix it up, have seafood for Christmas this year like the neighbors?"

"You've got to be joking—it's Christmas."

He said we needed a change. I said I'd ask the others.

My kids, my sister, my mom, my great uncle, all of them shrieked: "It's Christmas! Seafood is fine any other day of the year, but not Christmas."

My sister said she'd bring the turkey.

We are a family grounded in tradition, following the ebb and flow of patterns. Like the laws that structure the natural universe, tradition is embedded in our character and orders our existence. My husband and children follow the blueprints of custom and ritual that I have seamlessly woven into the fabric of their lives—traditions that have molded and grounded and anchored us into a cohesive family unit. My family has grown while I counted off Christmases—this family I began cultivating ten years after crossing my first Rubicon.

Christmas has always been my favorite time of year. In an ideal world, it creates an image of perfect balance, giving and receiving in an atmosphere of great love. I've worked hard to stress this principle to my children. I know some of it stuck, and it gives me joy to see them performing small acts of kindness, like buying gifts for underprivileged children without any prompting from me.

Yet the day strikes a distinctly melancholy note for me when the festivities wind down, and I'm left to take down the tree alone. That's when the ghosts of Christmases past drift in, after my college-age children leave to visit with friends, and my husband naps away his turkey and dressing and pecan pie.

"Just save the dishes until I get a little nap. Then I'll help you," Richard always says as he stretches out on the sofa.

"You go ahead. I'm fine." I say that every year.

"Leave the tree until tomorrow. It can wait." Before I can respond, his eyes are closed.

I can't explain to Richard why the tree must go today. I'm no obsessive neatnik, no, not at all. No perfectionist. I ignore dust on the furniture for days, and sometimes I leave dishes in the sink overnight. But leaving the tree up after Christmas makes me sad, a reminder of lives I never lived. I can't name the reason it affects me that way. Or perhaps I can. It's tied to the silly ornament I compulsively hide on the back of the Christmas tree year after year. It's been on every Christmas tree in my life since I was sixteen. Thirty-two years. Only an ornament, yet a symbol of the road not traveled.

Every time I put up the tree, I count the years since I reached that first fork in my life—my path. One way cut off, an immovable obstacle placed in the way, forced me in the other direction. Taking the path chosen for me, I was told I would forget the other in due time. But I have not forgotten. I never forgot.

I take down colored glass balls and lay them gently in their boxes. One or two are missing from each tattered box as the years have claimed their casualties. Once or twice I considered buying all new ornaments and putting up themed trees like some of my friends, but I can't force myself to break with tradition.

"Why do you hang onto all of this junk?" my cousin and best friend, Annie, asked me one time. "Your tree's always the same. Don't you get tired of this old stuff?"

I thought about it, and then I shrugged. "No, I don't."

I cast an affectionate glance at the eclectic array of decorations hanging from my tree, all of them either handed down from family or made by my children or given to me as gifts by people I love. I feel a rush of joy, getting out the same old things every year and putting them on my tree. They're like old friends, a collection of thirty-two years of memories. I started collecting them at sixteen. How could I even think of throwing them out?

Sometimes I ask my son, "Remember when you made this drummer boy in Mrs. Gentry's room in second grade?"

"Sure," he says. His eyes move on to the hand-painted apples. The gingerbread man. The glittery reindeer. "You still have those?" he asks, and I can tell it pleases him that I've saved his childhood. I hang it on the tree.

Each year Annie helps me with preparations for the

children's Christmas party at the hospital where I volunteer. "You're the poster child for tradition," Annie told me a few weeks ago as we wrapped gifts together for sick kids. Her expression was cynical as she looked at my tree. "Not to mention being sentimental to the point of sappiness." Annie works as a parole officer for the state, and she possesses not one sentimental bone in all of her body. Neither does she mince her words.

"If you want to rehabilitate someone," I told her as I stuck a red bow on Spiderman paper, "you'd better stick with your felons. You'll have more luck with them."

"You need some change," she said.

"It's coming," I told her.

"When?" She asked me.

"When the time is right."

"That's what you always say." Annie looked back at me and shook her head like she didn't believe me. "You're not the sacrificial lamb, you know," she said, picking up the scissors and slicing through a roll of Scooby Doo paper. "You can come down off your cross. Jesus already did that for you."

"You're mixing up Christmas and Easter," I said, laughing.

"It's all about the same thing," Annie said, "so don't change the subject. You deserve to do something for yourself for a change."

I hear the squeak of leather a moment before Richard sticks his head through the open doorway. He's up from his nap. "Why don't you sit down and rest?" he asks again. "The tree can wait a few days."

"It won't take long. I'm okay. I need to be busy."

He sighs. The leather squeaks as he settles back down on the sofa in front of the television. The ballgame is on mute, but it makes him feel better knowing it's playing there in front of him while he naps.

I take down camels and sheep and wise men, all handmade and painted by my sister-in-law the year before her brain tumor was diagnosed. I lay them gently in their box between layers of tissue paper, careful not to scratch their delicate surfaces. Next I take down the miniature painted wooden airplanes given to me by my friend who converted to Judaism, the priceless collection of handmade treasures created by my children, and the birds my mother-in-law brought back from Europe the year before she died. The crystal snowflakes my mother gave me. My grandmother's angels. Tiny olivewood nativities my minister brought me from Israel. A mélange of memories that fits together into a theme I understand perfectly.

"Stable as the Statue of Liberty," Annie says. "And as predictable," which, when translated, means boring and tediously conventional to Annie, a woman who loves change and excitement. A woman who's rid herself of three husbands.

"No sense keeping an albatross hanging around your neck, as far as I can see," Annie says after each divorce. After her second ex-husband, her daughter Emily's father, was killed in a motorcycle accident, Annie only sniffed and said, "Cleaned up a little riff-raff."

The last ornament to come down from the tree is a gold-toned bit of nostalgia, also the first in my collection. The color of the metal has dimmed a bit over the years, but I could no more part with it than I could get rid of one of my children's hand-painted apples.

Reaching into the tree, I gently lift the ornament off the branch. Holding it up by the hook, I watch the colored lights twinkle off its gold letters as it slowly twirls in my hand, creating a fleeting sense of magic in the worn, golden surface.

So young. We were so young the day we stopped to browse through the gift shop and found the display holding the ornaments. We looked through hundreds before we found an ornament to match each of our names. There were lots of *Jacks,* but I'd almost given up after half an hour of searching before Jack finally held up the small box with a *Georgia* ornament nestled inside it. So I bought *Jack* and he bought *Georgia,* and we laughed like kids at our silly purchases.

That was August. I could hardly wait for Christmas that

year to hang *Jack* on my tree. I thought for weeks what I might give him. At sixteen, I'd never bought a present for a boy. I carefully saved my money. I figured if I was going to spend the rest of my life with this guy, I should start things out right. I ought to knock his socks off with the first Christmas gift. I felt like the luckiest girl in the world. I knew exactly what I wanted to do with my life. And I knew who I was going to spend it with. I would finish high school, go to college, and then get married to Jack.

I watch the lights from the tree flicker on and off in the sheen of my *Jack* ornament for a moment. Then, after giving it a lingering caress, I wrap it in tissue paper and return it to the box. I gently place it on top of the other packages and boxes of ornaments in the big plastic container, and taking one last look, I close the top.

Richard asked me early on in our marriage, "What's this Jack thing?"

"An old family thing from way back," I said, and passed it off, but I cringed, knowing I should tell him.

When my children asked me about it, I just tickled them and said, "Didn't you ever hear of Jack Frost?" And I told them the story of Jack Frost, and then I told them about Frosty the Snowman. After that, they argued every year about who got to hang the Jack Frost ornament, and it sent guilty pangs running through my heart. Still, though, I could not part with *Jack*.

I wonder today, like every Christmas afternoon at tree disassembly time, whatever happened to Jack. He probably has a wife and kids. Did he ever make it to Atlanta? We were going to leave our small towns and live in Atlanta. Do his eyes still twinkle when he smiles? I loved his smile. I hope he passed that great smile to one of his kids.

I reach for a tissue in a box on an end table, and I wipe my eyes and blow my nose. For a few moments I indulge myself. Jack and I did not choose to follow different paths. The choice was made for us. I gave him up, kicking and screaming.

He was unhappy too.

I wonder what Jack did with his *Georgia* ornament. I wonder if he ever thinks of me, if he wonders what the road might be like if we had continued down the same path together. I wonder if he spares a thought for a girl who loved him once, or if he feels contented to live the life that opened to him down the path he followed. What would he think of a silly, middle-aged woman who still hangs a *Jack* ornament on her tree—an ornament she bought when she was sixteen years old.

I expand my moment of nostalgia to consider all of the people in the world who have faced divergent paths and had to make a choice. Are they at this moment, like me, looking at corny ornaments or ruined dinners or thoughtless gifts that must either be exchanged or relegated to top closet shelves—maybe thinking of a boy named Jack or Tom or Michael, or a girl named Georgia or Sally or Jennifer?

I unplug the lights, and the Christmas tree loses its magic and becomes only a dried-out Douglas fir. I slowly unwind the cords from the branches as I consider the new fork in my path that popped in front of me two weeks ago.

This new year is supposed to mark my year of change. My second Rubicon. After a quarter century of marriage, one kid just out of college, and another more than halfway through, I deserve it, the right to a little transformation, if there is such a thing. My kids are stable, both of them: Amy, newly graduated, about to settle into her career in Atlanta, and Will, happy and functioning well in Gainesville, nearing graduation. This is the family I've loved and held together, supported and anchored by the steel cables beneath my surface. Dedication, determination, and devotion, like lightning rods that divert a direct strike, have protected my family through all the storms, storms that required heavy giving and light receiving. Not a perfect world.

A week before Christmas, I decided to tell Annie about the job offer in Orlando. I'd decided to take it, knew I'd take it from the beginning. It was what I'd been waiting for, everything I'd wanted. I felt like a bird set free from a cage. Like I could breathe for the first time in fifteen years. Thank God. That was all I could think. Finally, after thirty-two years, no more sacrifices. Time for me.

I knew something was wrong when Annie walked in the door five days before Christmas. I'd known Annie all my life, her every expression, her moods. But I waited for her to tell me. I expected anything from her. Anything but cancer.

"I want to ask you a favor," she said slowly, dipping a cutter into flour and then pressing it into the cookie dough, lifting out a perfect star.

"Anything," I said. "You know you can count on me."

"If I lose this battle, I want you to think about taking Emily. I want her to have all this stability and tradition crap you've given your kids."

I met her stare, slowly looking into those somber blue eyes, understanding what the promise would cost.

"You're not going to lose the battle," I said. "Don't even think it." I couldn't entertain the thought of life without my best friend. Yet deep down inside, the price of another forced sacrifice was moving in on me, smothering me, and I was fighting back. Selfish, so selfish. But I had given up everything I wanted before. People say you forget. No, you store it all away, somewhere inside of you, but you don't forget.

"Everyone says that in the beginning, Georgia. But you and I both know a lot of people..." Annie leveled a frank stare at me. "Not everyone makes it. I need to know Emily will have the best chance possible at a solid life."

"I thought you wanted Emily to grow up knowing change and excitement." I looked at her, hopeful.

"Emily's enamored with all this tradition crap y'all do. Reading the Christmas story by candlelight from the Bible. The same tree every year with all that old trash. Easter sunrise service. Fourth of July cookouts with family everywhere. Your....," she waved her hand toward my living room, "museum."

I laughed at Annie's description of my antiques and heirlooms.

"Whatever it is. All that old family stuff you've got that's been handed down for generations." She ate a piece of cookie dough, leaving a ring of flour around her lips.

We worked in heavy silence for a few minutes before she spoke again. "Just promise you'll think about it. That's all I ask for now."

"Yes, I'll think about it," I said.

I was still thinking about it as I pulled tinsel off the tree and tossed it into a garbage bag. In the past several days, I'd put my hand on the phone three times to call the human resources manager in Orlando to turn down the job. The sinking sensation in the pit of my stomach stopped me each time. I thought I might die inside if I kept going like I'd done for the past fifteen years. I had to tell Annie, tell her that if Emily could be happy with me alone in Orlando in an apartment, then we had a deal. But how could I drag a fifteen-year-old who'd just lost her mom away from her friends and everything that was important and familiar to her?

What was I going to do?

Annie needed to live for Emily, but she was right. Everyone with cancer did not survive. Yet, I had sacrificed everything, and I wanted one time in my life that would be all mine. The choice was in my hands. But at what expense?

I vacuum up bits of tinsel and dry needles that have fallen off of the tree. Then I wind up the cord and push the machine back into the closet, closing the door quietly so I won't disturb Richard. Tomorrow he'll drag the tree, denuded of its grandeur, out to the street for the garbage collectors.

I walk into the living room and stand by the sofa, watching him breathe in easy, measured paces. Sighing, I turn and walk back to the bathroom, brush my teeth, and brush my hair. The light flickers on a strand of hair, and I put down my brush and separate out the individual hair shafts until I find the culprit. Unbelieving, I pull out a gray hair. A tiny wave of anxiety ripples through me as I consider the significance of the hair. Not vanity. Something deeper. I'm heading toward my forty-ninth birthday; still I have not gotten the thing I knew I wanted at sixteen. Always sacrifices. Life was messy; complications and barriers got in the way. Now a new complication has been placed in my path, just when I thought life was getting easier.

My sacrifices are measured out by Christmases. I never spent that Christmas with Jack. We were torn apart by circumstances beyond our control. I gave up graduate school twice; each time the hammer fell right before Christmas. Our first year, Richard got a job offer, the opportunity of a lifetime, but we had to move. I didn't want to move, yet he couldn't be expected to pass up a chance like that. The next time, I'd just passed the GRE when Richard got a promotion. We had to move right before Christmas. Once again, I couldn't expect him to pass up an opportunity.

I refresh my lipstick and retrace my steps back down the hall. Pulling my coat out of the closet, I walk over to the sofa where Richard sleeps. Placing my hand gently on his arm so as not to startle him, I say, "I'm off to the hospital to check on Annie." He grunts and rolls over onto his side.

The doctor had insisted on starting Annie's chemo immediately. She had a severe reaction to one of the drugs. While I was in the room, he talked to her about options and experimental medicine. It all spelled scary stuff to me. Annie looked scared too.

I need to give her an answer about Emily. I know that. I saw the urgency in her eyes yesterday, the unanswered question. She needs all her energy focused on the battle at hand.

I look back at Richard once more. I look around the house where I raised my children. Richard is settled in. Here. Established. Tired of change. Tired of moving.

Walking back through the living room, I pause and glance back at the dead fir tree, looking naked and alone without its finery. Then, on a whim, I turn around, open the box full of ornaments where it still sits in the middle of the floor, waiting for Richard to haul it back to the closet. I lift out the small box with my *Jack* ornament, and for a moment I hold it to my breast. Then taking a deep breath, I tuck it inside my purse before I walk out the door for the drive to the hospital to see Annie.

Hazel Polly Pope grew up in Laurel, Mississippi and moved to Mobile in the 1950s. She earned a B.A. in Communication and Marketing from the University of South Alabama. She is a member of the Mobile Writers Guild and the Quill Masters critique group. Two of her pieces, *Brother* and *A Picnic on the Haywagon,* earned honorable mentions from *Writer's Digest*. Her short story, *A House Full of Grandmothers,* appeared in *Christmas is a Season! 2008.* Polly and her husband live on a small farm in southwest Alabama. She draws the rich details for her stories from everyday life on the farm.

The Christmas Range Wars is a true story about farm life, especially at Christmas time. The antics of a rogue ewe and the fight for grass between the two masters of the farm are frequent occurrences. But, Christmas time always brings peace between the factions. I hope the story brings a smile to the reader's face.

Personal Essay

The Christmas Range Wars

Hazel Polly Pope

December through February are busy months on our Grand Bay, Alabama farm, because that's when our cows have calves and our sheep have lambs. For thirteen years, I have raised sheep and my husband, Buddy, has raised cattle. Buddy and I have engaged in range wars comparable to ones in the old west. Like the sheep in an old John Wayne movie, mine have always enjoyed grazing on the bright green rye grass planted for the cattle.

"Let's get rid of those sheep," Buddy argues.

"No way!" I come back.

Buddy's cattle are an English breed called Herefords—Polled Herefords to be exact. Polled means without horns. The cattle are red and white with big brown eyes. They're a gentle breed and not at all aggressive, but I've always kept an eye on Leo, our herd bull. He weighs 2,500 pounds and goes anywhere he pleases.

Buddy and I help each other with our respective stock. When a new calf is born, he tattoos the newborn's ear and pierces a plastic ear tag into it. The calf is funny looking with its plastic earring in one ear, but the tags identify the calves as belonging to our farm. It has always been my job to straddle the calf's back and hold its head while Buddy tattoos and tags it. Many times the calf lows when Buddy works on its ears, and I feel its mama's breath on my head as she watches over her baby.

Buddy helps me tag my lambs for identification purposes, and he gives the ewes injections for parasite

infestation. My sheep are also an English breed called Suffolk. They have black faces and stockings with cream-colored bodies. When the lambs are born, they are solid black but change over the first six months to look like their parents.

Although Buddy thinks it's silly, I always name my sheep after nieces and nephews. One year I named one of the ewes Charlotte. From the beginning, she was an escape artist and could get through any fence or paddock. She would ride a weak spot in the fence, pushing with her nose or forefeet until she created a hole that she could squeeze through. When she escaped, all the other sheep soon followed her.

Buddy plants fields of rye grass in October so it will be ready for the cows to eat by December. Charlotte seemed to be able to smell the new green grass even though it was several fields away in the back of our property. When I'd come out to check on the sheep and find them all gone, I knew Charlotte had led them astray. I would head to the back field with an empty feed sack and try to fool the sheep into coming back home. Sometimes it worked. Sometimes it didn't.

Buddy would get so angry. "Those @*&#*+% sheep are eating all the grass! There won't be enough for the cows and their calves!" And round and round we would go with him telling me I needed to get rid of my sheep. And me telling him, "no way."

One morning after breakfast, I heard the strangest noise coming from the sheep corral. A sheep was baaing, but it sounded as if it were coming from the bottom of a well. I walked out to the fenced-in area. Charlotte was walking around and around the sheep barn, baaing her heart out. When she came to the front of the barn, I broke out in laughter. Instead of putting the galvanized pail back when I fed them, I had left it sitting on the ground. Charlotte—ever the hungry ewe—had stuck her head into the pail to get the last kernel of corn. Her big head was stuck, and now she was crying. I held her neck and pulled the bucket free.

She seemed surprised to see sunshine and ran off to get into more mischief. The sun was shining warmly for a December day, and Buddy had turned the cows and calves into the green grass. I knew it wouldn't be long before Charlotte figured out a way to join them with the whole flock of sheep right behind her.

The year-of-the-bucket was also the year my grandson, Michael, was five years old and came to visit with us before Christmas. Michael and I stayed inside and decorated the house with wreaths and swags for the mantels. Buddy brought the nativity set down from the attic for us. Michael loved placing the tiny figures in the wooden stable. It was a ragtag bunch I had bought when Michael's dad, Billy, was small. If you turned the figures upside down, you would see a tag with *W. T. GRANT—5 CENTS* on each piece.

Billy, and now Michael, liked to play with the figures. Every day Michael moved them to another place. Many of the small figures had missing ears from Michael's teething. One day he sat the figures in the stable and called for my attention.

"Mema, I'm putting the bad sheep Charlotte in the front so I can watch her."

I smiled as I finished decorating the mantel. Even little Michael knew about Charlotte and her misadventures. Fascinated, I stopped to watch Michael load Mary, Joseph, the baby, the wise men, and bad Charlotte into the back of his Tonka pickup and drive them to Bethlehem.

When we heard the start of an engine outside, Michael and I ran to the front door. There was my son, Billy, and his skinny friend, Burt, starting to put the decorations on my three-story, live Christmas tree in the front yard. Twenty-five years ago when it was only six feet tall, I had bought the tree for our Christmas tree. After Christmas I planted it. I never expected it to live, but it did. Now my son and his friend decorated it every Christmas for my special present.

They borrowed a lift truck—commonly known as a cherry picker—from a friend. The truck has hydraulic gears that shoot a boom fifty feet in the air. Attached to the boom is a metal cage. Billy operates the gears from the back of the truck while Burt climbs into the cage and hangs the fifty-five-foot star on top of the tree. When we light the tree, I know everyone can see it from a mile away. I think it is beautiful, and I know many others who agree.

One night a few years ago when I went out to unplug the tree lights, I was amazed to see a group of young heifers gathered next to the fence that separates the tree from the pasture. They stood quietly, gazing up at the giant blinking star.

"Hey, Mom!" Billy yelled from the truck, bringing me back to reality. "I hate to tell you this, but from the cherry picker Burt says he can see Charlotte and her buddies over in Dad's rye grass."

I took off running with Michael right behind me and the feed bag in my hand. I needed to get those sheep back in their corral before Buddy found them. He would not be happy to see them devouring the cattle's precious grass.

A few days later, it turned exceptionally cold for southern Alabama, and the ewes had started lambing. It was really important to check on the pregnant ewes frequently because there was always the possibility that we would have to help deliver the lambs, which are usually twins. Every night Buddy and I took turns going out to the sheep barn.

One night just a few days before Christmas, Buddy said he would go out again to check on them, and I could stay in by the fire. When he was gone a long time, I began to think maybe he'd had to pull the lambs or had fallen or become ill.

I pulled on my old farm coat and found a woolen hat. When I walked out in the yard, there were a million stars in the black velvet sky. I could hear the soft *pie-whacking* of the guinea fowl in the limbs of the live oak by the back gate. I walked quickly to the circle of light coming from the sheep barn and heard a soft, encouraging voice and the baaing of a ewe. I crept in softly.

Buddy was kneeling beside old Charlotte. He had one of her twins, showing it where to nurse. The other lamb was trying to stand on wobbly legs. Buddy spoke softly to the lambs, giving a little laugh when they butted Charlotte's bag as they nursed. The lambs watched him with their dark black eyes, knowing he would take care of them.

Smiling, I slipped out of the barn and went back to the fire. Buddy had the situation under control. Another set of twins to add to the flock. Another set for Charlotte to lead astray.

Christmastime can even bring peace to the range wars.

Irene B. McDonald, who grew up in the Finger Lakes in New York, lives in Mobile. She earned a B.A. from SUNY (Albany) and an M.A. from the University of Wisconsin (Madison). Now a retired English teacher, she works with adult education at the University of South Alabama. She has published a book, *Language—All About It,* and has also published articles on Jane Austen in JASNA. Irene has enjoyed several federal grants that enabled her to spend a year studying Russian literature, a semester at Oxford, and a semester in Boise studying Victorian fiction.

Winter Light was inspired by a trip to Ireland where an archeologist lectured on Newgrange, which my husband and I visited. Having grown up in western New York's dark winters, I experienced the joy of anticipating spring, a feeling universal to all cultures.

Short Story

Winter Light

Irene B. McDonald

When the O'Donnells moved from California to Ireland, everybody joked that they were going back to their roots, though their grandfather and father, and even great-grandfather O'Donnell, had led happy lives, not in Ireland, but in Boise, Idaho.

Mr. O'Donnell's California computer firm was convinced it needed to open a European office. So here they were—Dan O'Donnell, his wife Maureen, and his three children, six-year-old Patrick, ten-year-old Maura, and twelve-year-old Sean—settled for a year, just outside Dublin, in a tidy village appropriately named Trim. Their names told everyone: we might be Idaho-Californians, but we're still Irish!

Because the firm hadn't considered the European Union and its attitude toward Americans, its profits were slow in coming, nobody's fault, really. But a new CEO decided to cost-cut. "Sorry to inform you...." he wrote, and in this way Mr. O'Donnell learned that his job was gone. In other words, as the locals put it, he was redundant. The letter arrived on the morning of December 19th. That evening he and his wife had a serious talk.

"What a Christmas present, Maureen, for you and the kids! It's at a time like this I wish I were single."

Patrick wasn't exactly eavesdropping. He'd never stoop that low. But he had sensed his dad's unhappiness, and with the concern of a sensitive child, he was about to rush into the living room to cheer him up. Maybe tell him a joke or two. Why can't elephants dance? Because they have two left feet. That sort of thing. Then be heard his father's bitter-sounding

113

words, "I wish I were single."

Suddenly he remembered the story of Hansel and Gretel, how their father, a poor woodcutter, could no longer provide them with food, and at the suggestion of his wife, took the kids in the woods to let them get lost. Of course, if Patrick had stopped to think, he would have remembered that in *Hansel and Gretel* the wife wasn't their real mother and that their own father was very, very unwilling to let them go. But Patrick didn't think. And so he didn't rush into the room to jump up on his father's lap and tell him a joke. Instead, he ran to Sean's room. Maura was already there. He could see they both looked worried.

"Should we go get lost in the woods?" Patrick suggested, vaguely aware that there were no woods around Trim. Well, maybe they could wander around the castle ruins he reasoned—there was a castle in Trim—and throw themselves in the dungeon. Their parents would return to California, unburdened. Of course, a good fairy or magician or even a green leprechaun would rescue them. Or maybe a friendly dinosaur.

Maura and Sean reacted to Patrick in their usual way. Such a puny little brother, so useless when it came to practical solutions.

"We could find the pot of gold at the end of the rainbow," Patrick suggested, playing his role to the hilt. After all, what were little brothers for? If they could only make dumb remarks, wasn't that the thing to do?

"Or find a gold hoard like some of the stuff we saw in the museum last year, gold collars and earrings and stuff. We could go out and dig up a bog somewhere."

Patrick, rarely at a loss for words, could keep up this line indefinitely.

"Or what about the hill of Tara? Don't you remember how Sean's book from Mr. Swann said that people were always hunting there for treasure?"

For the first time that night, his brother and sister laughed. Then Maura gave Patrick a soft shove. Sean whacked him with a pillow, but not too hard.

Despite its foolishness, Patrick's nonsense had its effect. Sean suddenly remembered the beech tree and the nearby cave he'd stumbled on a few weeks ago on his walk with Goldie, their Golden Retriever. He'd never told anyone, only Mr. Swann, his history tutor, who was interested in such things. Mr. Swann told him about these caves, cairns as he called them. They were very old, prehistoric, probably built well before the pyramids in Egypt, but nobody knew exactly why.

Could that cave or cairn contain a treasure? It was in a deserted spot. He doubted if anyone knew about it. He'd only found it because Goldie, chasing a rabbit, had dug away some ground, and then Sean had found that unusual stone, the one with strange spiral markings. But now he spoke cautiously. No sense in getting anybody's hopes up.

"Tomorrow after school let's explore to see what we can find. At least we can bring back some holly or evergreens to decorate for Christmas and try to get in the Christmas spirit."

They all agreed. Maura, The Practical, as she was known to one and all, offered to pack some food and see that they wore enough clothes and boots and woolen socks. In December, the fields of Ireland weren't like the California beaches. They'd discovered that early on.

By 4:30 the next afternoon they started their outing, Goldie leading the way proudly wagging her tail. Maura had left a neatly printed note: Gathering Christmas greenery. Back for supper.

They soon found the beech tree and the cave's entrance. Sean showed them the rock with the spirals. As they traced the designs with their mittened fingers, they sensed that the cave had some kind of magic in it, maybe even something to help their father. But no one said anything. It was the kind of feeling you kept to yourself.

Sean led the way, getting down on all fours to scramble through the small entrance. Patrick and Maura followed with Goldie who continued to sniff for rabbits. The narrow passageway was marked by upright stones. Suddenly Goldie caught a new scent. She zigzagged back and forth, returned to the narrow entrance, and began digging. She leaped up and down, scratched at the top of the cave, growled and whined.

"It's the gold hoard!" Patrick shouted. "And Goldie smells the scent of the dragon that used to guard it." He scratched his head and looked at Maura, "Can smells last that long? It must be at least 5,000 years old." The biggest number he could think of was a million, but it sounded too big. He needed something smaller, and he knew he must be close because he had overheard Sean and Mr. Swann talking about the caves.

When the O'Donnell children looked around, they found nothing but rocks, not any trace of a treasure. Goldie's frantic digging dislodged several small stones which fell across the entrance way. Suddenly a large bolder crashed down on the debris. Maura had brought a flashlight, or torch as she now called it after a year in Ireland. They examined what was once their entrance to the cave.

"I think we can push this mess out of the way," Sean said confidently.

They pushed against the stones as hard as they could. Goldie barked, jumped up and down, and dug furiously. Patrick slipped and banged his chin. The stones did not move. They pushed some more.

Sean still remained confident. "We'll just have to look for another way out. There must be one. Let's explore the cave a bit farther."

He sounded braver than he felt. He was glad Maura had a flashlight so he could see around him. But he didn't like the damp and cold feeling in the cave. He wished he'd brought some matches. A little fire would be nice.

They crawled along the passage, careful not to say what they were thinking. Sean worried about falling into a pit. Maura knew they'd stumble into a cache of moldering bones. Patrick was scared that instead of a gold hoard, they'd find a mess of snakes. Though people said St. Patrick had driven all the snakes out of Ireland, he knew his namesake—saint that he was—couldn't have truly gotten rid of *all* the snakes. A few clever critters must have survived—an occasional pithy python or a cunning cobra or two. He was sure they'd especially love a nice damp cave like this one.

They continued their slow, nervous crawl, and the three O'Donnell children found themselves in an open space. It was a kind of room, like a church sanctuary, the part by the altar. Even when they stood up, they still had plenty of headroom. Maura flashed her light around. They could see rocks piled up to form a tower. They had patterns cut into them. As Maura slowly moved the torch, its beams picked up the designs on individual rocks—swirls, vee-shaped chevrons, and diamonds. A few had circles decorated with petals and looked like a kindergartner's drawing of the sun.

But they saw no way out. They'd come to a dead end.

"Shine the torch all around and on the ceiling, Maura. Maybe some rocks have openings or are loosely fitted together," Sean said.

Maura made the light beam go up and down each rock. Patrick and Sean came closer to her and stood as still as the rocks towering around them. Even Goldie, for once, was quiet.

Suddenly the cave was dark.

Instinctively, the three children quickly locked hands and stood shoulder to shoulder.

"Maura, turn the torch back on," Patrick whispered.

"The battery's gone," Maura said. "I don't think I've ever put a new one in. It's gone dead."

Her last word echoed in the cave—*dead, dead, dead.*

Patrick, scared and feeling guilty because he'd brought them there, refused to cry. It was then that he saw a spot of light, a slender opening above the entrance.

"Look! I see a light!" He pointed even though it was dark.

"I see it!" Sean said.

"But it's not big enough to crawl through," Maura said.

But Patrick wasn't to be outdone. "I bet Goldie could get through if she squeezed a lot. And Sean can get her to do anything, at least most of the time. Give it a try, Sean. See if you can get Goldie to go through the hole."

Sean crawled back to the entrance and called to Goldie.

"Come on, Goldie. Here, girl! Here, girl!" But how

could he show her what to do? How could he get her to climb through the slit between the rocks?

Patrick knew how much Goldie liked singing. So he sang her favorite song, the one he'd been practicing all month with his choir at school.

"God rest ye mer-ry gentlemen, Let noth-ing you dismay," he sang as he sat down on the floor of the cave. Goldie nestled close. The other two children joined in: "O-oo tid-ings of comfort and joy."

They looked up. The light was clearly visible now, but night was not far off. Soon they would be in the dark again. Oh, if only dogs could understand human talk. Sean did his best, but Goldie wouldn't leave them. They couldn't get her to climb up on the rocks to the opening.

"If we could only get Goldie to leave," Maura said, "she'd bring back Dad. I don't mind staying here a while, but I've got to get home soon. Mom will need help with the Christmas cookies."

They tried. Oh, how they tried. Sean struggled to lift Goldie up to the slit. Maura carefully talked to her, explaining their dilemma. Patrick sang away. But Goldie, their ever faithful Goldie, would not leave them. Finally, Sean decided they would have to be mean.

"We'll have to do it," he said. "Sound mean. When I count to ten, yell at Goldie. Loud. Tell her to go home. First you, Maura. Then Patrick. You yell. Keep it up. I'll boost her up on the rocks and start to hit her."

Sean took a quick breath. "Okay. Let's go. One, two, three, four, five, six..."

He counted slower and slower. Finally he got to ten.

Maura shouted. Patrick screamed. And Sean lifted Goldie up to the slit in the rocks.

"Go home, Goldie! At once!" Maura shouted. Then added, "Please."

"Goldie, you're a bad dog!" Patrick screamed. "Bad dog. BAD dog! BAD DOG! YOU GO HOME, RIGHT NOW!"

When Goldie's body filled the slit, the cave was totally

dark again. Then suddenly, they could see the light and knew she was gone.

"I can't smell her either," said Patrick, wistfully. "I miss her breath, even though she needs mouthwash. A lot."

They talked about Goldie, and Mom and Dad, and Christmas and presents, and the tree, and Gramma and Grampa, and skiing in Idaho. How would Dad manage without a job? Would they ever see California again? Or even High Street in Trim? And the smiley lady in the bakery who gave them warm currant buns?

As darkness filled the cave, the children grew quiet. They huddled together and finally fell asleep. Sean leaned against a smooth stone. Maura, clutching her dead flashlight, rested against Sean, and Patrick curled up with his head on Maura's lap.

When Sean woke up, something was different. He saw a dazzling light. On the center stone in the big room was a sun design so bright it almost blinded him. Was it morning? How could sunlight shine like that in only one place?

Patrick and Maura stirred, opening their eyes. They too saw nothing but golden light reflecting off the stone. All at once Patrick began to sing, softly and slowly, "God rest ye mer-ry gentlemen, let noth-ing you dismay." The others joined in. "Remember Christ Our Savior was born on Christmas Day. O-oo tid-ings of com-fort and joy."

Many years later their father told his grandchildren their favorite Christmas story, in fact, their favorite story of all his stories—of which he had many. He told them how on the 21st of December, he raced through the green fields of Ireland following Goldie's zigzags. With him was Mr. Swann. As they came halfway through the field to a beech tree, they heard soft voices singing, "O-oo tid-ings of com-fort and joy, com-fort and joy. O-oo tid-ings of com-fort and joy."

Here Grampa O'Donnell always paused so long to clear his throat that his small listeners almost grew restless. But they stayed quiet. They wanted to hear the happy ending. They wanted to be part of the story in that mysterious place of dazzling light, to be there when their parents were small children and when everybody hugged and cried. They loved to hear about Goldie best of all. About how she jumped all over everybody again and again, licking their faces and wagging her tail until you would have thought it might drop off.

And Grandpa O'Donnell told them that not many years after Goldie had led him to his lost children, Mr. Swann had written about the mysterious cave, only he quite properly called it a cairn. Mr. Swann wrote in his book about the early builders and their evident knowledge of the winter sun, the winter solstice he called it. He described the designs on the rocks, and told how archaeologists guessed that all this had been made even before the Egyptian pyramids and may have been a way to mark the beginning of the new year. His book explained that the stones sparkled so brightly in the sunshine because they had white quartz on them.

And he gave full credit to the O'Donnell children from California for their remarkable discovery. Their picture, with Goldie of course, appeared on the back cover of a book that sold and sold and sold all over the world.

And then Mr. O'Donnell carefully pulled down that book, which most of the time resided high up in his best bookcase. He showed them the picture on the back cover, the picture of their parents, looking quite solemn as they hugged Goldie. He opened the book to page one, and they all recited along with him as he read those magic words.

"Winter light—the light mankind has always waited for, the light that comes to those who watch after the longest, darkest night of the year."

"Will it come to just about anybody who watches and waits?" A little fellow who looked so much like the little Patrick in the picture asked.

"Oh, most certainly," Mr. O'Donnell said. "That winter light will come to anyone and everyone. But they must wait and watch and always, always keep hope alive in their hearts."

"And maybe sing," the little one said, nodding his head.

"And maybe sing," Mr. O'Donnell agreed. "Oh, yes. Singing is always a good idea for those who wait and watch, especially if it's dark."

"Especially if it's pitch-black dark," added the little one. "Or anytime, like now."

And so they always finished up with their favorite song, the one Mr. O'Donnell and Mr. Swann, and Goldie, too, of course, had heard many years before as they rushed across the fields of Ireland in the winter light toward the big beech tree, "God rest ye mer-ry gentlemen, may noth-ing you dismay."

Mahala Church retired early from a career in healthcare and turned her attention to the art of writing. In her writing, she blends her education in Liberal Arts and Nursing with her love of the South. A 2008 Pushcart Prize nominee, her works appear in the *Emerald Ladies Journal, Sandscript, The Single Mother, Stumptail Monkey, Cup of Comfort for Grandparents, Encyclopedia of Alabama, and Christmas is a Season! 2008.*

Anything But Traditional is a fictional story dedicated to all the men and women who might feel tossed aside by those they love this Christmas. Although holidays often bring out the worst in all of us, holiday traditions serve as glue, holding families together and preserving their heritage. The story speaks of hope for the future at a time when personal loss appears overwhelming. In *Anything But Traditional*, a child leads the way out of despair.

Short Story

Anything But Traditional

Mahala Church

Shivering in the frosty emptiness of my living room, I watch the black night slip silently down the mountainside and the luminous dawn emerge over the mountain top. I know I should add more logs to the fireplace, but I'm mesmerized by the shifting colors in the sky and the beauty of the mountain as it reveals itself through my cathedral walls of glass. Wispy clouds scatter, while brush strokes of pastel pinks and baby blues blend across the canvas of a new Christmas morning.

From my roost on the top step of three that lead down to my bare living room, I huddle in the chilly silence, engulfed in sadness, while the birth of Christmas Day gently pours over the mountain, illuminating the deep greens of fir and cedar and pine. I sigh, disgusted that I'm watching this timeless miracle through a jaded eye. Normally I would be full of joy, watching Christmas force its way through the darkness, bringing the hope of yet another year filled with promise and tradition.

But this Christmas season has been anything but traditional for my family. It has been a season full of broken promises and discarded traditions.

Until now, the Christmas season had been my favorite time of year with its rich aromas, vibrant colors, and delightful days of sharing. Beginning with the first Christmas of my married life, I flocked every inch of our house with fragrant cedar and pine, and I embellished the house inside and out with yards of green and red ribbon, berries, and wreaths. Santa Clauses, angels, and candles of all sizes filled every corner of our mountainside home.

123

Every year our friends and neighbors poured into our home the first week of December for our tree-trimming party, which heralded the beginning of the glorious season. Decked out in their Christmas sweaters for the first time each year, they came ready to share in the pleasures of friendship and feasting.

Our Christmas tree, always twelve to fourteen feet high, had to be tethered to the wall with hooks to keep it steady as we drenched it with thousands of tiny, white lights, hundreds upon hundreds of ornaments, and my signature red and green checked bows. Finally, we topped it with our special angel, feathered wings spread wide, dressed in white velvet and pearls—our own elegant guardian.

I started baking and freezing deliciously decadent sweets in early November—cookies, cakes, fudges, and other candies—all ready to be packed into boxes for shipping to family and friends. Our house smelled like vanilla and butter for months.

The only sweet we were missing in the early years was a baby. Most of our friends had two or more children while we were mired in the wishing stages until eighteen months ago when our handsome son was born. His first Christmas was beyond anything I could have imagined. He loved the lights and grinned with happiness from head to toe when we carried him close to the tree. He didn't understand presents or why we celebrated the season in such grand style, but he loved to taste the goodies I baked. He reveled in the attention from our friends at a series of annual parties and rolled with glee in discarded wrapping paper and ribbons. His first Christmas morning, he saw only one thing, his *Talking Elmo.* He latched onto it and wouldn't let go. He giggled with delight when we squeezed Elmo's foot, engaging his recorded phrases to play over and over again.

Six months later, his first birthday party included Elmo plates and cups. He was thrilled with the birthday party—hats, streamers, balloons—and cried when everyone left. He wanted the celebration to go on forever. But the party was over.

My husband followed me around as I busily cleared away drooping streamers, bowls of melted ice cream, and deflated balloons. To my surprise, he told me he preferred the heat of the seaside to the cool of the mountains. He favored a walk on the beach to a hike in the woods. And most importantly, he fancied his partner's wife over me. I sat down when he made his last announcement. He told me he hadn't realized how much a child would alter our lives, and he didn't like the changes.

I cringed when he said *alter.*

"Wiping sticky fingers and a moist nose is repulsive," he stated matter-of-factly.

My six months of grieving started that afternoon while I watched the sun disappear in a last burst of gold behind the mountain. My ego became encumbered with a long list of *should-haves:* I should have known when he said it made him nauseous to watch me nurse the baby. I should have known when he refused to change a diaper. I should have known when he steadfastly refused to eat at the same table while our son was being fed.

He insisted we have our dinner after the baby had eaten and been put to bed, but gradually I was too exhausted at the end of the day to eat my dinner at nine. I needed to be in bed by then after a long day of parenting, housekeeping, and managing my on-line editing business. I tried to nap while our son was napping, but my West Coast clients were just starting their work day as I was lying down to rest. I couldn't afford for them to become annoyed by any delays on my part. My husband's law practice was floundering, and I needed to hang onto my lucrative business. So I ate at six with our son and left my husband's meal covered in foil in the warming drawer of the oven. Worn to a frazzle, I rarely heard him come home at night.

I stood at our bedroom door and watched him mutely pack his suitcases that afternoon. "Could you at least try to explain why you're moving out? I think ten years of marriage has earned me that courtesy," I finally managed to say.

"Don't edit what I'm saying here," he said, piling socks in a duffel bag. "I don't want to hear the silence of these Godforsaken mountains another minute. I don't want to smell another dung-filled diaper. I don't want to be entombed in red and green for another Christmas."

I cringed at the word *entombed*.

"I don't want to smell another sugar cookie baking. I never want to eat another bowl of homemade vegetable soup or a slice of apple pie from scratch, whatever the hell that means."

And he grabbed his coat and was gone.

He was right. Our lives *were* altered.

In the divorce papers, he asked for half the profit from selling our house and gave me full custody of our son. The papers, in eloquent legalese, stated firmly that he had no interest in raising our child. He practically dared me to file for child support or alimony. I didn't. Being an albatross is not my idea of a healthy relationship. Occasionally, I imagine him sitting at a seaside restaurant, eating steamed crabs and boiled shrimp with key lime pie for dessert.

I found out a week after he left that his partner's wife had gone with him. His partner never came by or called, just took a pistol a few weeks later and wordlessly went into the woods and ended his life.

I added him to my *should-have* list. I should have known how humiliated he was. I should have contacted him after they left. I should have invited him over for vegetable soup.

My stupor lifts as I glance at the section of glass in the cathedral wall that was replaced a few months ago after a vicious storm. A huge branch crashed through, saturating the carpet with shattered glass and pouring rain. I had no interest in replacing the ruined carpet, so I used a box cutter and sliced it into smaller pieces that I could drag, then hauled it away to the dump. I gaze around the room where we celebrated ten years of brightly colored, Dickensian Christmases. It is now an austere room with cold, gray cement floors.

I tried to ignore Christmas this year, but I found I couldn't do that to my son. He wouldn't know the difference, but I would. I did my best in the midst of feeling anger and grief. I covered a small patch of the icy cement in the living room with a round, green, braided rug from the guest room. I sat my oak rocker next to the rug. I bought a white, five-foot, artificial tree from the local thrift shop. It was missing the base, so I put it in the mop bucket and filled around it with wet dirt to hold it upright. In an odd twist of tradition, I have to remember to water it every day or it leans.

Tomorrow my son and I are moving to a smaller cabin on the mountain ridge. Thankfully, I have my business and can provide us a new place to live.

I sold nearly everything in a mammoth yard sale, but I kept back some emerald green ornaments, a couple of strands of twinkling white lights, a roll of green ribbon, and the white velvet angel, which I hope will create just enough delight for my son. I baked a batch of sugar cookie snowmen as a last hurrah to my country-sized kitchen and decorated them with butter icing and sprinkles. My son smeared himself as he licked the icing off first and enjoyed every bite. I lovingly washed his hands and face.

I hear the rustling of footed pajamas as the bright, winter sun lifts over the mountain top.

"Mommie! Mommie!" My son squeals as he runs down the hall, arms wide for me to pick him up. He stops in his tracks and stares at our Christmas tree unaware of the rocking horse a local carpenter made for him or the bright red rocking chair with his name painted on it. He sees only the beauty of Christmas in that pitiful tree.

"Pret-eee," he coos, snuggling into my arms.

"Merry Christmas, little man!" I pull him close in a big hug, so he can't see my tears. We cuddle for a few quiet moments admiring our special tree, and I drink in the smells of little boy that start to defrost my heart. Then he wiggles free and is off to admire his new wonders. I smile as the sun's rays make our white tree sparkle. I smile at the warm happiness alive in my son's face.

Next year, I'll fill our small cabin with loads of fragrant cedar and pine. We'll cover every inch of space with my signature red and green checked ribbons and light scented candles by the dozen. Rudolph will adorn my son's room again, and I'll fill our cozy cabin with the smells of vegetable soup, sugar cookies, and mint fudge. Christmas, the most cherished time of the year, is here again with all its resplendent joy and tradition.

Stefanie Wass, M.Ed., lives in Hudson, Ohio with her husband and two girls. As a freelancer, her essays have been published in *The Los Angeles Times*, *Seattle Times*, *Christian Science Monitor*, *Akron Beacon Journal*, *Akron Life and Leisure*, *Cleveland Magazine*, *Cup of Comfort for Mothers*, *Cup of Comfort for a Better World*, and five *Chicken Soup for the Soul* anthologies. Stefanie is a member of the Society of Children's Book Writers and Illustrators and is currently seeking representation for her first middle grade novel.

Stefanie's website: www.stefaniewass.com

Christmas Elf honors my husband, a man who not only embraces the spirit of Christmas, but also remembers to share it with others. It's not often that one encounters an elf—someone whose boundless energy infuses the season with laughter and love.

Personal Essay

Christmas Elf

Stefanie Wass

Need a hand around the house this holiday season? Someone to clean, wrap presents, and cook Christmas dinner? At my house, I have a Christmas elf—a magical guy infused with the season's spirit. With his help, I manage to make my way through tinsel and trappings, finding peace and meaning despite December's maddening pace.

My elf first appears at Thanksgiving each year. He helps bundle my two girls in jackets and mittens and then takes them on a wagon ride deep into the snow-covered Western Pennsylvania woods.

"Let's go pick out some greens for our wreath!" he gushes, jumping off the wooden wagon as it stops deep in an evergreen forest. As the girls gather pine boughs from the forest floor, the elf dashes about, bounding through the snow like an excited young fawn. "Look over here! Holly berries!" he calls. The girls' faces shine like holiday lights, glowing and ruby red.

"Can I help make our wreath this year?" my eldest asks, knowing full well the elf's standard response to all things Christmas: "Why, of course!"

Later in my uncle's barn, the elf sets to work helping my aunts and cousins thread pine boughs though metal wreath forms. "You can help make one, too," he assures my daughter, helping her add crimson berries and bright red felt bows to her creation. Smiling easily, he seems at home in this workshop, accepting the season with skillful, open arms. An hour later, my wreath is finished: a circle of Christmas love intertwined in fragrant, fresh pine.

131

By the first of December, our holiday helper kicks into high gear. "Time to get out the decorations!" he announces, ascending from our basement storage rooms with bins labeled Ornaments, Holiday Books and Music, and Christmas Crafts. Magically, the CD player, which I cannot ever get to work properly, starts playing Bing Crosby's *White Christmas* and Anne Murray's *Christmas Favorites*.

"Hurray! It's time to get out all the stuff!" The girls instantly start rummaging through candy-cane scented candles and tangled tree lights. Soon, they unearth treasures: plastic Santa-face stamps with red and green ink pads, golden jingle bell necklaces, and an oversized, stuffed gingerbread man. I stand back, feeling stress rise from the bins of decorations to my already aching head.

As I reach for a Tylenol, the elf whistles a tune, already having strung half the banister with imitation pine garland. *How did he hide those green twisty ties? They've vanished under boughs of plastic pine.*

"There! Looks nice, right?" he asks. I nod, amazed at his good cheer.

"Want to take a break?" I ask, hopeful for a bit of eggnog to ward off my throbbing headache. It pounds more than ever when I think of what's left to do: Christmas cards, shopping, meal planning, four recitals, three parties, and at least one cookie exchange.

"I want to get the outside lights on before it gets dark," he says. "Why don't you just come out after a few minutes and see how I'm doing?"

Shortly, the front porch twinkles. The doorframe, outlined in pine garland and glittery white lights, makes the perfect backdrop for my homemade wreath. A mechanical deer, complete with glowing red nose, softly paws the snow-covered yard. Two small evergreens, runty stumps guarding the front steps, now seem majestic, even proud, like a teenager illuminated by a little makeup. They seem to smile with their newfound importance. I smile as well, my Scrooge-like attitude melting under the season's radiance.

A few days later, my special elf hands me a gift-giving list, outlining possible purchases and shopping locales. "I think three presents per person is fine for this year," the elf says with a nod toward the troubled economy. "I'll shop for your mother, so you don't have to worry about that." A week later, *Simple Abundance*, a book of devotions, arrives from Amazon—a perfect fit for my spiritually-minded mom.

"Look what I found for the girls," he says after one shopping trip. He crinkles open several plastic bags filled with miniature-sized doll clothing.

"Take a look at this dude hat!" He laughs as he unwraps a small black beanie with the words *Dude* inscribed on the front. "This will fit perfectly on either the Webkinz Gecko or the Cheeky Monkey!"

Our girls, avid collectors of Webkinz stuffed animals, will be thrilled. I feel light and giddy, the burden of long lines and crowded shopping malls magically lifted from my shoulders.

One evening after the girls are in bed, the elf cranks up the radio and pours each of us a glass of Christmas cheer. Merlot, it turns out, helps gift wrapping speed. He sets up shop: a rainbow of ribbons, six tubes of festive wrapping paper, and eight rolls of Scotch tape.

"I'll wrap everything if you'll do the bow and labels," he suggests, already cutting a piece of red Elmo paper for my nephew's new Matchbox cars.

"Ho! Ho! Ho!" I write on the tags, amazed at my revelry. Maybe it's the Merlot or the carols playing on the kitchen radio, but despite the snowstorm raging outside, I feel warm and surprisingly settled. I take another sip of wine and soak up this Norman Rockwell-like moment. At my core, I am grateful for this evening, this season, and my exuberant elf.

To me, an elf is worlds better than Santa. Santa does not address Christmas cards, print ink jet, alphabetized labels, or purchase postage stamps. "I wasn't sure if you wanted Madonna and Child or Snowmen, so I got plenty of both," the elf says, avoiding any possible hassles.

Santa does not shop, wrap, and mail packages to far-flung relatives, weeks ahead of the big day. "I'll just stop by the post office during lunch," my able assistant smiles, throwing two boxes in the back of the SUV.

I am pretty sure Santa does not agree to walk miles upon miles through the snow-covered woods to select and chop down the perfect Christmas tree—Blue Spruce, over six feet tall, with a pointy, angel-worthy top branch.

Even if Santa does chop down a fresh tree, I am pretty sure he has help with the decorating phase. My elf, donning white surgical gloves for protection from prickly pine branches, insists on stringing the lights himself. I join him for the fun part—ornament and tinsel hanging. As I hang a glitter-covered Popsicle stick star, I think about my children. How lucky they are to be exposed to the elf's selfless giving.

Sitting down to Christmas Eve dinner—sautéed scallops and jumbo shrimp atop a bed of garlic mashed potatoes, I feel a little guilty. As usual, my holiday helper cooked a delectable feast. My contribution, a bag of pre-washed salad greens tossed with cranberries and pecans, looks sophomoric next to his artistically designed seafood. Fresh carrots jut out from the potatoes, a tower of goodness presented with flair.

"You outdid yourself again this year," my mom raves. I smile, but I am not fooling anyone. My secret is out: Elfin magic, delivered by a generous guy I deeply love.

Wearing khaki Dockers and a brown wool sweater, my elf looks surprisingly ordinary. No green tights or pointy shoes for this guy. Standing just over six feet tall, he doesn't fit the image of a munchkin or diminutive sprite. In fact, he looks like a middle-aged dad. As I spy a few wispy, white hairs on top of his head, I make a holiday wish: may we grow old together, sharing Christmas cheer for many years to come.

Years ago, I made the wisest decision of all: I married an elf. I couldn't survive the season without his boundless energy and loving heart.

J.D. Frost graduated from the University of Alabama at Birmingham. He is a member of the Coffee Tree Fiction Writers in Huntsville. He enjoys life with his wife, Donna, and son, David.

I write mysteries. That's not an easy well to draw from if you have the urge to write a Christmas story—which I did. *Snow Angel* is a reminder that not everyone is snug and warm on Christmas Eve. Some of us are in peril, and help sometimes comes from the most unlikely sources.

Short Story

The Snow Angel

J.D. Frost

Norm couldn't see any ice on the bridge in the center of the causeway. He held tight and let the cruiser roll on across. Lights danced off the choppy waters of the lake. Triangle Texaco was open. Until now, he'd thought all of Guntersville was closed. It was good to know someone else was at work. Nothing worse than being alone on Christmas Eve. He turned into the Triangle's parking lot and stopped at the ice bin—not a good spot on this night.

Frigid air came off the water. He pushed the pile collar on his puffy, nylon jacket higher. Though only steps from the door, he pinched the shiny bill of his service hat and sat it lower. His thin khaki pants felt like a tennis net against the piercing wind. He hurried inside.

"Deputy Fontaine," the woman behind the counter greeted him. She glanced at the closing door. The cold rushed in. "It's not fit to be out, is it?"

"No, it's not, Irene. This isn't like Alabama. My cruiser is warm enough, but a man on foot couldn't stand this long."

He stepped to the end of the counter and stripped off his gloves. "Everybody else is closed. I was surprised to find you here."

"People need gas and fresh coffee, especially on a night like this." She tucked red hair behind her ear, a lock that had strayed from her short ponytail.

Norm pulled a Styrofoam cup from the dispenser and placed it on the steel counter. He filled it with black coffee.

Irene went on, "Plus, why would I want off? Everyone in my life lives too far away, has left me, or is dead." As she

137

talked, she squinted through her bifocals at the cash register tape. "Christmas is for children, I guess. I love watching the little ones, but my sister's kids are grown, and I don't have any of my own."

"Where's Ajamian?" Norm asked, referring to the store's owner.

"I don't know, but you didn't think he was going to work tonight, did you? Just because he isn't Christian don't mean he won't take Christmas Eve off. No, I'll be pulling a double, getting off at six in the morning. Where's your boss?" She smiled.

"He and Mildred have gone to Florence to visit her folks." Norm knew Sheriff Loyd Johnson could go any place he pleased. He'd won four straight terms, destroying his opponent each time. If he wanted it, the job was his for life—people in the community had become that comfortable with him in the office.

"Well, he can't sheriff from up there. That means you're it—don't it?" Irene knew the chain of command as well as people on the force.

"That means I'm it. Acting sheriff." He didn't mind riding in the cruiser. Ticketing or serving papers didn't bother him, but he had no interest in bossing people around.

"Not much happening anyway," he told Irene. Just as he spoke, the phone on his belt buzzed twice.

He snapped it from its carrier. "Fontaine."

"Norm, I need you to 10-21r." The state of Alabama, following the lead of many other states, had directed everyone to use plain English instead of codes, but Wallace, perhaps out of habit or a sly sense of rebellion, found it easier to say 10-21r than "call the office." He pictured Wallace at the old metal desk, his Ichabod Crane profile hunched over the mic, intent on doing things his way.

Norm snapped the phone back on his belt. He dug a dollar out, threw it on the counter, and started for the door.

"Come back in a couple of hours," Irene told him, as he pushed through the door. "Maybe I'll find some eggnog."

Snow had started. The small icy flakes, driven by the

wind, streaked horizontally. Inside the car, he laid his gloves on the seat and dialed. "What you got?" he asked when Wallace picked up.

"I got a call a few minutes ago, sounded like a young girl. Said she left a baby in Shoreline Park. Then she just hung up—didn't leave a name or any information. We don't even have a Shoreline Park, do we Norm?"

"Patch in that call." It was simpler to listen to the call than to get details from Wallace.

He heard two clicks and then a young woman's voice. *I left my baby in Shoreline Park ten minutes ago. I can't take care of it. I don't want it, so don't bother trying to find me.* The young woman was crying, and the phrases came out between sobs and gasps. And just like that, the call ended.

"You think she means out by the state park?" Wallace was back on the line. For several miles, the state park bordered Guntersville Lake.

"Yes," Norm replied. "Did you get a number?"

"Yeah, she called from a pay phone in that plaza at the bottom of the mountain. You got the projects on one side, apartment city on the other, and the hotels are right there. She could've been from any of them."

"How many units we have on patrol?"

"Five, not counting you."

"Send three of them over to meet me at the state park campground entrance." The campground was a well known spot. It was also the start of a long run where the park and the shore of the lake touched.

"Send another car to the plaza where the call came from. If she's not there, tell him to cruise through those neighborhoods."

"Sheriff," Wallace said—Norm felt awkward at the use of the title—"my thermometer says eleven degrees. How long can a baby last out in this?"

"I don't know. Send me those units."

Norm flipped on his emergency lights but left the siren off. He drove quickly along 431. He turned right on Lusk Street, which morphed into Highway 227. Beyond the last residential area, fancy houses on hilly lots, the road dropped to the bottom of the mountain and snaked its way through the state park. Where the pavement leveled, there were signs, wooden arrows with destinations carved in them. One pointed toward Guntersville State Park Campground.

No one was on the road. He couldn't imagine anyone camping on Christmas Eve, especially on a night when an unforgiving cold front hovered over the area.

The edge of the water came up in his headlights on the left. He pulled over and reached for the hand-held spotlight mounted in the rack underneath the dash. He rolled his window down and flicked it on.

With the window lowered and driving slowly, he swept the bright light across the grassy area between the road and the water's edge. Snow was accumulating, but blades of grass were still peaking through the white. At the pier, he pulled into the parking area, turned the headlights off, and exited the car. Using his flashlight, he looked around the pier and the barbecue pit. He listened for some sound of life, but there was only the wind-blown water lapping at the shore. In the shallows at the edge of the lake, ice was forming. He hoped the mother had at least wrapped the baby.

Three patrol cars broke through the trees, their blue lights flashing. By the time he had returned to his vehicle, the officers had parked and were out of their cruisers.

"You see anything?" Lyons asked.

"No, but I've only looked here," Norm answered. "Wallace told you about the call?"

"Yeah, a baby left out in this," Lyons answered. "How long you think it will last?"

"It's probably a newborn. That's usually the case. So, I'd say we don't have a lot of time. Lyons, you and I will take the camping area. Drive to the other end of the camp sites. Start there and we'll meet in the middle. We'll have to do it on foot."

He looked at the other officers, "Williams, you and Hendricks go to Town Creek. Start at that bait shop and search the picnic area that runs from there to the end of the park.

You'll have to do it from the cars. Use your search lights, keep your window down and listen."

Each man headed toward his assigned territory. Norm parked at the gate. He saw the tire tracks Lyons had left, driving to the opposite end of the camping area. As expected on Christmas Eve, the guard house at the campground entrance was empty. Before getting out of the car, Norm dialed the office.

"Get Lister with the Rescue Squad on the phone," he instructed Wallace. "Have him call me. We need some volunteers to search along the lake near the hotels."

"They won't like that," Wallace replied. "Christmas Eve and all."

This being his first day in command, Norm didn't want to unload on Wallace. "No time to consider that. We've got a freezing baby." How Wallace could speak for the Rescue Squad, Norm didn't know. Personally, he'd always found them to be a dedicated, helpful group.

He directed his light along the grass and at the trash barrels that hung in pairs from a center post. He took a quick look in each bathroom. Norm could see Lyons in the distance, his light making the same sweeping motions. Neither of them had found anything. An hour and five minutes had past since he left the Texaco.

He called Wallace again. As he waited for the dispatcher to pick up, he considered the snow. In the back water, the wind had died down, but snowflakes big as saucers were floating to the ground. He heard Wallace. "What happened with the rescue squad?" he asked.

"Lister lives on the brow," Wallace answered. "It's iced up there. He put the Rescue Squad truck in the ditch trying to leave his driveway."

Norm wondered if the dispatcher had ignored or forgotten his request to have Lister call him.

"Lister's calling some of the guys in the valley," Wallace said. "They're supposed to call me back."

"When you hear from them, have whoever's in charge call me. Got it?"

"Got it," Wallace answered. "Hey, the temperature's dropping fast out there. It's nine degrees now."

"Play that tape again," Norm instructed, ignoring the comment about the temperature. Wallace didn't have to tell Norm it was cold—he was standing out in it.

As he listened closely to the tape, he remembered a paved walking path by the Highway 69 causeway. Maybe that was where she meant. It was a possibility. At the same time, someone needed to search the shoreline near the hotels. The walking park lay on the far side of the city. There was no way he could do both. Maybe the rescue squad would reach the hotels. He'd try the walking park.

Lyons was at his side now. Norm quickly described the park near the causeway on the other side of the business district. Lyons followed him out of the park. Norm switched on his running lights now and his siren. They were almost out of time. In his rear-view, he saw clouds of flakes billowing behind his car and Lyons dropping back, almost out of sight.

Norm braked at the causeway and turned left on Sunset Drive. He passed the recreation center and the tennis courts before pulling into the small parking lot where the walking trails began.

Lyons rolled to a stop beside his car. Both their windows went down. "Go across Highway 69 and search west. The trail wanders over there too. Go past the school, all the way to the end of it," Norm yelled toward Lyons, raising his voice over the engines and the wind, blowing hard near the water.

Lyons was gone. Norm grabbed two flashlights. His phone rang. He laid one light down and wrestled the phone from his belt. Maybe it was Lister.

"Norm?" Wallace said.

"Go ahead." He turned away from the wind.

"They've got two feet up in Florence. No let up, and it's coming this way. Do you want me to get Sheriff Johnson on the line for you?"

Norm doubted the dispatcher was listening to Florence weather on the radio—no doubt he had already talked to Loyd

Johnson.

"No need to call Sheriff Johnson," Norm said. "Has Lister called back?"

"Haven't heard from him."

"Get him on the phone. Tell him to light a fire under the guys in the city. I need those volunteers on the lake shore near the hotels. After you do that, contact Williams and Hendricks. When they're finished out by Town Creek, send them over to the hotels."

"Norm?"

"Yes."

"I called the hospital. The ER doc said a baby wouldn't last more than an hour in this."

"Just get Lister and the other officers."

He left the car idling, the blue light turning, and the headlights on. He started a sweeping motion with one of the flashlights, keeping the second light in his belt as a spare. From the street to the water was seventy-five feet. He couldn't walk the middle and see the curb and the shoreline. He decided to weave through the area, using the trash receptacles to mark his progress. He began at an angle from the street toward the walking trail.

Small concrete drains formed little scooped-out areas at the end of each section of trail. These little hollowed-out places made only slight depressions in the blanket of snow. All the pine cones, fallen branches, and everything on the ground was covered in billowy white. Norm saw something up ahead at the end of a section of trail.

As he approached, he heard a series of small sounds. He directed the beam of his flashlight toward whatever it was on the ground. That's when he saw it—the baby in one of the little depressions. He saw something else too, a small dog beside the baby.

"Hey fellow," Norm said in a calm voice, not wanting to rile the dog as he approached the baby. The dog only whimpered. Norm squatted. Perhaps the mother had laid the baby in this little scooped-out place, hoping it would afford some shelter from the wind. There was no blanket over the baby. The newborn was wrapped in two towels.

The baby's brows were pinched in a pained expression, but it wasn't crying. The sounds were coming from the small white dog, whose soft underbelly cradled against the tiny baby. "Good fellow," Norm said to the dog, and he lifted the baby in his arms.

"Good, good fellow," Norm cooed again to the dog. The dog stood and danced at the officer's feet, letting out two quick barks.

The baby had the tightly closed eyes of a newborn. Norm looked at the baby's face, a purplish color from the cold with lips more blue than red. He wrapped his arms around the bundle and jogged to the car, the dog yapping at his heels.

Norm slipped into the passenger seat of the cruiser. He turned the heat up and pulled his phone from its carrier. He called Wallace. Outside, the dog jumped, leaping for a peek in the window.

"Get me an ambulance out here on east Sunset Drive. I've got the baby. Tell Lyons to get over here." Norm held the baby against his chest.

"Alive?" Wallace asked.

"Alive. Get me that ambulance!"

Soon Lyons was there, standing beside the cruiser where Norm sat with the baby wrapped in his coat and the heater blasting on high. Ten minutes later the ambulance arrived.

Then, everything happened fast. A medic took the baby and rushed it to the emergency vehicle. The deputies could only watch now. In minutes, the ambulance lights were flashing, and the baby was gone.

Norm lifted the small dog while he and Lyons stood watching the flashing lights of the ambulance until it turned off Sunset and disappeared.

"You gonna take that dog?" Lyons asked.

"I got him," Norm said.

The two officers parted in opposite directions, walking to their cars. Norm looked down at the dog in his arms. He scratched the dog's ears. "If not for you, fellow, that baby would be dead.

Inside his cruiser, Norm switched on his overhead light. "Where's your collar?" He rubbed the dog's bare neck. "You must belong to someone. White as you are, don't you know you'll get lost in this snow?"

The dog hopped over to the passenger seat, surveying the landscape through the windshield and the side window. It appeared completely comfortable, as if riding in a sheriff's cruiser was standard fare.

Driving along Gunter Avenue, Norm saw the lights of Triangle Texaco still burning brightly. He parked again by the undisturbed ice in the ice freezer. He held the car door and waited for the dog to hop out his side. At the entrance to the store, he slipped through leaving the dog on the other side of the glass.

"Who's your little friend?" Irene asked.

"That's an angel," Norm responded. "A Christmas angel. Let me have two of those hot dogs and one bun, plain."

"That dog does looks like a snow angel, all that white. Let that little dog in. It's not like we're being swamped with customers here. I'm betting you want those hot dogs plain too," Irene said as she handed him two of the roasted wieners.

Norm opened the door, and the little dog bounded inside. The Sheriff broke one of the hot dogs and half the bread and let the pieces fall onto the tile floor. The dog ate quickly and looked up expectantly. Norm broke off another piece of hot dog and tossed it to him.

"Either you're one good tosser or that dog's a great catcher," Irene said and laughed.

Norm was about to toss a little of the remaining wiener when his phone rang.

"Sheriff," Wallace said, "I'm patching a call to you. Just a little problem this time."

"Fontaine here."

"Yes. I've lost my dog," a man's voice said. "I couldn't believe what she did. We were out for our usual evening walk right before it started to snow, and she just pulled out of her collar and took off. She's never done that."

"A little white dog, short legs and a long body?"

"Yeah, that's her. She answers to the name of Maddie."

"Maddie?" Norm questioned. He kneeled and patted the dog's head. "So you're a little lady," he whispered to the dog. A real little angel." The dog's tail went into rapid motion.

"I have her," Norm said. "We're at Triangle Texaco."

"We can't get out now. We're snowed in."

"Don't worry," Norm said. "I'll give her a ride home. We may be a few minutes though."

After Norm completed his call, Irene poured him a cup of coffee. Norm leaned against the counter and told her the story of the baby and Maddie, who was indeed a Christmas angel.

Delores (Dee) Jordan, a retired schoolteacher, recently published her first novel, *In and Out of Madness,* under the pen name N. L. Snowden. The novel is available on Amazon, Barnes and Noble online, and from Sneakaboard Press. Dee writes a column about the life of a published author for a California e-zine called *Active Voice.* She also does book reviews for the *Alabama Writers' Forum Online,* and she writes articles dealing with mental illness for *New York City Voices.*

Burning of the Yule Log emerged from my struggle with bitter feelings after my divorce. I attended church and did indeed have a miraculous healing of my broken heart. I've turned my experiences into fiction and added a few strange twists to the season as the protagonist and her daughter give gifts to Odin, burn the Yule Log, and cope with much personal misery.

Short Story

Burning of the Yule Log

Delores (Dee) Jordan

I wanted no part of Christmas that year. I didn't want to remember our family traditions, and I didn't want to worship a God who had heaped such misery upon me. I drifted back from the mailbox turning over what was obviously my first Christmas card of the season addressed to Bob and Helen Strange. I didn't have the heart to open it and see the smiling faces of the George family with their bragging letter of how wonderful the past year had been. In fact, as I walked by the trashcan, I ditched it.

Bob, my husband of twenty-five years, had left me for a younger woman and cleaned out our bank account. Since both of our names were on the account, it was legal and there was nothing I could do about it. As if things weren't sorry enough, I had to call my daughter and tell her I had more bad news—I had ovarian cancer.

The doctors had stressed the importance of positive thinking in order for my body's immune system to aid in treating my cancer, but how could I think positively when I looked at the world through a waterfall of constant tears? Nothing was as it should be, even my vision made things out of focus or doubled the images.

My world had collapsed.

When Sarah came home from college, it would be even more of a shock—the obvious empty chair at our Christmas dinner table, the lack of a video camera capturing us as we opened the presents, and that famous grin on her father's face. I just couldn't face trying to fit the square of our lives now into the circle of what it used to be.

149

"Sarah, we won't be celebrating Christmas this year."

"Mom, that's okay. I don't feel much like having Christmas with Daddy gone anyway." When I didn't respond, she said, "Mom, are you okay? Something besides Daddy's leaving is bothering you. I hear it in your voice."

The question made me realize the complete magnitude of my misery, and I broke down crying. Between gulps, I managed to get out, "Honey, I've been to the doctor, and he told me I've got ovarian cancer. You know how I feel about chemo and the horrors of the treatments. I'm opting out and going to live my life the best I can for as long as I can without the effects of chemo and radiation making me sicker."

"No, Mom, please...for me, please go through the treatments. I've lost Dad. I couldn't bear losing you too."

All my fears of needles and throwing up melted with that plea from my daughter. She was right. I was being selfish and not thinking of her. Trouble was, even with the treatments, no one could guarantee me a long life.

"Sarah, you know how I hate—"

"Mom, call me Randgrith, my Asatru name. I'll be strong enough for both of us. Please give yourself a chance."

"A chance at what? Crying all of the time because I'm so lonely and jealous?"

Despite my words, I knew I had to make an honest attempt to live, for her sake if nothing else. "Okay, you win. I'll do the chemo, Sarah—I mean Randgrith. I'll call you by that name, but you'll always be Sarah to me. Will you pray to Odin for me? My God has written me off and no longer hears my prayers."

I'm an Episcopalian, and I don't believe in the Bible literally. At that moment, I didn't believe in any part of it. It was just a bunch of myths like the Viking myths of the Asatru or the Greek and Roman myths.

"Of course I will, Mom. Listen, I know things are going badly for you right now, but I have a big favor to ask of you."

"I can't make any promises now," I said, "but go on and ask me."

"On the twenty-second through the twenty-fourth of the month, a few of my friends from high school want to rent a cabin in the mountains and have a reunion. I can't believe it's been over a year since I graduated."

Was she going to come home and then leave me alone? How could she?

Then I remembered that she was young and living her life in spite of everything, even the news that I had cancer. A perpetual optimist, she probably figured that the treatments would actually cure me. I loved her enough not to dash all her hopes and ruin her holiday.

"Okay, but make sure you won't drink and drive. Stay at the cabin and party. Don't get in a car with anyone drinking."

"God, Mom, I'm not sixteen. You know I'm responsible. Quit preaching to me."

With a quiver in my voice, I said, "Okay, you can go."

"I'm sorry I fussed at you, Mom. I know this has been hard on you, but please try to stop focusing on the negatives. Focus on what you have that many mothers would give anything to have—a daughter who loves you and respects you."

I realized she was right, and I also realized the perfect way to show her how much I appreciated having a wonderful daughter like her. I was a Christian, but Sarah declared herself a pagan, so I decided that before she went on her trip, we would celebrate the lighting of the Yule log on the Winter Solstice, a very big Asatru event that praised Odin for his favors. I figured it would really help her through the holiday season and would help bolster my attitude. A pagan god was better than no god. She'd never bought the Bible thing anyway. Maybe she had been right all along. Her religion had imperfect gods and goddesses that messed up all of the time. I liked that. How could anyone say God was perfect when marriages ended and He allowed people's lives to be cut short?

"Thank you, honey. When you get home for the holidays, I have a big surprise for you. I think you're going to love it."

"Come on, Mom. I need some good news now. Tell me."

"Okay, baby. When you get here, we're going to decorate and burn a Yule log on the Winter Solstice and do away with all that Christmas crap."

"Oh, Mom, you're the best! Can I invite some of my Asatru friends over for the celebration?"

"Sure. I love you, Randgrith, more than you will ever know."

"I love you too, Mom."

We never hung up the phone without saying we loved each another.

Most Christians don't know that Yule Tidings are an old Viking tradition. I knew that these two things would make this so much easier on Randgrith. She'd wanted to share her religion with me, and now she could. Our holiday celebration would be more like a *sumbel* where there would be a lot of bragging and gift giving to Odin. Being with her friends at Christmas would help remove the sting of her father's abandoning us.

Since she didn't arrive until the twentieth, we had a lot to prepare for the Yule celebration before the Winter Solstice on the twenty-first. First, we had to find a log big enough to burn for twelve hours. In the days of old, the log had to measure in size big enough to burn for twelve days, not twelve hours. Second, we'd have to make the log acceptable to Odin by decorating it before we burned it. Sarah would be tired from the long drive back home, but celebrating Yule would energize her.

As she walked through the living room, I watched her freeze before going to her room to put away her things. I saw her shoulders shake and knew that seeing her father's recliner missing from the room brought home the truth that he was indeed gone. Of course, this unleashed a new open faucet of tears from me. Watching my daughter's pain was worse than the pain I'd felt at losing him.

"Randgrith, this is why we'll not do Christmas ever again. I want to share your religion, but mainly I don't want to endure mine and all the emptiness it now represents."

She turned to me and we held each other, each lost in our memories of her father—both good and bad.

"Put your things in your room, then let's go to the woods and get our log."

I worried that we'd not be able to drag the Yule log out of the woods, especially with both of us so defeated emotionally. Then I remembered: By damn, we were two strong women, weren't we? We both vowed not to shed another tear over the man who'd deserted us. We got up, dressed in layers because it was cold outside, and headed out.

Inside the dusty barn that smelled of sweet hay and horse manure, we grabbed ropes, halters, nails, and a hammer. We walked out into the cool, crisp air and trekked to the woods to look for *the* perfect log. Of course, our curious horses followed us, along with three dogs and our pot-bellied pig that thought he was a dog.

Deep inside the woods, we spotted it, an omen that we were on the right track. Most fallen trees are long and thin, but this one answered the call of destiny. Obviously, the log used to be the trunk of a good-sized tree, so it would definitely burn for twelve hours. However, we knew immediately that we would never be able to drag it to the house.

Fortunately, we had horses. None had ever dragged anything, so we had to choose the horse least likely to spook and try to run away. Sarah's half Lipizzan had the strength to drag the log, but he also was the one most likely to turn aggressive if he got scared. The Hapsburg kings had bred Lipizzans to be warhorses, so they attacked rather than ran.

We settled on my black-and-white gaited gelding named Skywalker. The problem was, we had no harness and wondered if we could trust Skywalker not to hurt himself or us in the process of dragging the log to the utility patio. Also, how could we burn the log in our cozy fireplace since it was far too big and heavy for us to get it into the house?

I bridled Skywalker, then we looked around for some makeshift way we could hook up the horse to the log. Between ropes, a hammer, a chain, and an old mule collar that had hung in our barn for years, we devised a way to pull the log. The plan was to use Skywalker's love of food as the Skinnerian reward for taking one or two steps and pulling without lunging and taking off.

By then, it was dusk and difficult for us to see, but maybe that would work in our favor. We caught the other horses and put them in the barn so they wouldn't cause any problems over the feed we'd have in the bucket. I put the collar on Skywalker, and he acted indignant. He shook his head with his curly black mane flying, trying to sling it off.

When I brought out a handful of sweet feed for Skywalker, he settled down. His prehensile lips felt like velvet to my touch. He was smart and seemed to know he had a mission, so he peacefully walked with us to the log. By a miracle, we managed to nail loops that we tied more rope to and tied the chain to the log so Skywalker could drag it.

The log was so big that I had to guide Skywalker with bit and bucket while Sarah pulled with a separate rope. Skywalker leaned into the collar and the log inched forward. I could see the whites of his eyes and knew he was about to hightail it out of there. He kicked out at the log with both hind legs and sent chips flying. Lucky for us, we were both standing to his front and side, so the blows never threatened us. Still, I feared he'd hurt himself.

Again, a handful of feed worked its magic on him. We spent a good thirty minutes taking two steps at a time as we convinced Skywalker that the huge monster behind him wouldn't hurt him. Just as the stars came out, our hero dragged the log up onto the utility patio.

Since Sarah was already exhausted from the long drive home from school, I told her to go inside and rest while I took care of Skywalker and prepared him for his much-deserved rest in his stall.

When I finished, I walked by the giant log on my way inside and was so proud of what the three of us had done. Who needed a man in their lives—not us! Well, Skywalker was a male, so I guess we depended on one after all.

While I built a fire in the fireplace, Sarah said, "Be right back," and went to her bedroom. When she returned, she handed me a bottle of wine. "Mom, that's mead. It's an ale made from honey, and it's what the Vikings used to drink. I shopped all over before I found a store that carried it. We need to chill it overnight. Oh, and one of my friends, Gunar, is coming in tomorrow. He said he hunted yesterday and killed a deer, so we'll have venison roast instead of turkey."

The next morning, we woke up in a merry mood to make the giant log acceptable to Odin. Sarah—Randgrith as she would be called for the celebration—decorated it with flour, sugar, pinecones, and oak leaves. I mentally photographed the image of her dressed in a toboggan cap with her long chestnut hair hanging down her back, squatted down shaking flour along the log's top. She'd gotten that beautiful, thick hair from her dad, but her stormy blue eyes were my gift to the sacred union that had produced her. A huge lump nearly choked me with so many different emotions.

Next, we each put a photograph of something important to us on the log as a symbol of our gift to Odin. Of course, mine was a photograph of my husband and me kissing on our wedding day. I gave Randgrith her privacy as she placed it out of sight between the tinder. Around the Yule log were the smaller branches and kindling used to ignite the gigantic log.

Since the Winter Solstice celebrated the shortest day of the year, the ceremony we performed at dusk was a short one.

"Hail to Odin for the meat that he provided from our hunt yesterday."

"Hail to Odin for the sweet mead that we drink in celebration of the Yule."

"Hail to Odin for the family and friends gathered here to honor our god."

With each "hail" we took long drinks of the mead. I quickly began to feel tipsy because I wasn't normally a drinker. We exchanged unwrapped gifts as the mighty log caught fire.

We all watched in awe as the flames leapt in a dance of blue, orange, and bright yellow. When the photograph caught fire, green joined the pallet because of the developing fluids used in the photo. The kaleidoscope of colors, along with the star-filled sky, astounded us. Since it was getting colder, we retired to the house where the kids told tales of their own greatness as the Vikings of old had done.

Randgrith was grinning, bragging, and drinking more mead. I had fun at first, then a horrible loneliness set in, as well as a swelling anger. I realized with a hateful bitterness that I had lost both my husband and my best friend, and I had cancer on top of all that. I resented the hell out of his leaving me, and I resented God for my disease. Bitterness eclipsed the feelings of thankfulness. I had Randgrith home celebrating with me, but now about to leave again.

Gradually, the kids' laughter brought me out of my reverie. However, I felt there was something empty in my life besides my broken heart, and I knew something was missing. Nothing could satisfy me—not the Yule celebration, not even Sarah and her friend. My anger turned to hopelessness verging on depression.

To our delight, the log was still smoldering the next morning. Odin had accepted the gifts and showed us his pleasure. Soon, it was time for Sarah and Gunar to leave and for me to continue whatever Christmas celebration I could muster.

While Sarah was home, things weren't quite so bad, but after she left for her reunion, my depression threatened to overtake me again. I looked in the mirror and saw sagging skin from losing thirty pounds in two months. An ugly old woman stared back at me—my acerbic mother who had been cold and hateful to me all of my life. I didn't want to turn into her.

I had to do something to keep myself from falling into the abyss of depression. Out of desperation, I made up my mind to go to the Christmas Eve service at church and try to right things between God and myself. I wanted freedom from the weight of my own emptiness.

The bells chimed to announce midnight. The church was ablaze with lighted candles, and the scent of fresh holly filled my nostrils. Candlelight made the altar even lovelier than in natural light as the warm yellows reflected off its sacramental linens. I was suddenly filled with a sense of awe and reverence that my God was big and powerful.

The priest gave the most touching service on Jesus' birth and what it symbolized in our lives. My hands shook with emotion as the message registered with me. After hearing the Christmas story and realizing the wondrous gift of a forgiving God, my anger turned to shame. Who was I to cast judgmental stones at God?

As I walked to the altar for communion, I became cognizant of Jesus' forgiveness to all who had betrayed Him. Of course I was no Jesus, but I knew that. With His help, I could forgive my ex and myself. I could also hope for physical healing and for spiritual rejuvenation. As I chewed the wafer and drank the wine, I prayed, *Lord, please find it in your heart to forgive me and show me how to forgive. I know I'm unworthy to ask you for anything right now, but if you'll light the way, I will follow.*

Immediately, warmth entered my heart. The hatred and bitterness miraculously disappeared. I literally felt God lift the burden of anger I carried, and I sensed my anxious face relaxing with a spirit of joy and love. His blessing gave me new hope. I wanted to live! Yes—I would fight my cancer with God's help. I was at peace for the first time in months.

I could hardly wait to tell Sarah I had a new awakening, and it had not come from Odin. It had come from the baby whose birthday we were celebrating. I would call Sarah and wish her, not a happy Yule, but a happy Christmas.

As I walked out the church door, I looked at the babe lying in a manger on the church lawn.

"Happy birthday, baby," I whispered. "Happy birthday."

Hillene Deaton is a retired librarian, but spent most of her working life as a full-time homemaker in a large extended South Louisiana family. One of five siblings in a Cajun family with Texas roots on her maternal side, Hillene is the second generation to be named after the Civil War Battle of Malvern Hill. After raising four children, Hillene joined a local writer's group to tell her daughter-in-law's story of living the American dream after fleeing from Viet Nam with her family. Hillene has started a project with her sister, also a writer, to record family stories for future children who will never know past generations unless those stories are preserved.

His Hands is an essay about a remarkable man, my father, Preacher Hebert, who stood six feet three inches tall and was a renaissance man in every sense of the word. This story is a child's view of a man, bigger than life, whose children were always fascinated watching his hands as he went about such things as making a wreath, stringing his lures, mending his nets, or making functional Indian moccasins for their playtimes.

Personal Essay

His Hands

Hillene Deaton

As the holidays approach, I think back with fondness of my father and to childhood Christmases so long ago. It was rumored that my father once held nine baseballs in his hand at one time, yet he could beat his sisters at playing jacks.

His hands could skin alligators, yet they could pick out the smallest splinter from a tiny finger.

His hands could tie the thinnest strings through his fishing lures and hand-sew leather moccasins to fit tiny feet.

We lived in a big, white, two-story house in the country. There were four generations of us living together: my great-grandmother, my grandparents, Mom and Dad, and five of us—three boys and two girls. Everyone grew excited as Christmas approached.

The day my grandmother went to the attic and began moving the boxes that held the Christmas ornaments signaled to us that Christmas was not far away. It was time for our annual trip across the river.

We made our plans and gathered our tools—baskets, cutting shears, handsaw, shotgun, and a long piece of rope. We were going Christmas tree hunting, and this was the time of year that we five children looked forward to with great excitement. The delicious smells coming from the kitchen assured us that it was going to be a full-belly Christmas.

Back in those days we had colder winters, so Mom dressed us like the little brother in the movie, *A Christmas Story,* when his mother encases him in his bulky snowsuit, boots, mittens, and hat. I think we too would have bounced had we fallen over. On top of all that, we had to wear life jackets because we would be in a boat on the river behind our house.

My three brothers were younger, so it was up to my sister and me to organize the younger ones. But we didn't mind. We were thrilled because we were going in Daddy's fishing boat. I had ventured out with him one other time to fish, and once had been enough. I talked the whole time and wound my line around a tree several times. When I had the line in the water, I made pretty designs by moving my fishing pole up and down in circles. Who knew that fish could hear, and that they didn't like a lure to be jumping around in the water? But this was different. This was Christmas!

In the boat that Christmas season, we crossed the river and started looking for the perfect tree. We searched the tree tops for mistletoe. When it was spotted, Daddy blasted away with his shotgun, raining mistletoe down upon us. My three brothers' job was to pick up the mistletoe and place it in one of the baskets we had brought with us.

When we spotted our favorite holly tree, Daddy cut off some of the smaller branches. We were very careful as we put them in a basket so as not to dislodge the beautiful red berries.

Trying to find the right Christmas tree elicited many opinions. My brothers wanted a tree tall and skinny. My sister and I wanted a tree fat and full. We compromised. Daddy spotted the top of a tree that was just right.

With much laughter and good-natured arguing, Daddy commandeered the handsaw and began cutting. He tied the branches of the tree together, and we loaded our treasure into the boat and crossed the river back to our side.

Grandmother had hot chocolate and cookies ready for the intrepid crew. The house smelled of baking, pine, and chocolate. We took our cookies and hot chocolate outside. We wanted to watch Daddy's strong hands as he carefully wove the holly branches around a clothes hanger that he had shaped into a circle. When he finished, we had a beautiful, real holly wreath to hang on our door for everyone to see.

We left the tree up until New Year's Day. By that time, although it still smelled of pine, the needles were beginning to fall off. By then our perfect Christmas tree looked pretty pathetic. The season was officially over when we put the ornaments back into their boxes and into the attic.

Fast forward to the next Christmas season. We prepared to go across the river to cut our favorite holly branches, gather our mistletoe, and find our Christmas tree. We piled into Daddy's boat and took off. As we stepped onto the other bank, what do our wondering eyes see? Not a reindeer or a sleigh, but a NO TRESPASSING sign: SAM HOUSTON STATE PARK! DO NOT CUT ANY TREES! PROPERTY STATE OF LOUISIANA!

No more beautiful wreaths. No more mistletoe raining down on us. No more friendly haggling over the best tree. We crossed the river back to our side in silence.

We were a dejected bunch that walked back into the kitchen. We gathered around Daddy to discuss plan two. After a lively discussion, and Daddy's absolute refusal to buy a tree, we took the handsaw, the length of rope, and a wagon, and walked out of our yard to the woods across the road from us. We found a tree, and it was all right, but somehow it wasn't filled with the magic of years past. We had lost the fun and excitement of our family's river search.

We had an evergreen tree in the yard, and Daddy cut some of the branches and made a wreath. We watched his large hands as they wove those beautiful pieces together. He hung it on our front door, and my sister trimmed it with a bright red ribbon. But that didn't feel as festive either.

Many Christmases have come and gone, but the ones I remember now are the Decembers when my brothers and sister and I got into Daddy's fishing boat with him and went on adventures across the river in search of our perfect Christmas tree. The excitement and fun of those trips were bigger than life.

I still have some of Grandmother's handmade ornaments that I put on my artificial tree each year. I have the ugly Santa with his reindeer and sleigh that used to scare us as children because when she would plug it in, the light made him look really weird. Some of the legs and antlers have broken off. Santa's light doesn't work anymore, but I put him out each year because it brings back the memories of Christmases long ago. And of hands we thought could do anything.

Dixon Hearne lives in southern California, but his work draws greatly from vivid images of daily life growing up along graceful bayous and river traces of northern Louisiana. He is the author of a new book, *Plantatia: High-toned and Lowdown Stories of the South* (Southeast Missouri University Press 2009), and co-editor of two recent anthologies of Southern fiction. Recent work can also be found in *Woodstock Revisited* and *Christmas Traditions*—both from Adams Media. His short stories appear widely in magazines, journals, and anthologies, including *Mature Living, Louisiana Literature, Wisconsin Review, Cream City Review, Big Muddy, Roanoke Review,* and elsewhere. He is presently at work on a novel, another short story collection, and a collection of essays. The author can be reached at: www.dixonhearne.com

A Cockeyed Christmas came to me almost fully realized and nudged my heart until I wrote it down. As a child growing up in West Monroe, Louisiana, I prayed each year for a white Christmas complete with snow angels, flocked trees, and world-class snowball fights. And then one Christmas it happened. For two days, we romped along the fields and snow-covered levees that traced our little nook of the world, knowing full-well it was a once-in-a-lifetime gift. And when the snow disappeared—almost as quickly as it arrived—an arctic blast moved in and settled upon the town for two solid weeks. It was roughest, of course, on the animals, especially the small and frail ones that depended upon seeds and nuts to survive. The present story is fiction, but it draws from an early observation about the devastating effects of weather upon the lives of wonderful creatures I simply took for granted.

Short Story

A Cockeyed Christmas

Dixon Hearne

The deep breath of winter reached Trenton, Louisiana early that Christmas of 1960. Dot Bailey's asters and hollyhock posed stiffly in rows like frozen wax figures—too perfect, too lovely. The heavy pines had begun to amputate their own limbs, snapping and falling to the hard earth below. Birds went silent as if spirited away to some other world. All creatures went quiet except the squirrels, still foraging for food on the frozen ground. It was the coldest, harshest winter in local history, sure to be a testimonial to human struggle and selfless vigor. Bobby Hart had come to spend the holidays with his mother's sister in one of the little hedgerow houses along the levee, ahead of the others who would join them on Christmas Eve.

"It isn't fair. Squirrels need to eat, too," Bobby sighed. "Can't we put some food out for them. They'll never make it till spring."

"We can't feed them all, child." Dot Bailey frowned. "God takes care of His creatures in His own way. They know what to do."

It was Bobby's first winter this far north. Winters in south Texas came only in cool snaps and drizzle—always a welcomed event. But Trenton, Louisiana was accustomed to the occasional discomfort of an arctic blast, too cold to snow, a concept Bobby, at nine years of age, could not comprehend. In all the movies and magazines he'd seen, there was always snow in the winter scenes, floating or whooshing past in flurries. Numbing cold, he now realized, could not be captured in a picture. It must be experienced.

"Take Eboo outside for a bit, Bobby," Aunt Dot said. "He needs to survey his property, fuss a bit at the cracking tree limbs—tell them to shut up." Eboo, our little Sheltie, stood up, ready to go when he heard his name

Houses in Trenton—even in town—sat on large lots, most dotted with fruit and hardwood trees and all now naked in the wind. Eboo took notice of the frozen ground—no more than three paws down at a time—and watched the sudden scurry of two squirrels arguing over a pecan in the distance. Cold or not, he warned them off his property with threatening yelps and bared teeth. One of them raced across the yard to a neighbor's tall elm, but the other one refused to go, engaging Eboo in a boisterous show of determination, squatter's rights.

"No, Eboo!" Bobby scorned. "It's just a baby squirrel." The squirrel turned full-face toward him, and Bobby could see that its eyes appeared cockeyed, and one of them looked as if it had been put out. It was pale and hollow. His heart leapt into his throat with pity and admiration for the creature that stood his ground in the face of certain defeat.

"Let's go, boy. C'mon, Eboo," Bobby cajoled the dog. "Time for your bone-bone. Let this one go, boy. He's seen enough trouble for one little squirrel."

Back inside, comforted by the warmth and security of Aunt Dot's love, Bobby could not shake the image of the pitiful, cross-eyed creature grappling for a few life-saving morsels in the frozen ten-degree world outside.

"Aunt Dot, can I have some of these walnuts to feed two squirrels we saw in the pecan tree? They look so hungry."

"Heavens no, child! I'm trying to get rid of those pesky critters as it is. They're the filthiest, messiest things God ever created."

"We can't let them starve," Bobby sighed loudly.

"Feed them, and they'll set up housekeeping. I'll never get shed of them."

"Just enough to keep them till the cold snap is past," Bobby pleaded.

"Absolutely not, and that's final, young man. It ain't like where you live, child, lots of land and trees all around to bed and board them. Besides, they eat up electrical wires and strip my summer fruit trees and keep me up all night in the attic or on the roof. You see why now, don't you, Bobby?"

"Yes ma'am," Bobby moaned, deflated and disappointed. But he knew his heart held quite a different reply.

Dot Bailey lived alone now since her husband, Truman, moved out. Truman had left only heartache anyway. He'd more or less just taken up residence and settled himself into a lazy life of expectations. If Dot loved him, it was a thing she kept to herself. Except for occasional smiles the two exchanged at family reunions and other get-togethers, one could only guess at their relationship. He was gone for several months before it was commonly known. Bobby was disinterested in all of this. He loved his Aunt Dot, with or without attachments, and he viewed the matter as any nine-year-old might, as something done and gone. That was that.

"Don't forget to leave the bathroom faucet on tonight, Bobby," Aunt Dot called as they prepared to retire from a busy day of baking and gift-wrapping. "Help me remember, too, child. The pipes'll freeze and bust for sure. And I can't fix 'em."

Bobby gave a lackluster nod okay, but he couldn't think about the water right now. He had other images in his mind, the quivering little squirrel so alone and tiny against the elements. He'd heard on TV that the temperature would reach zero degrees overnight. He tried hard as he could to imagine what zero might feel like as he studied the naked limbs of the giant pecan tree glistening in the moonlight outside his bedroom window. There was no sign of either squirrel now. No pecans, no nuts of any kind left to argue over. Aunt Dot said they sometimes even try to take Eboo's dry dog food from the back porch. "Take everything you got if you let 'em," she'd said.

By next morning, a line of clouds had moved in and thickened throughout the long day. Bobby shifted restlessly on the window bench studying the backyard through the frosted frames while Aunt Dot puttered endlessly in the kitchen— mixing, stirring, conjuring sweet holiday treats. In three days the rest of the family would arrive, their first Christmas at Aunt

Dot's house—fifteen in all, from Bobby's parents, Robert and Sarah, to aunts and uncles, to a stair-step of cousins. All of which set off new concerns for Bobby. Would they try to catch the squirrels? Harm them? Throw rocks? Cousin Brodie was a cruel boy who once tied a cat's tail to a street sign and watched him rush into traffic and spring back when he hit rope's end. And there were other reasons, other meanness among his cousins, all of whom he loved with a cautious heart.

As the day for the cousins to arrive grew closer, Bobby fretted and couldn't sleep. A blurry shadow formed in his head, slowly giving way to the image of tiny gray and brown features so real he could reach out and stroke the soft tufts along the squirrel's neck and tail. And then a pitiful face, a mess of crooked teeth and crossed eyes and one eye not working at all—the little thing shivering and gnawing on an imaginary acorn and staring, just staring back at him.

As he lay awake, he heard the mantel clock strike twelve, the hour of ghosts and goblins and things that go bump in the dark, all too real and menacing. The eerie cold and moonless night conjured other sad images, too. And these sad images would not do. The helpless must be helped.

Bobby moved stealthily through the house so Aunt Dot would hear nothing as he made his way out onto the back porch. In his freezing hand, he held a sock filled with walnuts he'd pilfered from the pantry. The stinging breeze had now returned, and moon rays freckled the yard, just enough light to find his way across the hard ground to the pecan tree. Quickly, he deposited the nuts, shaping them into a heap. Surely his friend would find them first, before the other, larger one laid claim or stole them all away.

When he went back inside and crawled into his bed again, it was the worry about whether or not the little squirrel would find the walnuts that finally wore Bobby's tired mind to sleep.

Rising early was routine in Aunt Dot's household. Bobby rose and lurched for the door, making his way to the kitchen window, still frosty from the deep night.

"What's so important out there you can't get washed up and dressed first?" Aunt Dot demanded to know, hands on hips. "You're not still looking for them squirrels, are you? I'd shoot the things before I let you get attached. They're wild and dirty and cause disease. Ain't much good to eat neither." She made a wringing gesture with her apron and frowned. "Now get yourself ready for breakfast. I got cocoa waiting for you on the table."

"No ma'am...I mean, yes ma'am, I'm coming," Bobby stammered, scurrying toward the bedroom.

"One egg or two?" Aunt Dot called, still muttering to herself about the squirrel situation. "Maybe fry up a mess of squirrel," she mused. "Breaded."

Once dressed and back in the kitchen, Bobby moved his plate and cocoa mug to the end of the table where he had a clear view of the back yard.

"Now, you see there?" Aunt Dot said, pointing out the window with her spatula. "They're gnawing to beat the band out there. Eating up the roots on my pecan tree! Ain't a nut left on that tree, so I know it's the roots they're chewing."

BAM went the back porch door. "Scat! Scat, I say!" Aunt Dot yelled, shaking her broom in the direction of the squirrels. But neither squirrel moved an inch. Domestic noises no longer scared them.

"You see! They'll have you cooking and cleaning for them if you let them. Lazy critters oughta be in the woods instead of my backyard." She stood stiff, cold hands on her hips again, shaking her head with exasperation. "I'm calling the pest control and have the things killed or relocated."

Bobby listened attentively and without protest. He had caused the eating frenzy out back. But it was no pleasure to see his Aunt Dot so upset. Neither was it pleasing to watch the larger squirrel hoarding and glutting, leaving only the scraps for Cockeye. It was even sadder to him that he could do nothing more to help the needy creature. He worried through the day with the burden of his guilt and the fear of Aunt Dot's phone call to the pest control. But it was a call she did not get to, for they spent the entire day once again wrist deep in cookie dough, icings, and chocolate delights. Other treats filled the house with smells of cinnamon and allspice.

Nowhere in the day was there time for her to entertain an unpleasant thought. Aunt Dot was lost to holiday joy—not Uncle Truman, nor the weather, nor the pesky inhabitants in her backyard. It was a pleasantness she maintained in the ensuing two days till the arrival of other family members who'd driven long distances to join them.

Encouraged by Aunt Dot's happy mood, Bobby continued sneaking small gifts to the old pecan tree, careful not to deplete an entire bag of pecans or black walnuts or filberts. But he knew it must halt when the others arrived, especially his cousins.

And arrive they did, with noisy merriment, warm greetings, and round hugs on Christmas Eve. And all came toting festive boxes and bags and covered dishes of unimaginable good tastes. They'd brought Santa's gifts as well and piled them high round the giant spruce Bobby and Aunt Dot had dragged from a local tree lot the week before and transformed into a regular Rockwell painting. It was the perfect gift for his mom and dad, Bobby thought. It was easily the prettiest Christmas tree he'd ever decorated in all his nine Christmases, right up to the bright gold star Aunt Dot had fashioned from old foil wrapping paper.

The cousins had also brought their mean and selfish ways—at least Brodie and Tina had. Being the eldest cousins, they immediately assumed all power, delegating none to the younger cousins. This included playing Santa for the gift exchange later in the evening. But there was no room for animosity on Christmas Eve, with all its joy and promise. Besides, Brodie gave up his Santa hat quickly as he unwrapped his first present—an air pump pellet gun he was warned not to shoot till he got back home. There were dolls and games and toys of all manner, clothing of every size and color, small appliances, a new pipe that Bobby had bought for his dad. Every family member received a heap of precious I-love-you gifts. Things that kept eyes popped wide through the night. And there was one more special Christmas gift Bobby had to deliver under cover of darkness, while the house slumbered in deep anticipation of more Christmas joy.

Christmas morning brought the household to life, eager to greet the day, with no one aware of Bobby's secret. Grown-ups congregated in Aunt Dot's spreading kitchen, all hands eager to help with breakfast. The kids, some still in pajamas, chose up rooms to play with their Santa gifts—all except Brodie and Tina. Brodie begged his parents to let him take his new gun out back and *play-shoot*, and it being Christmas and all, they finally agreed.

Never one to do as he was told, Brodie emptied the shell box of pellets into his jean pockets where he could retrieve them at will. Brodie never made a threat he did not deliver on, and the kids all knew it, so no one dared report his disobedience to his parents for fear of a good licking.

Pump-pump-pump went the pellet gun to an easy tightness—then POW! The pellets flew toward the elm tree. Another, slower round of pumping followed, then POW again, this time at the pecan tree. A sudden movement drew all eyes to the base of the tree. A quick pump-pump and POW threw another scatter of lead toward the trunk, sending Bobby's two squirrels scurrying to the back side of the tree.

A fourth round of pumping followed, marking time for one of the creatures to show itself again. All eyes remained fixed on Brodie's target—a teasing flash of brown and gray. Pump-pump-pump-pump strained the gun. Brodie took slow, deadly aim, and held the squirrel in his gun sight, grinning with delight. POW went the volley, aimed squarely at the gnawing little face poking from the right side. The packed shot split the icy air with a rude loudness that echoed in every direction.

The pellets found their mark. There in the distance they all witnessed Brodie's first kill. Some of the cousins ran to see, others held back. At first Bobby could not move. He could not accept the sudden demise of a creature he'd come to care so much about. He fled in a fury down the block, across the empty schoolyard to where empty lots gave way to a thinning wood. There was much to ponder. Much to regret.

Back at the house, no one mentioned a thing. Most of the children soon forgot altogether in the merriment of Christmas and their new treasures, things that could quickly cure any child's worry or sadness. Bobby sat on his anger and pretended to be happy the remainder of the day, even in the face of Brodie's swaggering and winking. Brodie had tossed the dead body into a neighbor's yard, and Bobby knew in his heart he could not look at the pecan tree ever again. He could not bear the pain of discovering that it was Cockeye. He prayed for the deceased and left it at that.

He would remain with Aunt Dot for another week after his parents, aunts, uncles, and cousins finally loaded their cars with countless treasures of mutual love and returned to their separate lives in other places. And a cloud of loss settled quietly over the once-festive house, rather like a warm oven empty of all its sweetness and goodness. Aunt Dot turned inward, reflective, perhaps lonesome. But for whom? Family? Her mother and father? Uncle Truman? Bobby wasn't sure.

Old enough to sense her feelings of sadness, he recalled Christmases past when she and Uncle Truman were the ones who drove away on Christmas evenings, the days when everyone gathered at Granny and Grandpa Parker's house in Minden. Then after Grandpa died, it was just Granny's house alone. They gathered there until Granny's last year. Bobby watched with squinted eye as Aunt Dot puttered in the kitchen long after the last group had gone. He knew now what real sadness was. He wished desperately to tell her.

"Now wasn't that the best Christmas we ever had, Bobby?" Aunt Dot called out from her kitchen at last. "Everything was just perfect. Not a scrap left over to freeze or reheat. We ate so much we won't need a bite till New Year's Eve," she giggled. "We'll have to bake you a fresh batch of Snickerdoodles tomorrow, Bobby. That Brodie beats all when it comes to sweets. He must of ate two dozen cookies today alone."

"No ma'am. I mean yes ma'am," Bobby replied.

"Bobby, that's the second time in two days you seem to be lost when I'm talking to you. Something on you mind, child? You homesick?"

"No ma'am. Just daydreaming I guess."

They left it there, but Bobby thrashed the covers through the night, replaying the hateful killing: the aim, the firing, the tiny body falling to the frozen earth in a lifeless clump. And morning brought but more sadness and renewed guilt. He could not hold back his terrible secrets any longer. He would tell Aunt Dot about the stolen nuts from the pantry, his feeding them to the squirrels against her orders, the killing—all of it. He could live easier with the burden of her disappointment than with the knots of guilt and pain that had taken over his heart and mind every waking hour. But once again, his courage was diverted.

"Come here quick, Bobby!" Aunt Dot called suddenly from the back porch. "Hurry up, child. I want you to see this. And don't slam that door," she whispered as he approached. "It's loud as gunshot in cold weather." She stood frozen in place, except for a movement of her right hand pointing toward the pecan tree. "Now stand real still, Bobby, and just watch yonder."

He could barely force himself to look upon the tree. A rush of dark images overtook him, and he flinched.

"Shh! Look out yonder, child. You ever see a cross-eyed squirrel? I swear that pitiful thing is cockeyed as they come. And got one eye dead and frosted over. See him?"

A well of feelings rose up bringing tears to Bobby's eye. His heart pounded and raced. "Yes ma'am!" He'd prayed for this, promised God he'd give every Christmas present to needy children in exchange for Cockeye's life.

"Ugliest little thing I ever saw. Skin and bones." Aunt Dot giggled again. "Lord what a pitiful creature you done made here."

Bobby's head spun with hope that she wouldn't mention pest control.

"You pitiful thing. I ain't got no use for you, but I 'spect you ain't long for this world anyway," Aunt Dot

173

proclaimed. She then turned to Bobby. "Ain't even worth a call to get rid of him. I'll just let the Lord take him when He's ready."

It was a prayer answered, something Bobby never truly expected.

"I've lived with other useless creatures," Aunt Dot said at length, a statement Bobby sensed was a reference to Uncle Truman. "But I ain't taking you in and have you take over," she said as if she spoke directly to the little squirrel. Cockeye stared steadfastly in their direction, at least they thought he did. "Besides, you need to learn to make it on your own."

Bobby slept peacefully that night, even with his terrible secrets. He decided the secrets could wait a while to be told.

Morning brought with it a break in the clouds and enough warming rays to melt the ice from Aunt Dot's asters. A noisy woodpecker announced his *all-call*, bringing small creatures out into the light. Aunt Dot stared out the kitchen window at Eboo's bowl on the bottom porch step. Another larger bowl sat next to the oven where Eboo took his meals in bad weather. He did not care for freezing conditions and always hurried back when he'd finished his business. Lately, he'd shown no interest at all in other residents out back, not even Mrs. Cain's black cat that pawed at him from a fencepost.

Bobby edged close to Aunt Dot. Now he saw what was holding her interest out the kitchen window. It was not Eboo's bowl, but what was in it. In all this time she'd never once mentioned missing nuts from the pantry. Could she have known all along that he was a thief and a liar? That he disobeyed her? Her eyes drew wide as Cockeye worked cautiously toward the bowl.

Bobby glimpsed his dear aunt's tender confession in her eyes now. He was not the only one feeding the little cockeyed squirrel. He said not one word. He just stood next to his aunt, watching the little cockeyed squirrel edge toward the winter feast.

CJ Petterson is the pen name of Marilyn Johnston. After she retired from a career in communications at a Fortune 500 company, Marilyn began writing for pleasure and settled in Mobile, Alabama to be near her family. Her work has appeared in *Christmas is a Season! 2008* and in Adams Media anthologies, *Christmas Through a Child's Eyes* and *Cup of Comfort for Divorced Women.* She is a member of Sisters In Crime, the Society for Children's Book Writers and Illustrators, and a charter member of the Mobile Writers Guild. CJ Petterson is hard at work editing two action-adventure stories and digging into her third novel, a young adult fantasy.

In *Hobbes House*, a lonely child meets a scared fox, and a dead father's tragic secret is revealed to his angry daughter. When Merrill Cowper rents her lake house to strangers, she learns that the best Christmas gifts don't always arrive wrapped in pretty paper and tied with a bow. Sometimes, they don't even arrive on Christmas...or Boxing Day.

.

Short Story

Hobbes House

CJ Petterson

*For rent: Lakefront 2 BR log cabin, fireplace,
open floor plan. Off-season rate $325/wk.*

Merrill Cowper re-read the ad she took off the laser printer and decided that $325 wasn't too much to ask for a lake rental in the winter months. She'd negotiate down a bit if necessary, because she'd get double that in the summer. Using manicure scissors, she snipped the bottom of the page into uneven strips, penned her cell phone number on each sliver, and jogged over to the Student Union to get a posting authorization before the office closed.

Even though it was midweek, missing from the Union was the usual low roar of voices. Most of the students had already vacated the Samford University campus the week before Christmas. Mentally kicking herself for not posting the notice in September when she still had a good chance to rent the place, she tacked the ad in the middle of the SU bulletin board. She tore off one of the strips to get the ball rolling and stepped back to read the other ads stuck like a collage to the corkboard.

"Anything interesting?"

Merrill glanced in the direction of the man who appeared at her side. Tall and dark haired, her exact opposite, she guessed him to be in his early thirties. A freckle-faced boy about eight or nine stood next to him, his thumbs racing across the keys of a Nintendo game.

"If you need a statistics tutor or a term paper typed, you're in luck," Merrill said.

"Guess I'm out of luck then." He ran his finger across

her ad copy. "Or maybe not," he said as he pulled off a phone strip. "Wonder where this is?"

"Oops." She scribbled on the ad, *near Center, Alabama.* "It's about an hour and a half from here. I'm Merrill Cowper." She stuck out her hand, "and that's my ad."

"Bradley Warner, and this is Bradley Warner the third, Trey." His hand was warm and noticeably softer than her own which she quickly retrieved. Two days of working at the lake house had taken its toll. When she rubbed her palms together, she could feel the blisters starting to firm up. They'd be hardened into calluses soon, but at least the soreness would be gone.

She bent down to Trey's level. "Hi, Trey," she said and held out her hand. "Nice to meet you."

The boy didn't take his eyes off his game.

When Merrill dropped her hand and straightened up, his father took away the toy. "Trey, say hello to Miss Merrill."

"Hullo," Trey said with a scowl then snatched back the game.

"He's a little tired and cranky. We just drove in from Atlanta."

"A long trip always makes me cranky, too," she said. "The house is really clean. It's on a small private lake about thirty minutes from Centre as the road turns. If you're a fisherman, there's pretty good bass fishing even in winter if we get a few warm days."

"Is the fireplace the only heat?"

She shook her head. "Electric wall furnace, and there's a backup generator if a storm knocks the electricity out."

"When can I see it?"

"As soon as you like. I posted pictures on Facebook." Merrill ripped off another phone slip, scribbled the website address, and handed him the scrap of paper. "Here." Then she wrote it on the ad as well. "That's what I get for being in a hurry."

"I'll check it out."

"When did you want it?" *Not a good idea to let a potential customer get away without some kind of commitment.*

"Christmas Eve to New Year's Eve. My turn to spend the holidays with my son." The boy dodged when his father reached out to tousle his coppery hair.

"Can we go, now?" Trey asked. "You said you'd take me to McDonald's. I want to go now."

"One of my favorite places too," Merrill said.

The boy ignored her, and his father sent her a small, apologetic smile and a one-shoulder shrug.

She wondered if being tired was the boy's whole problem. There seemed to be something more.

"Okay, son. Thanks, Ms. Cowper."

"The place is still available that week, Mr. Warner," Merrill called as they turned to walk away. "I'll need a $100 deposit."

"I'll give you a call," Bradley said, waving the phone slip.

"Merrill," she murmured, "now that's what I call timing."

Three days later, after Bradley Warner had decided to rent the cabin and paid the deposit, Merrill stood in a numbing icy rain on the porch of her grandmother's condominium. She pushed a cold finger against the pale glow of the doorbell and quickly stuffed her hand back in her coat pocket. Shivering in the raw wind, she eyed the balsam wreath hanging on the mahogany door. Like the imitation velvet ribbon which had frozen to the wreath, her blonde ponytail was fast becoming a Popsicle. Just as she reached to ring again, the door squealed ajar, and a pair of gray eyes that mirrored her own peered out under the gold safety chain.

"You called," Merrill said, her voice a single flat note.

Pursed lips stretched into a strawberry-colored line across the pale face in front of her, and then the door shut. Merrill listened to the chain rattling off its hook. When the door swung wide, her seventy-four-year-old grandmother, Elisabeth, stood behind it, wielding it like a shield against the cold air.

"Well, don't stand there like a lump. You'll catch your

death. Come in. Come in," her grandmother said and tugged on Merrill's coat sleeve, pulling her into the living room.

Elisabeth closed the door behind her and re-hung the safety chain. "Please try not to track water on the floors," she called over her shoulder as she shuffled away, her mauve cashmere dressing gown swishing across the marble tiles.

Merrill slipped out of the thin, black raincoat that did little to keep the cold from seeping through her thick sweater and blue jeans. She shivered as she draped the wet garment over a curled hook on the brass coat tree and left her rubber-soled clogs on the Oriental throw rug next to the door. Massaging warmth back into her arms, she padded in red wool socks toward the tiny, back part of the kitchen area that Elisabeth called The Gathering Room. Lights in the condo were dimmed or turned off, and the winter thermostat was set at its usual sixty-three. Merrill knew it wasn't because of any save-the-environment precepts. Elisabeth saved her money to collect the trappings of status—sterling silver, fine china, art, diamonds, antiques. Investments she called them.

"I can't stay long, Grandma. I've got a lot of work to do."

"I've asked you not call me that, dear. It sounds so coarse."

"Sorry, *Grandmother*. What was it you needed?" She started to move one of the stacks of ornament boxes that filled the tapestry-covered seats of both fireside chairs.

"Don't bother with that, dear. The decorators are coming tomorrow to finish up. Sit here." Elisabeth patted the cushion next to her on the small, chintz sofa facing the fireplace. She toggled a button on a remote, and the gas fire log flickered to life with a soft whoosh.

Merrill looked around for another place to sit, but finding none, folded onto the sofa, tucking her feet under her.

"I do so enjoy all the colors and bustle of Christmas," Elisabeth chirped brightly, "but by the time Boxing Day arrives, I'm more than ready for order to be restored."

"You're probably the only person in Alabama who calls December 26 Boxing Day."

"December 26 is really St. Stephens Day. It's known as Boxing Day only when the day after Christmas doesn't fall on a Sunday, which it doesn't this year."

Merrill wanted to say, *You call it sharing information. I call it reinforcing how stupid you think l am.* But she held her tongue.

Elisabeth poured tea from a custard-colored Baleek teapot embellished with a sprinkling of hand-painted, emerald-green shamrocks. "This teapot was your great-grandmother Merrill's. You were named after her, you know."

"I know."

"She brought her traditional English Christmas with her when she arrived in Savannah. Gifts were never to be exchanged on hallowed Christmas Day, unlike the American heathens, she used to say." She started to pour a second cup of tea.

Merrill shook her head. "No thanks." She didn't want to take anything from her grandmother, not even a hot cup of tea. "You didn't say what you needed when you called," Merrill said.

Elisabeth squeezed a lemon wedge over her teacup and brushed her pale, wrinkled fingers across the crisp fold in a white linen napkin. "I called because some of my Christmas dinner guests can't make it at four o'clock this year. I wondered if I changed it to five, would that be convenient for you?"

"Actually, I'm not coming for dinner. Judy is coming over so we can work on our theses. I'll stop by on Tuesday. That *is* Boxing Day after all."

"Not last year, and now not this year. Christmas is the traditional time for gatherings of our family and friends."

"Judy is a friend." *You're not going to lay a guilt trip on me.*

"Bring her along, then."

"We won't get any studying done. Besides, traditions should evolve over time."

Last year was the first Christmas without her father, and Merrill had decided to spend it at the cabin. Her grandmother had declined to join her, choosing instead to play hostess at her usual Christmas dinner. It had been a lonely Christmas. Merrill stared into the low, uneven fire warming the room. It crossed her mind that even a roaring fire couldn't thaw her grandmother's icy crust.

"Was that all you called about?" she asked after a long silence.

Elisabeth's cup tinkled lightly in its saucer when she picked it up. "I think you should sell the lake house."

"Not now. Not ever," Merrill said with a violent shake of her head. "Daddy left Hobbes House to me."

"That bequest was not one of your father's smarter decisions."

Her grandmother's criticism sent a flush of anger through Merrill, as though Elisabeth had scratched a match head into flame. The retort exploded out of her mouth. "He may have been your son, Grandmother, but he was *my* father. Can't you let up on him even now?"

Elisabeth dipped her lips to her teacup and sipped. "Derek tells me the place is vacant, has been for months, and needs a lot of work. Where will you get the money?"

Merrill let out a soft resigned sigh. "Derek is your stockbroker, Grandmother, and he knows diddly-squat about my house. Lake properties make good rentals. In fact, I'm headed over there to open up the place because a man has rented it for next week."

"Oh my dear, I wouldn't waste my time." Elisabeth's mouth curled down slightly. "He'll certainly change his mind when he sees the place. It's unlivable, no more than a squatter's cabin."

"He's already seen it. You haven't been there in years. Daddy made it a wonderful, year-round home before he..." Memories choked off her words.

The hours she'd spent playing go-fer, handing her father hammers and nails, were her most cherished memories. At first, Elisabeth often joined them, bringing iced tea in a jug and tomato sandwiches to eat in the cool shade of the pines.

For a brief moment, Merrill thought she saw a veil of

pain cloud Elisabeth's eyes. Then it was gone.

"I told your father he should have sold the property after your mother ran off to God knows where with that golf person at the country club."

Merrill noted the dig with silence and a bowed head. *She left because of you, and if Daddy hadn't needed me...* She left the thought unfinished because remembering pulled a shroud of pain over her. *I just wish she'd told me what was going to happen. One day she was here, the next she was gone. Just gone.*

After her mother left, her father often spent weeks away from home. When he did take Merrill to the cabin, it was only for an afternoon. Elisabeth stopped going altogether. Merrill was into her teens before she could believe her father when he told her she was not the cause of her mother leaving. So, if it wasn't her fault, and it wasn't his fault, the only one left to blame was her grandmother. She just didn't know why exactly.

"Why would anyone in their right mind rent a cabin on a cold lake in the dead of winter?" Elisabeth asked.

"I didn't ask."

"Perhaps you should. Except for a few year-round residents, that part of the lake is quite abandoned this time of year. What if the man's into something illegal?"

Merrill felt a little jolt. Elisabeth raised a point that she hadn't considered. "I doubt it. Mr. Warner just wants to spend the holidays with his son."

"Warner? Of the Virginia Warners?"

"Don't know. Didn't ask. Don't care. And I am not selling Hobbes House," Merrill said, looking her grandmother directly in the eye.

"I do wish you could see reason. You are just as obstinate as your father was."

Merrill checked her watch. "I have to leave." She stood and air-kissed her grandmother's cheek.

Merrill hadn't driven out of the condo's parking space when she started crying. January 6 would be the two-year anniversary of her father's suicide. "Why, Daddy? Why?"

By the time the tires of her ten-year-old Honda Accord crunched onto the graveled parking space in front of the cabin, the rain had quit, but she sat there with the engine idling for several minutes. "Won't get finished sitting here," she muttered, turning off the ignition and listening as the engine hiccupped and shook to a halt. "Okay, Jonathan," she said and patted the instrument panel. "I get the message." She'd have to use some of the rental money for a tune-up.

It took two hands to lift the red plastic, five-gallon gas can out of the trunk then she reached back for a cardboard box full of cleaning supplies. She wanted to take one last lick at the kitchen and bathrooms. Leaving the gas can by the bumper, she keyed open the front door of the cabin, and stepped into the dark interior that smelled of lemony furniture polish with just a hint of the mustiness that comes with being closed up for a year. She knew a good swipe of bleach and some air freshener would take care it. The flip of the light switch was useless. She'd forgotten to call the power company to turn on the electricity. No problem, she thought. I've got gasoline for the generator, and Bradley and mini-Bradley won't arrive until tomorrow afternoon. I'll get it turned on in the a.m.

When her eyes adjusted to the dimness, she set the supplies on the gray Formica counter and went back outside to get the generator started, turn on the water pump, and haul in some firewood. The temperature at the lake would turn frigid when the pale sun disappeared behind the pines. She wanted to get a fire started as soon as possible.

"Rats!" About a dozen sixteen-inch-long oak logs lay in the space between two pine trees where a four-foot high eight-foot long stack of logs was supposed to be. She'd also forgotten to order a load of firewood. Her fingers were white with cold when she got back into the house with an armload of split oak and a pocketful of fatwood kindling.

Even before the blazing fire had warmed the cabin, Merrill worked up a sweat wiping down the last of the kitchen cabinets and disinfecting the sinks and the toilet. She tossed the faux Oriental throw rugs onto the porch, put on her coat, and followed them out. After sweeping them down, she left them draped over the railing while she mopped the tile floor of the combination kitchen-dining-living room.

Last on her to-do list, she pulled a string of tiny Christmas lights out of the box and hauled a kitchen chair out onto the porch. Using the chair as a makeshift ladder, she ran the Christmas lights across the cup hooks her father had screwed into the ceiling of the front porch. Testing the lights would wait until after the electricity was on.

It was a velvety black eight p.m. when she put fresh linens on the beds. She took a shower then wiped down the tub with a bleach and water solution. She draped one set of new, multi-striped towels over the side of the tub and put three more in the tiny closet. Muscles aching, she brewed a mug of green Chai tea and wrapped in the down couch throw, sat cross-legged on top of her sleeping bag in front of the fireplace. The house was as ready as she could make it.

Overwhelmed that she was stomping on her father's memory by renting the house to strangers, she began to sob. *Sorry, Daddy.*

***

Schneider's Tree Service had dumped a face cord of wood on the ground near the pines and was following the power company truck out of the drive when Bradley Warner's red Dodge Ram 1500 pickup drove in. Merrill waved him in. *Timing is everything. The pickup is a surprise though.* She had been sure he'd drive a fancy sport utility vehicle or some big butt import sedan.

"Hey there! Welcome to Hobbes House."

"Any relation to Calvin and...?"

"One and the same. My favorite cartoon. Well, that and Charlie Brown."

Trey dropped down out of the pickup pointing in the direction of the pine trees. "Look. A wolf."

Merrill saw the bushy tail of a fox disappear into the grove of pines. "It's a fox, Trey. He's looking for something to eat. Probably a field mouse in the woodpile."

Bradley walked up with a suitcase in each hand. "Don't

try to get too close to him, Trey. He's a wild animal and might bite."

"Your father's right." She took a longer look at Bradley. Almost black hair, clear blue eyes, a warm, broad smile that revealed a slightly crooked front tooth, close to six-feet tall, good-looking. *My gosh. I'm looking at Prince Charming.* "Did you have any trouble finding the place?"

"Not at all. Your good directions and a GPS made it easy. Map quest showed gravel and dirt roads so I brought the pickup just in case."

Of course, he'd have more than one car. "Great. Let me show you around."

"Grab your backpack, Trey."

The boy was walking toward the pier. "Aw, Dad. I want to see the lake."

"We will in a minute. Let's get our stuff in the house first." He turned to Merrill and spoke quietly. "It's his first Christmas without his mother. She's in Atlanta. Said she wanted to spend some alone time with her next victim." He paused a moment. "Sorry, that was a pity-party shot," he said.

Merrill's lips parted in a little *oh.* "Sounds like hurt to me."

"Not for myself. For Trey."

"I understand." *More than you know.*

Merrill walked her renters through the cabin and saw to it that Bradley knew how to start and bank the fireplace. "If the temperature is forecast to drop into the twenties, leave the cabinet doors under the sinks open. Keeps the pipes from freezing. Any questions?"

"Nope, I think we're all set."

"I left my cell phone number on the kitchen table if you need anything."

"Wait, there is one thing. Is there some place we can get a small Christmas tree and decorations to go with those pretty lights you strung on the porch? Nice touch, by the way."

Her face warmed at the compliment. "There's a Grab 'n Go Market about five minutes from here. Stocks everything. Go to the blacktop and turn left. You can't miss it." She slipped on a green barn coat. "I'll stack the firewood while you're gone and then get out of here," she said, as she pulled a pair of tan deer hide gloves out of her coat pocket.

"Got a pair of gloves for me?"

After a moment's hesitation, Merrill smiled. "I think I can find a pair."

He shrugged on his coat, helped Trey into his, and followed her out. She opened the trunk of the Honda and pulled out a pair of her father's gloves. "These should fit."

Fifteen minutes into the task, Bradley noticed Trey was gone. "Trey," he called. He whistled through his teeth.

Merrill remembered Trey's fascination with the lake, and dread squeezed her heart with a cold hand. "I'll check the pier," she said.

Then they heard the boy scream, and both started running. When she rounded the corner of the house, she stopped and grabbed Bradley's arm to hold him back. "Wait!"

Crouching at the end of the pier, snarling, teeth bared, the normally shy fox was ready to attack. Trey had somehow managed to get between the fox and the animal's escape route.

"It feels trapped, Bradley," Merrill said. "It's likely to attack if we get any closer."

"Don't move, son. Stand. Very. Still," he commanded, and then whispered to Merrill. "I'll kill it first."

"Not before it bites your son." She needed to give the animal a way out. "Maybe...Trey, don't look at the fox," she said softly. "Just back up."

The child was petrified, too terrified to move.

"Back up, son."

The boy took a step and stopped.

Bradley started to move towards his son, but Merrill grabbed his arm. "We're too close. Back away."

"Not without—"

"If we back away, maybe Trey will follow."

Bradley stared at her intently for several seconds then slowly moved away from the pier.

"Trey, the fox is afraid of you," Merrill said. "That's why he's growling. You have to get out of his way and let him get past. Back up slowly."

"I'm scared." The boy was crying softly." I can't see backwards."

"One step at a time, Trey," Merrill said. "A baby step."

The boy took a step, found safe footing, then hurriedly took three more steps before his foot slid off the pier. He toppled screaming into the water.

Bradley lunged forward, but Merrill held him back. "Wait! The water is only about a foot deep right there." Trey's arms flailed and splashed then he sat up sputtering.

The fox raced down the pier and into the trees. Merrill, nearest to the pier, reached Trey first. She grabbed his uplifted hands and pulled him into her arms. He clung to her, shaking violently and sobbing into her neck. Bradley peeled him out of her arms and ran back to the cabin where he wrapped him in the down throw.

"Bradley. I think he's in shock. We should take him to the hospital and get him checked out."

After Bradley deposited Trey on the front seat of his pickup, Merrill held out her hand. "I'll drive."

He handed her the keys, slipped in beside his son, and pulled him close.

***

When the resident on duty in the emergency room pronounced that Trey was fine and released him, an ambulance crew was wheeling a gurney down the hall toward them.

"Grandmother!" Merrill cried when she recognized the ashen face of Elisabeth under the oxygen mask. She spun around and followed the EMTs. "What happened?"

"Who are you?" The EMT with a long dark braid asked.

"I'm her granddaughter. Her only family. Will she be all right?"

"Probably a heart attack. You'll have to check with the doctor for more information."

The nurse guided her out of the curtained area. "You'll have to wait in the waiting room. We've called her regular doctor, and he should be here any minute."

"But—"

Bradley put his arm around her shoulders and walked her through the ER doors. "Let them do their jobs, Merrill. Come on. We'll wait with you."

For the next hour, Merrill sat with a Bradley on each side of her, each of them holding a hand. As worried as she was about Elisabeth, Trey's obvious concern for her touched her deeply.

The ER doors swung open, and Merrill jumped to her feet as her grandmother's physician strode toward the trio in the waiting room. "Dr. Hardy, how is she?"

"She'll be okay. She's a tough old bird. We'll keep her two or three more days. When she goes home, she'll need someone to stay with her for a while. I'll arrange for nursing care unless you—"

"We don't get along. Actually, I think she hates me or at least she should. I've been pretty nasty at times. I think I'd be more hindrance than help."

He nodded slowly. "She doesn't hate you, Merrill. She loves you very much. I've been Elisabeth's doctor since before you were born. Your father's, too. She constantly brags about you. Even when she was dealing with your father's manic depressive episodes, your well-being was top-most of her priorities.

"What do you mean manic depressive? If Daddy was depressed, it was because his wife left him and his mother treated him like a child or a...a lap dog! Always telling him what to do and when to do it."

"Because if she didn't, he wouldn't take his medicine so he could drink. He'd go on binges and hide away in the cabin for weeks at a time."

Shocked, Merrill's voice dropped to a whisper. "She always said he was away on business trips."

Dr. Hardy shook his head. "After your mother left, he couldn't hold a job. He fell deep into a clinical depression."

"She was ashamed?"

"Not at all. Elisabeth only wanted to protect both of

you."

Merrill's memories began to reveal the little cracks in the perfect world her mind had created. The hours her father sat staring into the fire. The times he threw his tools when things didn't go as he planned. When he put his fist through a cabinet door, she'd blamed it on his frustration and loneliness after her mother left. Now it made sense. Her mother left because she couldn't deal with his illness. But Elisabeth—she was his mother—she couldn't leave, and she couldn't make him better. *How awful. What have I done?*

"When can I see her?"

"Right now. She's awake."

"When you arrange that nursing care, set it up for just a couple of days so someone can show me what to do. I'll stay with her for as long as it takes."

"What about school?"

"Not a problem. I can take some time off."

Merrill pushed aside the curtain and stepped close to the hospital bed. Elisabeth was a small bump under the sheets—her carefully coifed hair now a swirl of tangles, her makeup-free face ashen. When Merrill collected a thin hand in her own and caressed it, Elisabeth's eyes opened.

"Merrill, I'm sorry. I put a damper on your Christmas holidays."

"No, you didn't, Grandmother. It's okay. The most important thing is that Doc Hardy says you'll be okay." Tears rolled down Merrill's cheeks. "He…he told me about Daddy's illness. I am so sorry. All these years I've blamed you. Can you ever forgive me?"

"Nothing to forgive, my dear."

"Why didn't you explain?"

"There was nothing anyone could do, and I didn't want to burden you. You were just a child." She sighed and closed her eyes. "And now I've ruined Christmas for everyone."

Merrill swiped at her tears and sent her grandmother a smile. "No you haven't, Grandmother. We'll just stretch Christmas holidays into two weeks this year. If you're feeling well enough, we'll make it a celebration of life and have

Christmas dinner on Three Kings Day. I'll arrange it with your friends, if that's all right with you."

Elisabeth's eyebrows knit together then relaxed. "Sounds like a charming idea. You did say that traditions need to evolve."

It was nearly ten o'clock when they parked on the gravel at Hobbes House. Trey was snoring softly as his father carried him into the warm cabin and tucked the bed covers around him.

"Been a long day, Merrill. You look exhausted. Why don't you stay here tonight?"

The thought of driving even the short distance to her grandmother's condo seemed daunting right then, and the fireplace was so inviting. "I think I'll take you up on that. I've got my sleeping bag in the car."

"No, you take the bed. I've got the couch."

"Thanks, but sleeping in front of the fireplace is where I usually am this time of year."

"Give me your keys. I'll get the sleeping bag for you."

When he returned, she was brewing green Chai tea. She unrolled her bag in front of the fireplace, sat on the couch next to Brad, and reached for her mug.

She took a sip and felt the warmth make its way down her throat. "This is one day I wouldn't want to repeat, except for reconciling with my grandmother."

"I'm with you on that. Merrill, what you did with Trey—"

"I didn't do anything."

"No, I mean when you hauled him out of the water, he clung to you so tightly."

"He was scared."

Brad nodded. "At the hospital, when he wouldn't let go of your hand, that's not like him."

"He's a lonely boy, Brad."

"When you get back to school, could I call you?"

She ducked her head so he couldn't see the pleasure in her eyes, but she shook her head. "I'm not ready, and

191

Grandmother…" Her voice trailed off.

"Of course, but maybe when you're ready, I was thinking maybe two friends could get together sometime. To talk. Maybe over a hamburger. You know, a couple of buddies."

"Sounds like something that could happen, sometime." After a few silent minutes, she murmured, "You didn't get your Christmas tree."

"That's okay. My Christmas present wouldn't fit under a tree."

"Neither would mine." She tapped her mug against his, toasting a new beginning.

"Merry Christmas."

Jean Loeb Reiner is a second, almost third, generation native Mobilian. Her grandmother came here at thirteen. Jean loves Mobile, and it usually plays a part in her novels. Jean has been published in the *Mobile Press-Register* and in *Single Mother*. As Aunt Jean, she has created a CD to assist single or working parents help their children to quietly and quickly fall asleep. She has performed on almost all the theatrical stages in Mobile and has many best actress awards. She also has a large part in the movie *Soultaker* that was shot in Mobile and has been on the Syfy Channel many times.

In ***Dear Santa*** a little boy sits down to write Santa a letter. The unusual aspect of this letter comes from the fact that he is telling Santa not to bring him any gifts. The young boy also has an opportunity to reflect on Jewish and Christian holy seasons.

Short Story

Dear Santa

Jean Loeb Reiner

Eight-year-old Josh Simpson walked into the delicious smelling kitchen. His mom was bent over a floured cloth covered with pale, wet-looking dough that had been sprinkled with pecans and cinnamon. He watched her lower the rolling pin in her hands to the countertop. Josh had always enjoyed watching his mom bake. She started to roll the dough into a long log.

"Mom," Josh said, "Mom, can I talk to you for a minute?"

Ruth pushed away the hair that had fallen onto her forehead with the back of her hand that still had flour on it. That lock rarely stayed where it belonged, especially when she was baking.

"Okay, son. I can give you about two minutes." She smiled down at her son. "I need to cut the pastry and bake it. You do want bulkies, don't you?"

Josh licked his lips. "You bet!" He hesitated a second, but when Ruth tilted her head, he continued. "Mom, I need something to write on. Can I have one of Dad's yellow pads?"

A smile touched Ruth's lips. "Taking after your dad already, huh? Of course, honey." She wiped her hands on a towel, reached into a drawer, and handed Josh a yellow legal pad. "Will I be allowed to read what you write when you finish?"

"Sure, Mom." Josh took the pad, reached for a pencil on the desk and ran to his room.

Sitting down at his desk, he chewed on the pencil, then on his bottom lip. He squirmed in his chair and pulled on his head of curly brown hair. Suddenly, he sat up straight and placed the pencil to the pad of paper.

> *Dear Santa, I'm writing you this letter*
> *because I don't want to hurt your feelings.*
> *You seem like a nice, kind person, so I*
> *wanted to explain why I don't want you to*
> *worry about bringing me any gifts. You*
> *see, Mr. Santa, I'm Jewish, and I will get*
> *gifts for Chanukah. In fact, I'll get one*
> *each night for eight nights. I know some*
> *Christian children get more than eight*
> *gifts, but they open them all at once. I only*
> *open one gift a night, but I can pick out*
> *the one I want to open.*

He stopped writing for a second, and bit his lip again. His hand rushed through his hair before he continued with a deep breath.

> *You may not be familiar with Chanukah,*
> *so I better explain. Once many years ago,*
> *there was trouble for Jews in...*

Ruth put the rolls in the oven and took a Coke out of the refrigerator, finally able to sit down a few seconds before she started to clean up. Her mind took her back to Josh's request. He was such a good boy, but she couldn't imagine who he might be writing to. She decided to call Philip and tell him that Josh wanted one of his legal pads. She and Philip had worried so before they had a child. There had been slight disagreements on how to raise a happy, well-adjusted child in a home of mixed religions with a Jewish mother and a Catholic father, but they had decided to worry about that later.

They had fallen in love in college. Mixed marriages were happening all around them. Some worked out, some didn't. Both sets of parents asked the young couple to finish college, and if they were still in love, the parents would support the marriage. They finished college, still very much in love. Philip had insisted he would have to have a job before he could get married.

Ruth understood and supported his decision. She wanted to get a job, too. They were lucky, and both were hired right out of college. Their marriage took place very soon after. Their wedding ceremony was conducted by a reform rabbi and a Jesuit priest. They felt very married.

One night, after they had been married for five years, they were in bed, and Ruth turned to Philip and said, "I want to have a baby. Are you ready?"

Philip sprang up and said, "You bet. Oh, honey, when did you decide this? I've wanted to talk to you and bring this subject up, but I didn't know how to begin. Are you sure you're ready? You know, you may have to quit work."

"I know, I know. That's not the problem."

"Okay," Philip held his breath. "What's the problem?"

"When we have children—and you heard me say when—what religion will our children be? She felt her brow creasing with worry. "Please tell me what your feelings are about this? I know we talked about it a little in college, but now it has become a possibility, or should I say a probability."

Philip used his fingers to smooth the wrinkles on her forehead. "I never really thought about it. I just always assumed I'd have Catholic children."

Ruth felt as though the wind had been knocked out of her. "And I always knew I'd have Jewish children. How do we settle this? I love you so much, but have we made a mistake getting married?"

"I didn't realize you were so strong in your beliefs," Philip said. "Why do you feel our child should be raised Jewish?"

"Well, in the Jewish religion, if the mother is Jewish, the child is automatically Jewish. The father being Jewish won't make a child Jewish, only the mother. So, I always thought that if I had a child, it wouldn't matter what I did, my child would be Jewish because I am."

"As a Catholic," Philip said, "I was taught that children

197

are very important to the church. They have to study the catechism in order to learn the doctrines of the church before they are considered Catholics. I never understood what you just said about your religion. I thought they had to have Bar Mitzvahs to be Jewish."

"At thirteen years of age, a boy or girl can have a Bar or Bat Mitzvah. That makes them accepted as an adult in the community, but it doesn't make them Jewish. With our children, I would make them Jewish. I don't know if they will practice the faith, but they will forever be Jewish." Ruth heaved a large sigh when she finished.

"I'll love our children as I do you," Philip said. "Your being Jewish has only brought me joy. So, I would think that if my children are Jewish, if they are good kids, I'll love them, too. Maybe even if they're not real good, I'll still love them like crazy. Like I love you."

Ruth got on her knees in bed and threw her arms around Philip. "Oh, darling, I love you so much. Thank you, thank you."

And so, Josh had been raised Jewish knowing his dad had a different religion. Josh had always been told that all religions were good if the people were charitable, kind, and good. He'd also always gotten Christmas gifts *and* Chanukah gifts. This year, his Sunday school teacher had told him the story of the Maccabees and why Chanukah was celebrated for eight days, and it made a big impression on the boy.

Ruth knocked on Josh's door. "Can I come in?"

"Sure, Mom, come on in."

Ruth had brought a glass of milk and a freshly baked bulkie for Josh.

Josh took in a deep breath. "Gosh, Mom. You brought the smell of fresh baked rolls with you. You know I love them, and I'm ready for a break anyway."

"Are you having a problem with your writing?"

"Kinda," Josh said, "but I think I can work it out. It's not as easy as I thought it would be."

"You know I would be glad to help if you want me to."

"I know, but I've just got to do this myself. When I finish, I'd like you to read it. Okay?"

"Of course, darling." Ruth stood, looking at the child that she and Philip had created. She was so proud of him. She loved his looks. He had her hair and eyes, and Philip's mannerisms, mouth, and cleft in his little chin. And like his father, he thought of other people. She smiled, looked up, and prayed, *Thank you, God, for this wonderful small person. I pray that one day he will be a wonderful adult that we'll always be proud of. Thank you again for our son.*

Josh looked up at his smiling mother and shook his head. "Mom, I really need to get back to work. You can have the empty plate and glass if you want, or I can bring them down later if you're not going into the kitchen now." His brow furrowed like Ruth's when she was concentrating or worried.

Ruth bent and kissed his forehead. Josh brushed the kiss off with his hand. Ruth knew that was a habit of his and not meant to hurt her feelings. He always brushed kisses off. She put them there anyway. "Someday, you're going to meet a girl, and you'll hope she kisses you."

"Sorry, Mom. I guess I was just thinking hard. You're not mad, are you?"

"Never," Ruth answered as she left the room.

Once more, the pencil became a pacifier and ended up in Josh's teeth as he contemplated the story he'd heard at Sunday school, and suddenly the pencil took flight in his fingers and landed on the yellow paper.

"Yes!" When he finished writing, he read it aloud.

Once, many years ago, there was trouble for Jews in the town of Modin, not far from Jerusalem. A bad king called Antiochus wanted all of the Jews to give up their religion and worship Zeus. Even though the Syrian army fought a small band of Jews led by Judah Maccabee, the Jews won. They went to Jerusalem and found the holy Temple had been destroyed, so they rebuilt it. They searched for

*oil for the menorah. There was only enough oil
for one day, but after it was lit, it burned for
eight days. So, Chanukah means Festival or
Dedication of Lights. We add one candle to light
the menorah each night until all eight are lit.
That's why we celebrate for eight days.*

*My Sunday school teacher said this was the first
time a war was started and won for religious
freedom. So, Santa, thank you anyway, and I still
appreciate the gifts in the past, but don't worry
about me anymore. Besides, I thought if I got
Christmas gifts too, someone who is not Jewish
might get left out. I don't want that to happen.*

*Your friend,
Josh Simpson*

That evening after dinner, Josh proudly handed his
legal pad to his dad. "Thanks, Dad. Mom said it would be okay
if I used your paper. I wrote a long letter, and I'd like you to
mail it for me, okay?"

"Sure, son, I'll be glad to. Mom told me you were
writing, and that we would be able to read it when you
finished. Is that still a go?"

"It's real important to me, so please don't laugh or try
to make me change my mind. All right?"

"We'd never do that. You should know us better than
that," Philip said. He read the letter first and then handed it to
Ruth. There were tears in Ruth's eyes when she finished, but
Philip had a wide grin on his face.

Josh said, "You're laughing at it."

"Oh, God no," Ruth said. We're so proud of you and
your ideas. You're so thoughtful and kind."

After Josh went to bed, Ruth and Philip talked about
their son. They were so proud of him.

"You know," Ruth said, "after Josh was born, and the
doctor said I couldn't have any more children, I was angry with

God. I didn't know then the wonderful gift he had given us. I thought that maybe he was angry with us because we married out of our faiths. But look what a blessing he has bestowed on us. God couldn't be angry. He loves us, and he knows that though we may say it in different ways, we both love Him."

Kay Grafe lives with her husband, Roy, on a farm in Lucedale, Mississippi. She worked for the George County school system for twenty-eight years: six as a high school history teacher and twenty-two as a speech pathologist. Thirty-five years ago she began writing a column titled *Grin 'n' Bare It* for a local paper. In 1995, *Grin 'n' Bare It* was picked up by a statewide magazine, *Today in Mississippi.* She has also received a First Place award in the Mississippi Press Association's Better Newspaper Contest. Kay has been described as Mississippi's Erma Bombeck and, in addition to writing, is also a frequent after-dinner speaker throughout Mississippi. Kay's first book titled *Oh My Gosh, Virginia* is a compilation of her favorite columns and is scheduled for publication in early 2010. She is also working on a novel which she plans to complete in 2010.

The Worst of Christmases, the Best of Christmases is a personal essay based on true events in my life. It's the story of dealing with illness, death, loneliness—all during the holiday season. It takes place when and where it happened, in rural Mississippi during the 1940s.

Personal Essay

The Worst of Christmases,
the Best of Christmases

Kay Grafe

Being an only child during the forties wasn't easy. Back then most couples had large families. I had cousins who served as replacement brothers and sisters, but it wasn't the same. Every night when Mother and I said our prayers, I asked God for a baby brother.

"You talk to Him, Mother," I'd say. "Tell God to send us a boy like Edda Jane's brother, Jackson. I like him cause he won't let anybody say mean things to her. If I had a brother, he'd beat up Huston when he tells me I'm skinny."

Mother always smiled and prayed alongside me, "God, you heard Kay's prayer. If it's Your will, let it be so."

"What does 'Your will' mean?" I asked her.

"It means that since God created us, He knows what is best for His people, so if He thinks we need a baby in our family, He will answer yes."

In 1945, when I was six years old, three amazing events came to us. May 8, V-E Day, marked the end of the war in Europe. August 14, V-J Day, marked the end of the war in the Pacific. July 4, Mother told me she was pregnant.

Of course, she didn't come right out and say *I'm pregnant.* In those days, not in a million years would adults use the word pregnant in front of a child. It was a delicate subject that parents weren't prepared to broach.

The day I learned I was to be a big sister, I was sitting cross-legged on my mahogany, spindle bed that matched the double bed of my parents. My bed was a single and was four giant steps away from my parents' bed. I liked my bed snug

203

against the west wall where there was a picture of a little girl about my age, standing in a corner with her collie dog. They were being punished for stepping on her mother's daffodils. My parents' bed was on the east wall of the room, next to the double window. I'd watched Mother crochet my white bedspread to match theirs. I was very proud that the spreads were alike.

I had arranged my paper dolls in a circle on the bed, and I was talking to them about a dog named Tippy.

"Kay," Mother called, "come in the kitchen. I've something to tell you."

Mother wore her best grin when I walked into the kitchen. "What would you like more than anything in the world, Kay?"

Without hesitation, I said, "A baby brother."

She leaned over and kissed my forehead. "Well, I can't promise a boy baby, but I promise we are going to get either a girl or boy."

My happiness spilled over in the form of a strident squeal. I was thrilled to my core.

Mother laughed. "Kay! You'll break a window pane screaming so loud."

I remember saying over and over, "It's God's will! It's God's will!"

Mother crocheted booties, caps, and sweaters for the baby. I made chains out of construction paper, cut out paper dolls, and drew pictures to help decorate the baby's room.

"Honey, we'll have to put the baby's bed where your bed is now. You can have the guest bedroom like a big girl. We'll hang the picture of the little girl and her dog that you like so much in your new room, and you can hang the pretties you made over the baby's bed."

By early December, almost all of our preparations were complete, including the baby's layette.

"When can I move to my new room?" I asked Mother one day.

"Oh, I suppose we'll wait until the baby arrives to move your bed into the guest room."

That was on Friday, December 7, 1945. It was early morning, and I'll never forget the date, because the whole city of Forest had a day of prayer and remembrance that afternoon for our servicemen who had been killed at Pearl Harbor. It was at the courthouse square, and it was packed with people and soldiers wearing uniforms.

It was the same day, but barely nighttime, when Mother got sick. Daddy helped her to bed, and I stood outside the bedroom door with Daddy and my grandmother, Mama Jennie, as Dr. Sam examined mother. My grandfather, Daddy Tom, sat by himself in the kitchen, and I could hear a soft whisper of crying coming from the room.

When he opened the bedroom door, Dr. Sam said, "Kay, why don't you wait in the kitchen with your granddaddy for a few minutes?" As he said those words, he reached for the telephone. He sat down in the chair next to the telephone table in the hallway and dialed.

I heard the familiar scraping noise as Daddy pulled down the hideaway stairs and climbed up into the attic. He called, "Mr. Tom, will you come here please?" I watched from the kitchen doorway as Daddy passed the valise down to my granddaddy and backed down the stairs. Our bedroom door was still closed.

When Daddy had maneuvered the stairs in place and pushed them back into the ceiling, I stepped into the kitchen away from the bedroom door. He went into our room with the valise, and Mama Jennie followed. Daddy came back out quickly and said a few words to Daddy Tom that I didn't understand. Then he looked at me.

"Come here a minute, Sugar Plum." He'd called me by that nickname all my life. "Your mother's pretty sick, so an ambulance will take her to the hospital in Jackson. I'm going to go with your mother. Mama Jennie will stay here tonight with you. But I'll telephone tomorrow and let you know how your mother's feeling."

Before I had time to think about the baby, Mother called, "Kay, come in the bedroom a minute."

I hurried to the bedroom, and Mama Jennie closed the

door behind me. Mother was standing between the two beds in her pretty blue silk bathrobe. The valise was open, and her nightgowns and underwear were folded neatly on one side. On the other side were a pair of house slippers and a box of Johnson's Baby Powder that we'd bought for our new baby.

"Where's the baby's layette?" I asked as I rummaged through the valise.

"Come close, honey, so you can hear me," she said, sitting down on the side of the bed. She wrapped her arms around me and pulled me close. "There's something wrong with the baby and with me, so I want you to understand that we probably won't get our baby after all. Now, I want you to be a good girl while I'm away and help Mama Jennie. Do you understand?"

My tears were falling faster than a summer's driving rain. "But, it's God's will!" I cried. "It's His will. He can't take His will away."

"Be quiet a moment, Kay. Just listen to me."

I jerked away from her. "You're lying! When you come back home, bring our baby too! Please don't leave him there at the hospital. Please, please!"

I didn't hear my grandmother come into the room, but she was down on her knees beside me. She wrapped her arms around me tightly, but I squirmed to get free.

"No! Turn me loose! Let me go!"

"Wait!" Mother said sternly. "Be still and pay attention, Kay. God knows the baby is sick and wants to take him or her back to Heaven."

Still crying, I stopped moving and surrendered to Mama Jennie's arms.

Mother said, "It's not God's fault. It's my body that can't carry the baby any longer."

I remembered how she had placed my hand over her dress and let me feel our baby kicking over the past months.

She went on. "I'll show you why my body can't carry the baby any longer."

I was shocked when she pulled her robe back so I could see her stomach. It was swollen, ugly and black, with red streaks crisscrossing back and forth over her skin. I thought for a moment her skin would burst open and spill the baby on the floor. They took her in an ambulance to the hospital.

When it was over, I stood at the graveside service on a cloudy bitter afternoon and watched two pallbearers place the tiny, white satin coffin atop an aperture covered with fake green grass. A metal frame sat beneath the grass, cradling the coffin. Mother was too sick to go to the funeral, so I stood between Daddy and his mother, Mama Fannie, as they held my hands in theirs. All my grandparents, aunts, and uncles stood near the small white box like statues.

I stared down at the chest that had two small handles on each end. When I looked up at Daddy, he closed his eyes, but I saw the wetness beneath his lashes.

"Can I see my brothers before they go to Heaven?"

Daddy nodded and motioned to a man who walked closer and opened both ends of the coffin. There lay tiny twin boys. They were wearing blue flannel pajamas and blue crocheted caps.

After the funeral, Daddy went back to the hospital, but not before he told me that Mother was too sick to come home for Christmas. She had developed phlebitis, a serious illness in those days.

I was granted special permission to visit Mother in the adult wing where children weren't allowed. The doctor said I could stand at her open door for five minutes, with a nurse to oversee this arrangement.

I rode from Forest to the Mississippi Baptist Hospital in Jackson in Daddy Tom's black Ford with my grandparents and Mother's sisters. It was a long hour's drive.

While I waited in a vacant room next to Mother's, my heart pounded so loud that I took a pillow from the unmade bed and held it against my chest. When a nurse entered the bathroom from the adjacent room, she emptied water from a large silver bowl into the toilet. I could see the back of Mama Jennie's flowered dress as she stood at the foot of Mother's bed. I tried to peek around the nurse's white starched apron, but she quickly flushed the commode, returned to the room, and closed the door in one smooth motion. I didn't have time to see my mother.

I thought that if I could just hold my mother's hand, I would tell her I loved her, and she would get better and come home because I didn't want her to die like my baby brothers. I waited as long as my legs would let me, then I walked into the bathroom and slowly turned the doorknob. There was a crack I could see through, but everyone was too tall for me to see over their heads, so I quietly closed the toilet lid and stood on top of it.

There was a strange woman lying in the bed with a mask over her nose, a long tube extending from her mouth, and a needle taped to her arm. There was a smaller tube leading from the needle up to a jar of what looked like water hanging from a tall pole. Why was she in the room with my mother? A white cloud floated over my eyes and blurred them, so I blinked several times. Then I could see. The woman's hair was black like Mother's and her left hand had the same scar where Mother had touched a hot iron.

That's when I fainted.

When I opened my eyes again, my daddy and a nurse stood over me, and I was lying in a bed without a pillow. My arm was wrapped in a hard white cast. My head was hurting, but I couldn't keep my eyes open to tell anybody. The next time I awoke, I was in bed at Mama Jennie's house, and she was sitting next to me.

I looked at her and then at my arm. "I didn't get to stay long enough. Is mother dead?"

"No, of course not. She's very sick, and that's why she looked so quiet and still. But she made it through the second surgery and will get better now. It may take a long time, but your mother will be okay."

"Will she get well by Christmas?"

Mama Jennie shook her head—a no.

So, not only did I lose my brothers, but in my young mind I'd lost Mother and Daddy and Christmas too. I took turns staying with both sets of grandparents, and they all tried to console me as best they could.

Those were the darkest days of my entire life.

My grandparents told me to be careful with a cast on my left arm, so all I did was sit at the kitchen table and watch Mama Jennie make fruit cakes and cook pies for the holidays. As Christmas approached, my grandparents assured me that Santa Claus would not forget me, but I didn't care. All I wanted was my mother.

There were whispers and mournful looks in my direction from family members, and I had the distinct impression that my mother was going to die. I didn't get to repeat my hospital visit.

I heard Mama Jennie talking to Aunt Sarah on the telephone one day. "The doctor said Kay is not emotionally stable, and he can't agree to another visit. A child shouldn't see her mother in that condition."

During the years before television, most six-year-olds believed in Santa Claus, and until then I had been a girl who loved to excite audiences made up of my friends and cousins with fables about Santa's magic sled led by reindeers flying above the rooftops. My words would gush like strong undercurrents into receptive ears. The other children screamed with delight and went away with extraordinary images to mull and repeat. As they retold the stories to their siblings and other friends, some would ask, "How do you know this is true?"

Their answer would be: "Because Kay said so. She's been there."

When I had an audience, even if it was only our housekeeper, Mary Alice, I poured out stories on my favorite topic—Santa Claus. I made it clear that Santa didn't live in a town with other people.

"How's it you know so much?" Mary Alice asked.

"I've been there," I said, matter-of-factly. It's called the North Pole. It's sorta like the Forest Country Club. Not just anybody can go there. But I'm Santa's favorite in the entire world, and that's why I get to ride with him in his sleigh up to the North Pole. Only Santa, his wife, the elves, and reindeer live there."

I truly believed Santa's family was alone at the North Pole, because when I fabricated my stories, they took on a life of their own and were just as true as Edward R. Morrow's nightly radio newscasts.

I had convinced myself and anyone who would listen that the Clauses' living quarters were rainbow colored with candy trees and a wishing well where, with the toss of a penny, all wishes came true. Mrs. Claus was always in her kitchen, cooking up candy canes and silver bells in her large pots. I spent many lonely hours inside my head, imagining details of the North Pole's gigantic castle, toy workshops, and the bright red barn for Santa's reindeer. I especially liked the elongated red barn that I designed with stalls for each reindeer and their names engraved above the entrances. There was a fireplace with a crackling fire in the center of the barn, and the castle, where the Clauses and elves lived, had a fireplace in each of the fifty rooms.

On Christmas Eve of 1945, all my cousins and grandparents changed the usual family tradition and came to our house. Usually we went to Mama Jennie's and Daddy Tom's to spend the night and wait for Santa Claus.

But that year, I didn't tell any of my exciting stories about Santa Claus and the North Pole. I didn't participate in any of the games with my cousins. Instead, I sat alone in the new rocking chair Daddy had bought for our baby and rocked myself to sleep. I'd hoped my Daddy would come home from the hospital before I fell asleep, but he didn't make it. I had the impression that my mother's family was trying to make a little happiness for me, but instead of making me feel better, it made me even more afraid that my mother was going to die. My aunts, uncles, and cousins had brought cots with them, and they also folded thick blankets on the floor for beds.

Christmas morning when I awoke, I realized someone had put me in my bed. I heard noises outside—doors opening and closing, and a car engine either driving in or out of our driveway. I was afraid to get out of bed, so I pulled the blanket over my head until I heard Daddy speaking to me from the foot of my bed.

"Wake up, Sugar Plum. Santa Claus came last night."

"Daddy, you're home!" I threw the covers back from my head and leaped into his arms.

"I have a surprise for you," he said. "Not only did Santa come, he brought someone with him."

Hugging me tightly, Daddy carried me in his arms down the hallway and into the guest bedroom. Lo and behold, Mother was propped up in bed. Toys were arranged neatly on the floor around a Christmas tree near the bed, but I didn't even notice them for hours. All I wanted was my mother. I stood and stared at her in disbelief. She was still pale, but all the tubes and the mask on her face were gone.

"Be very careful not to shake the bed or bump her," Daddy said softly. I carefully crawled into the bed next to her.

Over the years, my relatives referred to 1945 as *that terrible Christmas,* meaning our twin babies had died. And that part was terrible. But to me it turned into my best Christmas.

My greatest gift was my mother.

Joyce Sterling Scarbrough is the author of three novels—*True Blue Forever*, *Different Roads*, and *Symmetry*. She also has four short stories accepted in three upcoming anthologies. Joyce writes full time and does freelance editing. She's the president of the Mobile Writers Guild and is active in the Quill Masters critique group. She lives in Mobile, Alabama with her three children and husband of twenty-six years.

Journey of a Thousand Miles is a tribute to all the women and children who—unlike me—are not blessed with a life free of abuse. I guess the unfairness of it all touches me more around the holidays when I'm surrounded by my wonderful family. If the message in my story helps even one woman find the courage she needs to take that first step, I will feel as if I'm worthy of the gifts God has given me.

Short Story

Journey of a Thousand Miles

Joyce Sterling Scarbrough

Curtis had hit JoElla in the past more times than she could count, yet she had never considered leaving him until that day the week before Christmas.

Nothing he'd done before had seemed so terribly bad to her, at least not compared to everything JoElla's mama had put up with from her daddy before he ran off and left them when JoElla was twelve. Besides, Curt had to put up with a lot too. God knew she wasn't much to look at, and she was so dumb that she probably wouldn't have finished high school even if she hadn't gotten pregnant and had to drop out her senior year. Curt also worked really hard at the shipyard to take care of her and the baby, and that was a lot of pressure on him. So what if he drank too much sometimes and came home in a bad mood? JoElla had learned when to leave him alone so she wouldn't provoke him.

But this time was different.

The Thursday before Christmas, Curt promised they could go get their tree when he got home from work. Most of the lots would have them reduced by then, so JoElla was hoping they could get a fir instead of the usual pine. After she finished her housework, she spent the day stringing popcorn, making garland out of construction paper, and singing carols that delighted eighteen-month-old Cassie.

JoElla loved the way her little girl clapped her chubby hands and bounced whenever she sang. And she thought it was pretty smart for a child that young to recognize music and know what to do when she heard it. Maybe with the right encouragement, Cassie could grow up to play in the school

213

band and maybe even get a music scholarship. JoElla had wanted to be in the band herself once, but it hadn't worked out.

The first sign of trouble with Curt was when he was an hour late getting home from work. JoElla tried to convince herself that it must be the holiday traffic holding him up. That had to be it. He wouldn't go to the Crossroads Club on a weeknight, especially when he had promised her they could get the tree when he got home. But when he finally arrived at seven thirty, JoElla smelled the whiskey on him as soon as he came in the front door. Since getting mad wasn't an option, she questioned him under the pretense of concern.

"I was worried sick about you, Curt," she said, taking his lunch pail and hanging up his jacket. "You said we were gonna go get the tree tonight as soon as you got off, so I was scared to death that you'd had a wreck in all that Christmas traffic. Where've you been?"

He walked past her without so much as a glance and fell heavily into his chair in front of the television. JoElla hurried over to help him take off his heavy work boots.

"Don't worry 'bout where I been," he said, his words noticeably slurred. "I'm here now, ain't I? What's for supper?"

"I'll heat you up some of that stew I made yesterday," she said. "I got some biscuits left over from this morning too."

He grabbed her arm before she could walk away. "Why ain't it already heated up?"

"I thought maybe we could.... Oh, never mind. I'll go get it heated up for you now, Curt. It won't take but a minute."

He didn't release her arm. "You thought maybe we could what?"

She didn't want to make him mad, but she knew she couldn't get away with not answering. "I just thought maybe we could get a hamburger or something at the Burger Hut after we got the tree. You know, make a special night of it." She looked at him with a querulous smile that died when he shoved her toward the kitchen.

"We can't afford no damn hamburgers! The shipyard cut our bonuses in half this year without so much as a word of warning. Blamed it on the damn economy!" He kicked one of his work boots viciously across the room then sat with his head in his hands.

JoElla put a hand on his shoulder. "I'm sorry, Curt, but try not to worry. We'll make it all right. We'll just get a little pine tree and forget about the fir. I already got some decorations made that we can—"

"Didn't you hear me, Jo?" He stood and grabbed her by the shoulders, his red-rimmed eyes boring into her along with his fingers. "They cut my bonus in half! We can't afford no damn tree either."

"But, Curt, even if you only got half your bonus, it should be enough for a little tree."

He shook her roughly. "Don't you get it, you half-wit? I already had that money spent!"

Ordinarily, she would never dare to question him when he was mad, but she was too distraught to check herself. And the possibility that he might have spent it on her or the baby never entered her mind.

"Spent on what, Curt? It was supposed to be for our Christmas!"

JoElla's head struck the edge of the coffee table when she fell after Curt hit her, so at least she didn't feel the pain of the other blows until later when she came to.

Curt was gone when she opened her eyes again. He'd put Cassie in her high chair in front of the TV before he left. JoElla was glad that at least be hadn't left her free to roam around the apartment without anybody watching her. She told herself that meant he was trying to be a good daddy.

She got up slowly—the only way she was able to get up. Curt must have kicked her a couple of times in the thighs before he was done, but she reckoned that was better than getting kicked in the ribs like he'd done the time that he'd forgotten he bet on a football game and thought she had taken money out of his wallet.

Cassie had what looked like a soggy Ritz cracker clutched in one of her hands and was mesmerized by Sponge Bob on the television, so she didn't cry to be held when JoElla finally managed to stand up. Good thing, because she would have been afraid to carry her while her legs were so shaky. She went into the bathroom and reluctantly looked in the mirror to see how bad she looked this time.

There was a gash on her forehead at her hairline where her head had struck the table, but it didn't look like it had bled much. Her top lip was cut and starting to swell, but it didn't look too bad either. It seemed her legs had gotten the worst of it, and that would be easy to hide, so she actually felt relieved. She washed her face and went back to check on Cassie.

"C'mere, baby girl," she said as she removed the high chair tray and lifted Cassie into her arms. "Sponge Bob went bye-bye, and we need to get you some real food for supper."

Cassie put a chubby index finger on her mama's lip and said, "Boo-boo."

JoElla's eyes had been dry until then. She never cried anymore when Curt hit her. She'd learned a long time ago that it only made him angrier and made her feel worse later from having swollen eyes along with any other injuries. But when her little girl leaned over to kiss her busted lip, JoElla's eyes filled with tears. She tried to wipe them away before Cassie saw them.

"Yep, Mama got a boo-boo. Silly Mama." She tickled her daughter and got a giggle as usual, but she wondered how much longer she would be able to distract her so easily. Cassie would soon be old enough to understand how her mama got hurt.

JoElla pushed the thought from her mind the way she always did. She busied herself fixing Cassie a grilled cheese sandwich and some tomato soup, trying also not to think about where Curt might have gone and what kind of mood he'd be in when he came back.

After Cassie finished her supper, JoElla carried her into the bathroom to put her in the tub. She heard Curt's key in the front door just before she turned on the water.

"Get in here, Jo!" He yelled. "I got something to show you!"

She hurried into the living room with Cassie in her

arms. In one hand, Curt held a scrawny Christmas tree nailed onto two crossed boards. In the other he held a half-empty bottle of Wild Turkey.

"Look what I bought for you," he said, his speech so slurred now that JoElla had trouble understanding him. "Spent good money we don't have on it too, so you damn well better 'preciate it!" He thrust the pathetic-looking thing at JoElla, and she hurried to take it.

"Thanks, Curt. It'll be real pretty after I get it decorated." She set it down in front of the window and turned to take Cassie back down the hall.

"Well, what're you waiting for?" he demanded, falling into his chair. "Go on and get it decorated. You was so hell-bent on getting it."

JoElla stopped but didn't turn around. "I need to get the baby bathed and put to bed first."

"Fine," he said, and she could hear him taking a swig from the bottle. "Just hurry up and get back in here."

"I will, Curt."

She cringed as she walked down the hall, because she could tell from his tone what was coming. While he finished the bottle of whiskey, he'd start thinking about what he'd done earlier and get mad at himself. He'd start crying and telling her he was sorry, then he'd want to put his hands on her. She sure didn't want him to, but if she didn't let him, he'd hit her some more.

She tried to take extra long to get Cassie into bed, hoping Curt would pass out before she finished, but he was still working on the bottle when she went back to the living room. He was staring at the Christmas tree and turned to look at JoElla, and she could see the tears in his heavy-lidded, bloodshot eyes.

"You think I like not being able to provide for my family, Jo? You think I wanna spend my whole life crawling around in ship hulls?"

"I know you work hard, Curt," she said.

"I was gonna use that bonus money to go in with Dougie on buying an oyster boat we saw for sale over in Moss

217

Point. Guy who owns it says he's too old to work it anymore, but two able-bodied men like us could make a killing on oystering." He paused to take another drink from the bottle. "I used the rent money last month to give Dougie part of my half. That bonus money was gonna catch us up."

"Oh, Curt..." JoElla caught herself before she said anything critical, even though she was terrified at the trouble they were in now. "Maybe it'll be okay. I can look for a job as soon as Christmas is over."

He ran a hand through his hair and squeezed his eyes shut. "I'm so damn stupid. What made me think I could ever be anything different than my old man—just a grunt living from paycheck to paycheck?"

Despite everything, it broke JoElla's heart to see him like that. She walked over and put a hand on his arm. "Don't say that, Curt. You done real good by me and Cassie."

"You're even stupider than me if you think that." He looked up at her, and she could see the change in his expression. Too late she realized that he'd suckered her again. Before she could move away, he pulled her down onto his lap.

She knew better than to try to get up, but she said, "I need to get the tree decorated."

"You can do that later." He took a drink from the bottle then put it to her lips, but she shook her head and turned away.

"You know I can't drink that, Curt. It makes me sick."

He laughed and took another drink before setting the bottle on the floor. "Makes me sick sometimes too, but I don't let that stop me."

He turned her face back around and kissed her. When she winced, he touched the cut on her lip with his finger.

"Why do you make me hit you, Jo? You know I never mean to hurt you. Don't you?"

She didn't know it by any means, but she said, "Yeah, Curt. I know."

He started to unbutton her blouse, so JoElla closed her eyes and bit her lip, despite how badly it hurt.

Later, while Curt snored beside her in the bed, JoElla lay awake trying to get up the courage to ask him for the only thing she really wanted for Christmas—an electronic music maker for toddlers that she'd seen at the toy store. She knew Cassie would love it, and she truly believed her little girl had musical talent that just needed to be encouraged.

Curt would say they couldn't afford it, of course, but JoElla hoped that if she told him she could go door-to-door in their apartment complex to see if anyone would hire her to clean for them, she could make enough money to buy the toy for Cassie and help them pay the rent too.

He stirred in his sleep, so JoElla took advantage of it and said, "Curt, you hungry? I can go fix you some of that stew now if you want." She never understood how he could eat after drinking, but he always did.

He stretched and yawned. "Yeah, gimme a couple of biscuits too, and put some apple butter on 'em."

"Okay, sure thing." She threw on her robe and hurried to the kitchen, thanking her lucky stars that they weren't out of apple butter. She'd wait until he was eating before she asked him about getting the toy so that he'd be in the best mood possible.

He came in the kitchen a few minutes later and shielded his eyes from the overhead light. "Can't you turn on something that ain't so blinding, Jo?"

"Sorry, Curt. I'll turn on the light over the stove. Here's your plate all ready for you. You want milk with it?"

"Yeah, that's fine." He sat on one of the stools at the small bar next to the stove. After taking a couple of bites, he said, "This ain't bad at all, Jo. Thanks."

Her hopes soared at his good humor. "I'm glad you like it. I got a piece of apple pie saved for you too if you want dessert."

He nodded without looking up from his food. "You ever know me not to want dessert? Specially pie."

She smiled and went to get it for him. When she set the pie on the bar, she said, "Curt, I wanted to tell you that it's okay about the money. I already got you something for Christmas that I been saving for since August, and I didn't want nothing for me anyway. But there is something I wanted to get for Cassie."

He looked up and started to shake his head, but she hurried to go on before he could say anything.

"Just hear me out, Curt. I think I figured out a way we can do it."

He sighed and went back to eating. "How?"

JoElla took a courage-boosting breath. "Well, I was thinking that I could go around to the other apartments in the complex and ask if they want any cleaning done. You know, to get ready for Christmas."

He looked up at her again. "People ain't gonna have money to spend on nothing like that."

"Some of them will, Curt. The ones having parties and stuff. And they're gonna want their apartments cleaned before people come over."

He thought about it and looked interested. "How much you think you could make?"

"I figure I could clean two a day and still be able to get my housework done, so I think I could make at least a couple of hundred dollars. It'd be plenty enough to buy Cassie's toy and help make up the money for the rent too."

He shrugged and continued eating. "I guess it'd be okay. We gotta get the rent money somehow."

"And I can buy Cassie's toy?" JoElla held her breath after the question.

"What kinda toy is it?"

"It's a music maker for toddlers. The box said it would help with their fine motor skills and..." She paused to think. "Oh, and their hand-eye coordination."

He scoffed as he sopped up the last of the stew with his biscuit. "What the hell does she need any of that for? Just get her a toy broom and a mop so she can start learning to be like her mama."

His words hit JoElla in the gut harder than if he had kicked her. The funny thing was that all the times he really had kicked her, it hadn't made her mad nor opened her eyes the way it did for him to talk about their daughter with such disregard, as if she were nothing special at all instead of the precious treasure that she was.

And the worst thing was that he was right about Cassie, but not about what kind of work she was destined to do. If she grew up in this house with him for a father and saw her mama getting hit over and over and taking it, Cassie wouldn't have a chance of ever being anything different. The image of the way Cassie already cowered whenever Curt was yelling about something, even though it wasn't directed at her—not yet anyway—made JoElla finally see just what she was teaching her daughter to become, the same way JoElla had learned it from watching her own mother.

And that was when she knew she had to leave.

She muttered something to Curt that maybe he was right and busied herself cleaning up the kitchen, but her mind was busy with something a lot more important. She had to figure out the best way to get both of them away from Curt's abuse. JoElla finally saw her situation for what it was. She couldn't go on making excuses for him just because he worked hard. She had to get Cassie away from him.

If she never did anything else for the rest of her life, she was determined to make sure that Cassie learned not to ever let a man hit her. It was the best Christmas gift JoElla could give to herself or her little girl.

The following night, JoElla and Cassie sat with a group of women and children around a huge Christmas tree at a women's shelter in Mobile—a shelter for victims of domestic violence. Like JoElla, many of the women had bruises, black eyes, or busted lips, but there was something else they all shared as well.

In this season of light, a glimmer of hope shone in all their eyes.

Editor's Choice

From

Christmas is a Season! 2008

Four pieces from the 2008 anthology were nominated for Pushcart Prizes. The staff wanted to run those four pieces again this year, each with an editorial note. Enjoy!

Jen Calder grew up on a farm in Upstate New York and attended Syracuse University, where she earned a B.A. in Russian Studies and an M.A. in International Public Administration. She began writing fiction at age 41, and studied craft at Fairfield University, Yale University, and the Bread Loaf Writers' Conference at Middlebury College. Her work has appeared or is forthcoming in *The Blue Guitar*, *The Chaffin Journal*, *Musings,* and *Talking River Review.*

Christmas Dinner is not a long story, but it has taken me more than ten years to understand what I saw in the ripostes among siblings and the swirl of cats in an overheated kitchen. Dynamics within families, often established during youth and reverted to in adult gatherings, can subtly exclude and alienate. Like story, they conceal as much as they reveal. The irony of the pain engendered by those closest to us seems most ironic at Christmas, and fiction seemed the best vehicle to show what I could not tell.

Editor's Note: Jen Calder's short story, *Christmas Dinner,* is about events we all know, yet the story is filled with surprises. Everyone has experienced the disappointment of holiday family gatherings frequently tinged with undercurrents of individual grievances. Calder doesn't *tell* us the specific nature of the singular hurts, she allows us, as readers, to discover them, festering just below the surface. While the story is powerful, the telling of it is understated, quiet—we're allowed into the over-heated kitchen to listen and observe. And those cats! We shudder as they stroll across countertops and sniff at the food. The last line is the clincher—we know this is a family that has lost its way. Yet, the story whispers rather than shouts.

L.B.P.

Short Story

Christmas Dinner

Jen Calder

My sister Beth drove up from Washington last night. Her job allows her half days before holidays. I arrive just before four. My sister Sarah has used the tractor to plow the driveway at some point earlier in the day, but wind heaps a solid drift across the left side as it sets up a circular howling pattern around the little farmhouse. The December sun sets, lengthening shadows about the yard and marbling the sky along the horizon in mauve and frozen pink. I smell burning pine from the chimney smoke as I plod through the drift to get to the back door, allowing myself a fleeting sense of elation at making first tracks in the white, unbroken surface. They have not heard my car pull in. A string of red and green Christmas lights has been tacked around the door, and most of them blink on and off. A few are duds, and these catch the failing light on the horizon to glow pink-gold. I step into the kitchen's damp air, heated now by an inefficient wood-burning stove that affords uneven warmth.

The room smells of smoke, turkey, and the fetid odor of cats. Cats sprawl together in twos and threes in proximity to the wood stove, which crackles and hisses smoke from the wind's downdraft. Sarah sits in front of a little TV, the remote in her left hand, a glass of wine in her right. The weather station blares. She wears a T-shirt that declares *Work Is the Curse of the Drinking Class*. It plainly discloses the absence of any undergarment.

"Oh good, Jodi." She looks up at me. "You made it. Now I can drink serious." She hefts herself out of the chair and moves toward the oven door, stooping low to peek into its

225

interior and examine the turkey's progress. A cat scrambles onto her seat and settles into a tight ball. A puff of smoke escapes the oven and Sarah blinks, wiping her eyes with the back of her hand. "Glad you could take a day to be with your family. Rough trip?"

"Hit your lake-effect snow about an hour west of Albany. But the traffic wasn't bad. Everybody else gets where they're going earlier on Christmas, I guess. Hospitals can't really close…"

"You'd think the goddamned weather station could have called this one," Ma snarls. Ma sits at the kitchen table bending over a box of mushrooms, holding a little paring knife and a mushroom inches from her eyes as she whittles the outer layer of skin from the mushroom's crown. "We've been watching it all day, trying to guess when you'd get here."

"Sorry. I would have called, but nothing was open along the highway. Not even McDonald's. What can I do here?" I shift about, look for a clear space where I can place my travel bag, finally decide it'll be out of the way just inside the door. I remove my coat and hang it over the back of a chair.

"Not much." Beth reaches into the freezer and pulls out trays of ice, opens them into a bowl. "You timed it right. Turkey's about done and we're just starting the mashers. Ma's working on the gravy mushrooms there. Get a drink. We've already started."

I pull the fridge door open, search the crowded shelves, and retrieve a Budweiser. I look around for a place to sit. Cats occupy every chair. I consider the counter, where I used to sit as a girl while my mother bustled about fixing supper, but the surface is cluttered with serving dishes and an assortment of pans. I position myself at the edge of one of the chairs, taking care not to disturb the sleeping cat. The cat protests in any case, letting out a plaintive meow at being forced to share his space.

I sip my beer and consider the porcelain statue of Jesus on the crucifix hanging from the opposite wall. His shoulders are cloaked with greasy dust, and cat fur catches in the thorn crown on top of his head. Ma used to keep Him spotless. An artificial Christmas tree, about two feet tall, is positioned beneath the statue. It's draped with silver and gold tinsel, and the cats have been at it, because strands of tinsel have been dragged all over the room.

Sarah slices the mushrooms and stirs them into the gravy, presses the wooden spoon to her tongue to evaluate its taste, liberally adds wine. Beth removes the turkey from the oven. Ma, having completed her mushroom chore, leans heavily against the side of the refrigerator for balance, using a chopstick to stir ice in the martini she mixes in a jelly jar.

"I hate carving. This is the only time I wish we still had a man in the family," Beth grumbles. She rips off a piece of turkey skin and drops it to a hairy yellow cat. The cat sniffs it, abandons it. Beth steps on it as she leans over to take a drag off the cigarette she's left smoking in a saucer.

"Can't count on 'em for much in life," Ma says.

"Not if you want anything done right," Sarah adds.

Ma tests the martini for dryness, pours it into a crystal glass she's had chilling in the freezer and, martini in hand, works her way to the nearest chair where she pushes the resident cat onto the floor. Cats circulate, barely missing entanglement in Ma's feet. One climbs over the turkey platter. Beth pushes it aside with the carving fork.

"Give me the juice from the carving pan," Sarah orders, mixing flour into the mushrooms. "And open more wine, will one of you?"

"I don't know." Beth sucks a different finger between each word as she arranges the turkey on a platter. She extracts the wishbone, lays it on the windowsill to dry. A cat licks it. She rolls up her left sleeve with a greasy hand, brushes her hair from her eyes, picks up a knife for a final attack on the carcass. "When you had David living here, he helped out with fence posts and the hay, at least."

"Yeah, well... he was better at what he did by day than by night. Who needs 'em. Hand me the gravy ladle from the cupboard over your head—and try to get both the white and dark meat on the same platter. Means one less dish to clean up after."

"Don't worry. I work for the government. I know how

to pile things up." Beth finishes arranging meat, pushes the platter to one side of the counter.

I have the bottle of wine, and I struggle with the cork screw. Sarah laughs. "Never could line things up straight, could you Jodi?"

I place the bottle between my knees, lever the cork and pull. The cork lurches from the bottle in a loud *pop*, wine splashing after it. Cats rush over to investigate, sniff with distaste, scuttle off again.

"Your David was okay," Beth muses, wiping her hands on her pants. "Only trouble was, he wanted kids, and I don't think he had the genes to improve upon the line."

"I hate big meals like this," Ma grumbles, swirling the ice around in her glass with her forefinger. "The women always get stuck cooking all day, spend hours cleaning up after, all for a half hour of over-eating. Your father always insisted on it, but why not? He was the lazy beneficiary. Thank God none of you girls chose to marry and carry that burden."

I want to believe in Christmas. I want to believe in love, and the warmth of family, and the traditional rituals that bind community. We'd agreed, no gifts. The whole commercial side of Christmas undermined the spirit, the idea behind the observance. Instead, we would all make an effort to be here. Together. I try to redirect the conversation. "So, Ma. What a day, eh? Sure didn't expect this storm."

"Makes no difference." Ma considers the olive in her glass, apparently decides to let it soak a little longer before she eats it. "I'm trapped in here no matter what the weather does."

Sarah's lips tighten, and she reaches for the bottle of wine I've placed on the counter, tops up her glass. Beth opens a can of cranberry and offers, "Poor Ma. Snowfall sure is pretty when it's coming down like this, though."

"Too damn cold. I ache all over in weather like this."

Beth and Sarah exchange glances. Beth's eyes reveal no emotion. Hoisting the platter of turkey, she moves toward the back room that serves, when company comes, as a dining room.

"OK, we're ready." Sarah picks up the gravy ladle and

follows Beth to the next room. "You can help Ma to the table."

I offer Ma my hand and pull her up from her chair. She teeters as she stands, and her drink slurps over the top of the glass as she grasps my arm. She steadies herself and bends over to take a sip, so the remaining contents will not be endangered by the journey. I feel her weight against me as we start our way into the next room. I smell the smoke in her hair and the ever-so-faint hint of rose toilet water she has always worn—that she wore when she used to tuck me into bed and listen to me "pray the Lord my soul to keep."

Sarah's voice carries back to us. "And somebody has to come up with a blessing, 'thanks be to God that we're gathered here together this day,' or some such. You can do that much, Jodi."

We pass by the crucifix, and I keep my right arm around Ma as I bend down for a piece of gold tinsel. I wind it through the thorny crown, then run my fingers over the little plastic tears on the cheeks.

Mahala Church is one of the founders of the Emerald Coast Writers and of the Mobile Writers Guild. A business editor and writer with extensive experience in medical management and team dynamics, she retired early and turned her attention to the art of writing. She brings her education with a B.S. in Liberal Arts and a degree in nursing plus her love of the South to her writing. Her work has appeared in the *Emerald Ladies Journal, Sandscript, The Single Mother,* and *Cup of Comfort for Grandparents.*

Wonders Never Cease is a non-fiction essay dedicated to the wonder of childhood and the mystery of Christmas, which often brings out what I call bonus characteristics in people. The story speaks of a simpler time in the history of our country, a time when family fellowship and a belief in magic were enough to make Christmas special.

Editor's Note: While Mahala Church's *Wonders Never Cease* is a personal essay, it presents itself with all the rising action of a short story. The reader bumps into a surprise around every corner. Church perfectly captures the wonder of a small child at Christmas. The details are rich, the resolution well earned. *Wonders Never Cease* is an example of the personal essay at its best. While Mahala Church serves as an editor at Excalibur Press, she had no idea this piece was selected until after the nominations were dropped in the mail. Congratulations Mahala!

L.B.P.

Personal Essay

Wonders Never Cease

Mahala Church

When I was four years old, my parents decided to spend Christmas with my father's family in North Alabama. My brother Billy was almost a year old and my grandparents hadn't seen him yet. He weighed only three pounds at birth, and in 1949 there were no neonatal intensive care units. He had been very sick but now was thriving, and my parents looked forward to showing off their miracle baby.

Mother had taken Billy and me to have our picture made with a department store Santa a few weeks before the trip, and the picture sat in our living room as a daily reminder of the tricycle Santa had promised me. Old enough to understand that Santa would magically enter our living room and leave presents, I could hardly wait. We had a small Christmas tree, sparkling with multi-colored lights and glass ornaments and a red felt advent calendar with candy canes in little pouches for each day until Christmas. After dinner we were allowed to have our candy treat as a reminder of how many days were left until Santa arrived.

The day before we departed, my mother took down the Christmas decorations and packed them away. She said Christmas would be over by the time we got back home, and she wanted to leave the house ship-shape. When Daddy took our undressed Christmas tree out with the trash, a tremendous fear hit me. Santa wasn't coming. Somehow I had missed Christmas. No tricycle for me. A torrent of tears rushed down my face as my parents tried to reassure me.

"We're having Christmas at Granny and Grandpa's, remember?" My father said. "Santa will visit you at their house

231

and bring the tricycle he promised." He hugged me tightly until I fell asleep still not completely convinced that Christmas would come.

Like every trip of my childhood, we left in the dark of early morning. Daddy carried me half-asleep to the cavernous back seat of our Plymouth where I slept through the first few hours of travel. When I awoke, I was still in my flannel gown and robe with thick socks on my feet. My mother had swaddled me and Baby, my favorite doll, in heavy blankets. Baby had honey blonde curls painted on her head and crystal blue eyes. We both stared up at the blue sky and worried about missing Christmas.

The drive to my grandparents' farm took a whole day. My brother Billy rode in the front seat so my mother could keep him warm. I could hear her softly reading to him from Golden Books. I had my own stack of picture books in the back seat, but I wasn't interested. I was still worried about whether or not Christmas would come.

As we wound our way around mountains and traveled farther and farther from home, my apprehension grew. At breakfast, I picked at my pancakes. My parents tried to cheer me with promises of snow angels, roasting marshmallows, and playing with my cousins, but my mood remained gloomy. I pelted them with questions.

When exactly had they let Santa know we wouldn't be home on Christmas Eve? Would Santa remember Billy, since he was too small to ask for anything? What if Santa left my cousins presents but forgot me?

The minute we pulled into my grandparents' yard, the front door swung open and my grandparents and Aunt Grace spilled out. I jumped down from the back seat of the car, and immediately announced in a loud, clear voice how worried I was about missing Christmas.

My Aunt Grace, the family's old maid, lived with my grandparents. Without children of her own, she lavished love on each of her nieces and nephews. Optimistic and chuckling as always, she reached for her new nephew while doling out reassurances to me.

"Don't you worry, Sweetmeat. You're going to have a Christmas you won't ever forget. That jolly old elf, Santa, always comes to our house."

My short, round grandmother hurried toward me, a crocheted black shawl draped over her open arms. The hems of her flour-sack dress and white apron fluttered across the top of her cotton hose and lace-up black shoes. She gathered me into her chubby arms with a tight squeeze. Smelling faintly of flour, sugar and vanilla, she pressed me to her generous bosom. "I talked to Santa, and he assured me he'd be here," she said.

My grandfather, clad in his usual overalls and checked flannel shirt, wore his customary gray fedora, covering his slick bald head. A dyed-in-the-wool curmudgeon, he studied me from under his hat, issued his usual "humph," and tromped back into the house with a load of luggage.

Once inside, I didn't see anything that looked like Christmas. There were no decorations, or greenery, or angels. Nothing.

"Where's your Christmas tree?" I asked.

"Young lady, you're not half-way through the door and already stirring up trouble," my father said. "I don't want to hear another word from you about missing Christmas or Santa or anything. Hush for a change and watch what's going on around you."

"We'll have a tree soon enough," Granny said.

The next morning, everyone got busy. All of my grandparents' children and grandchildren were coming for the Christmas Eve feast and, with only four days left, we all had a lot to do. Daddy and Grandpa took the shopping lists written by Granny and my mother and headed into town. Momma put me to work checking the pecans and walnuts to make sure all the shells and bitters had been removed. She chopped dried apples and peaches while Aunt Grace chopped up nuts for cakes and candy.

I continued to pepper Granny and Aunt Grace with a never-ending barrage of questions. Where were the decorations? Did they remember to tell Santa about Billy? When did they tell Santa about me? Did we need to remind

233

him? Mother threatened to tape my mouth shut at one point, but my beloved grandmother kept telling her to be patient.

Two days before Christmas, my dismay over the missing tree led to a trip into the woods with my father and grandpa to find a Christmas tree. I talked continuously as we hiked. Why didn't we get a tree at a tree place like at home? How were we going to get it back to the house without a car? Could we take back some pinecones for decorations? Was Daddy sure Santa was bringing me a tricycle? Even the rich sights and sounds of the thick icy woods, squirrels and rabbits scampering around, and the rich aromas of pine and cedar weren't a salve for my worried soul.

Grandpa glowered at me from under the brim of his hat and shook his head with annoyance as he stomped through the frozen underbrush in his heavy brown boots, examining one tree after another. Daddy carried me on his shoulders at first, but his patience soon wore thin. He pulled me down and plunked me thigh deep in the snow, promising me a discussion with a switch if I didn't close my mouth and keep it closed.

My short legs, encased in a bulky snowsuit, made walking in the snowy woods a tricky business. More than once, my father had to pull me back onto my feet as I stumbled over the thick underbrush.

When my grandfather spotted a tree to consider, he'd circle it several times and then stand silently looking it up and down, waiting for my father's response. Finally selecting a tree, they wrapped it in an old sheet and tied it with string. My grandfather cut the tree down with his axe, releasing the enticing smell of cedar into the air.

Daddy picked me up and swung me around, exclaiming it was the most beautiful Christmas tree he'd ever seen, but it didn't look or smell like a Christmas tree to me. We'd always had a fir tree, and this tree was totally different.

I held my stance as the most melancholic child on earth. I hadn't seen any Christmas cookies, or fudge, or divinity, or candy canes, or red ribbons at Granny's house. No turkey thawing in the refrigerator. And now a strange tree from the woods. Nothing looked or smelled familiar.

With a heavy rope tied around the trunk, my father dragged the tree back through the woods. The sheet kept the tree from picking up leaves and other debris off the ground. My grandfather and I silently plodded behind. When I stumbled and fell, Grandpa plucked me from the ground and put me back on my feet, never saying a word.

Back at the house, everyone oohed and aahed over the tree while Grandpa stood it in a galvanized bucket filled with dirt. My parents and Aunt Grace decorated the tree while Billy and I watched from Granny's rocking chair by the fireplace.

They draped strings of popcorn and red berries around the limbs and tied old tin ornaments and cookie cutters with brown string onto the branches. Last to go on the tree were the plastic icicles that were supposed to glow in the dark. Aunt Grace had ordered them from Sears's catalogue and was quite proud. I whispered to Billy that what they were doing was not the real way to decorate a Christmas tree.

There were no shiny glass ornaments sparkling in the lights or silver tinsel icicles hanging all over the tree. For that matter, there were no lights. Granny said they used to clip tiny candles to the branches until they almost burned the house down when Aunt Grace was a little girl. Fortunately, my mother had thought to bring a string of electric Christmas lights, which brightened up the tree just a little. I was convinced that even if Santa Claus did find me, he would never leave presents under such an ugly tree. The worst part was its bare top, the forlorn thick stem jutting from the treetop, aghast in its nudity.

"Where's the angel?"

"We don't put an angel on our tree, Sweetmeat," Aunt Grace said.

At bedtime, my heart ached. I stared at the pathetic tree in the dark corner. When I got to the *Please bless* part of my prayers, I added the woebegone Christmas tree to the list.

Christmas Eve morning, the sound of crackling bacon woke me. The savory aroma seeped into the front room where I slept on a thick featherbed piled high with patchwork quilts. I glanced at the dull Christmas tree and wiggled from under the quilts. Dragging a quilt with me, I slowly pushed open the swinging door to Granny's huge kitchen. She pulled me into one of her bottomless hugs and sat me in a chair by the potbellied stove. I watched her cut huge slabs of bacon with an enormous cleaver and place them in two sizzling-hot, cast-iron skillets.

I smelled coffee bubbling in the speckled enamel coffeepot on the stove. From the pie safe, granny retrieved the large wooden bowl she'd made biscuits in for over forty years. "Are you going to make cookies in case Santa comes tonight?" I asked.

"Ain't no 'in case' to it. The tea cakes with cinnamon are already made and in the cupboard. All you got to do is pour him some milk." Smiling, her dark brown eyes mirrored mine.

With her fingers, she dug a deep hole in the center of the flour in the bowl and added pinches of baking powder and salt and a splash of buttermilk. Quick as lightning, she mixed the dough with her right hand while holding the bowl steady in her left arm.

"Now you remember when you're making biscuits for your family one day that handling the dough too much makes the biscuits tough," she said. "You got to fluff it quick, like it's red hot." She pinched off blobs of dough between her thumb and forefinger, lightly patted them into circles, and placed them in huge cast-iron skillets. Finally, she spooned hot grease from the sizzling bacon over the top and heaved the skillets in the oven.

The kitchen door swung open and Aunt Grace shuffled in. She maneuvered her ample body onto one of the straight-back wooden chairs. Reaching down, she rolled her cotton stockings up from around her ankles one by one and tied them in knots on the side of her knees to hold them up. She forced her feet into bulky black rubber boots and heaved herself upright.

"It's so cold, Bessie may give me ice cream this morning," she said and kissed me on the top of my head.

"Merry Christmas, Momma, Sweetmeat." Pulling a thick wool jacket from the pegs by the back door, she disappeared into the dark and cold.

When Granny began to break eggs into a large tan bowl, she sent me to wake up my parents. I climbed up beside my mother and Billy in the bed and told her that Granny said kin folks would be pouring in by droves before long, and they would be hungry as bears.

Still troubled, I asked again about Christmas. "Do you really think Santa will find me tonight?"

My mother, never a morning person, shocked me by her loud voice and expletives! I had never before heard her use profanity. I shot off the bed and back to the safety of my grandmother in the warm kitchen.

Granny and Momma were putting breakfast on the table when Aunt Grace, bright red cheeks puffing steam from the cold, blew through the back door. Grandpa banged in from the back porch, carrying a tin bucket of fresh eggs and a full coal bucket. "Mornin'," he mumbled and headed for his place at the head of the long table.

Just as he did every morning of his life, he removed his white coffee mug from its deep saucer and gently poured some of the steaming black coffee into the saucer, never spilling a drop. Then he added fresh cream and some sugar to the remaining coffee in the mug. He methodically cut his thick strips of bacon into bite-sized pieces and deliberately laid them on top of his scrambled eggs. Pulling his biscuit into two halves, he poured two heaping spoonfuls of milk gravy on each side. Now he was ready to eat. The only time I ever saw him vary the routine was when Granny fried ham for breakfast. Then he ate red-eye gravy on his biscuits.

Whatever the reason—perhaps my pre-breakfast tiff with my mother—I never mentioned Santa once during that meal. However, I made up for lost time while Aunt Grace and I washed dishes. She stood me on an upended short barrel, wrapped a dishcloth around my waist for an apron, and let me scrub away at the plates and cups and saucers. I can't imagine what a mess I must have made, but I felt so grown-up and proud to be helping. And Aunt Grace never once told me to be quiet.

We decided to put Santa's cookies on one of my grandmother's precious pink plates and his milk in one of her green Sunday glasses. When Aunt Grace told me that as soon as I went to sleep that night, Santa would come down the chimney with my toys, I was completely baffled. Having been admonished repeatedly to stay away from the fireplace, I was quick to point out that Santa would catch on fire. My aunt explained that entering down the chimney wouldn't be a problem because God had made Santa so he wouldn't catch on fire.

Grandmother bustled around us in the kitchen working on the feast to come. Mason jars were emptied right and left. She issued a directive for my grandfather to go to the smokehouse and bring back a whopper of a smoked ham and some fat-back for cooking vegetables. Then she had him wring a couple of chickens' necks. Aunt Grace bundled me in the quilt to go outside and watch the headless wonders run around the yard. She was laughing so hard, I started giggling. It never occurred to me that the chickens weren't enjoying this spectacular event.

As the day pushed forward, relatives from all over Alabama arrived. Everybody dressed in their Sunday best, which for some was a new pair of overalls. My grandfather never changed from his customary outfit, but my grandmother got spiffed up. Granny wore her black dress with the white lace collar and, of course, one of her snow-white aprons. Part Cherokee Indian, she usually wore her jet black hair in a long braid coiled in a bun. But this day, she wore a smoothly coiffed chignon shaped in a figure eight. She even strapped on her black lace-up heels. Aunt Grace stayed in her felt house shoes all day, but after Granny shamed her, she broke down and put on a cranberry and green flowered dress with a full skirt. All the women found something to do in the kitchen while the men gathered outside to smoke and talk cars.

Children ran everywhere, and the main topic of discussion was Santa. The older ones no longer believed in Santa and tried to convince the rest of us to let go of our belief. Some of my cousins wondered along with me if Santa would find me so far away from home. Grimfaced, my grandfather told my older cousins to hush up all this Santa business or they'd see coal in their stockings. That was a concept I'd never heard of, and it sent another shiver of fear running through me.

By the time we settled down to the feast late that afternoon, the mantle and all the tables and chests were festooned with greenery, and pinecones, and curling ribbons that relatives had contributed. Pecans glazed in butter and sugar, along with fudge, and divinity were in little bowls everywhere. Presents piled under the Christmas tree as more and more relatives arrived.

I was allowed to eat at the children's table, which was a great treat. The kitchen tables groaned under large bowls of pole beans, creamed corn, turnip greens, mashed potatoes, bread and butter pickles, spiced apples, pickled peaches, pinto beans, green beans, biscuits, gravy, and cornbread. Oversized platters of baked ham, fried chicken and fried steak emptied quickly. Most of us had to wait a few hours before eating some of the luscious desserts—yellow cake with caramel icing, apple cinnamon cake, peach and apple pies.

After supper, packaged in layers of itchy wool, children and parents piled in the back of Uncle Carl's wagon for a hay ride. We snuggled in tight bunches under cotton quilts and wool blankets. The sound of crunching snow echoed in the night as the mules' hooves clomped across the frozen dirt roads. Staring into the velvet sky where millions of frosty stars twinkled back at me, I begged Santa Claus not to forget me.

As if by magic, a streak of silver light arced across the sky.

"Look, it's Santa Claus and his reindeers flying!" I shouted.

"I saw him too!" My cousins chorused.

Back at my grandparents' house, the children shrieked in unison as we ran through the door. "We saw Santa in the sky!"

After a cup of warm cocoa and now convinced Santa knew where I was, I nestled deep into the featherbed and slept the trusting sleep of a four-year-old.

As I awakened the next morning, the lights on the Christmas tree twinkled in the early dawn. I lay quietly snuggled under warm quilts and stared at a golden star encrusted with little shimmering jewels shining down from atop the Christmas tree. As I leisurely gazed around the room, I noticed a lumpy red stocking hanging from the mantle.

Then it hit me. It was Christmas!

I plowed my way out from under the stack of heavy quilts and yelled for the entire world to hear, "Santa's been here!"

I must have jumped two feet when I heard a deep voice say, "Mornin'." I hadn't seen my grandfather sitting in his rocker across the room.

For just a few seconds, I forgot the trepidation I usually felt around him. I was focused on my new red tricycle sitting under the tree. Then a sparkle at the top of the tree caught my eye.

"How'd the tree get a star?" I asked.

"What with reindeer flying and all, who knows?" he said.

"Where did the red sock come from?"

"It's not a sock. It's a stocking. Santa left it for you," said my taciturn grandfather. He walked over and took it down from the peg. Without a word, he handed it to me.

I emptied the stocking on the hearth rug while Grandpa stirred up the fire. The oddest things poured out—an orange, a few walnuts and pecans, a Brazil nut (my favorite), a quarter, and an enormous peppermint stick almost a foot long.

I looked up at my grandfather. "Santa usually leaves me chocolate and whistles and stuff like that—never anything like this."

"I'll be," he said. And then I saw it. A tiny smile played around his lips right before Momma, Granny, Aunt Grace, and Daddy carrying Billy in his arms, poured into the living room.

The last time I discussed this trip with my mother, she was well into her seventies. She told me my bothersome behavior disappeared the minute I found my tricycle under the tree on Christmas morning. To this day, no one knows where the glittering star that topped the Christmas tree came from, and my red stocking, well, to the best of my knowledge, it's the only one that ever hung on that mantle..

Joan Stidham Nist is Professor Emeritus at Auburn University and has lived in Alabama over half her life. She interrupted her doctoral program to raise four sons, with occasional teaching through the years at Indiana University, Eastern Michigan University, and Austin College (Texas). Most of her professional publications are scholarly. Since retirement, she has focused on memoir and poetry. Professional awards have enabled her to spend summers in Germany, the USSR, China, and New England. She has lectured for the Alabama Humanities Foundation and the Hawaii Humanities Committee, the latter allowing her to return several times to her beloved Hawaii.

In *Memory of the Spirit of a Christmas Past*, I wanted to describe the strong spirit of Christmas 1941 in Hawaii. Though blacked-out, our nights shone with reassurance. We could clearly see the stars in our tropic sky, a reminder of the star of old, its faith and hope. Despite insinuations of sabotage, because of the large Japanese-American population, there was none. Rather, Christians and the Islands' Buddhists showed faith in each other. War denied us bright lights and holiday feasts. But we were free to go to church where we were inspired again by the simple Biblical birth-story.

Editor's Note: Joan Nist's essay, *Memory of the Spirit of Christmas Past*, is a rare gem of history and keen personal observations. What an opportunity to have someone who was there, and actually saw the planes fly over, tell us about the bombing of Pearl Harbor, December 7, 1941, and tell us about the Christmas season that followed. After this essay was published in *Christmas is a Season! 2008*, the Auburn, Alabama newspaper ran a full-page story about Nist's experiences in war-time Hawaii. Gnu's Room Books (Auburn) gave her a solo reading. Nist's style is straightforward, but the power is in her eye-witness account. What a joy to have published this essay!

L.B.P.

Personal Essay

Memory of the Spirit of a Christmas Past

Joan Stidham Nist

On December 7, 1941, I was fifteen, living in beautiful and peaceful Hawaii. That Sunday morning, a girlfriend who had spent the night and I were preparing for church and a rehearsal of our Christmas choir program.

Instead, we watched the destruction of Wheeler Field, visible downhill from our house. Wheeler was the major Army Air Base north of Pearl Harbor. Instead of hymns, we heard the hum of a Japanese plane which broke off from squadron formation to fly reconnaissance up our way. It turned back before reaching us, but the plane was so low that we could see the pilot's head, encased in leather helmet and goggles. And we recognized the red sun insignia on his wings.

Christmas came only eighteen days later. But in 1941 Hawaii, preparations were bleak. Martial law had been declared immediately after the attack. People were in shock and fear, wondering whether another air strike—or even an invasion—would come.

Grocery stores were depleted. Most of Hawaii's food, then as now, was imported and food supplies weren't getting through. Allotments were made. We ate a lot of canned corned beef hash those early days after the Japanese attack.

We also began blackouts, covering any lights at night. At first, my mother made curtains only for the bathroom. That meant no evening lights by which to read or write in the living room or bedrooms. Our lives were up with the sun and to bed at sundown.

As the nights went on, people were allowed outside into their own yards after dark—no farther by military decree. But in our family, we played it safe and stayed in after sunset. The town was patrolled by home guard whose members were understandably nervous. Some nights we heard shots. Trigger-fingers were at the ready, and men could mistake wanderers for parachutists.

We returned to church the next Sunday, but the young male choir members did not. Most were servicemen from Wheeler or Schofield Barracks. The young men were all on duty because there was apprehension that the enemy would return, knowing it was our holiday season. Hadn't they attacked on a Sunday, our day of worship and rest?

In the early weeks, we were the first U.S. civilian population to be mass-fingerprinted and issued identity cards. At the same time, we were given gas masks. Those cumbersome relics from World War I had carbon-filled canisters which supposedly would filter poison gas from the air. They were heavy, ugly, smelly, and uncomfortable—physically burdensome and mentally a constant reminder of the threat of deadly gas.

There was no school. Nor did our Leilehua High School return to civilian control. Literally on the other side of the fence from Wheeler Field, the school buildings were taken over by the military.

In 1993, for our 50th Leilehua reunion of the graduation we never had, my classmates and I happily gathered. I saw again friends of Philippine, Chinese, Korean, and Japanese ancestry, all renewing old ties and filling in accounts of the divergent years. There was a pause of sad silence, however, to remember those not there for the reunion. Our class vice-president, forever twenty, had been killed in Italy. With other American servicemen of Japanese ancestry, he is buried in the National Cemetery of the Pacific in Punchbowl mountain crater overlooking Honolulu. His 442nd Battalion, composed of young Nisei—Japanese-Americans—is still the most decorated unit in American military history.

Instead of attending school, friends and I who had learned first aid, taught at the Red Cross Center. We also made bandages. The bandages were not for those wounded at Pearl Harbor. Those still needing care from that attack were being treated at Tripler, the large military hospital high in the hills above Honolulu. Our work was for the unknown future—both military personnel and civilians who might be wounded in the months ahead.

As sunny days and blackout nights passed in our new restricted way of life, Christmas spirit revived. We set up a small table-top artificial tree with a few ornaments and lights, lights lit only during daytime. Our exchange of gifts was small, some homemade, because the shops had little to offer. Ships could not allow much space for luxuries. And air cargo, just developing, was used for military shipments only.

A few letters from our mainland family had finally come through. (Incoming phone calls were not allowed until the New Year.) Dear Aunt Bessie saved a few of my letters, their envelopes slit and resealed with tape and certified by an official censor. In one letter, parts had been cut out, and in another there were blacked-out unreadable passages.

What dangerous information could I have given? Maybe I wrote: *The days are sunny.* They usually are in Hawaii.

I responded to Bessie: *Thanks so much for sending packages. I haven't received them yet, but am anxiously awaiting them.* At the end of my letter, I wrote: *May there be a successful peace as well as a successful war.*

On Christmas afternoon, we went to friends in Honolulu, using some of our car's precious gas. Fuel, of course, had immediately been rationed, reserved for essential workers. It was the first time I had been to Honolulu since December 7th. As the road wound past Pearl Harbor, I saw bombed and burned wreckage. I thought I could distinguish the remains of the blackened towers of the *Arizona,* already a monument to the thousand men still entombed in her sunken hull.

Early December 1941 had begun with tragedy and infamy. Wartime Christmas, with its blacked-out nights, had dampened some of our festivities. Mostly we simply greeted each other: *Mele Kalikimaka.* But we kept the spirit of the

245

holiday, and we held tightly to the wish for peace on earth and good will toward all mankind.

C. D. Mitchell has experienced the courtroom as a prosecutor, defense attorney, and a special judge. He has built houses, worked as a bouncer, a short order fry-cook, as well as a tracklayer and bridgeman for the Southern Pacific and Union Pacific Railroads. As a boxer he finished with a 45-5 record with 38 knockouts. He now teaches creative writing and literature at the University of Alabama, Tuscaloosa.

After *The Tree* was written, Clayton relapsed again. Arkansas Children's Hospital could do no more, so St. Jude's stepped in. After an experimental procedure involving a stem cell transplant, Clayton went back into remission. When he clears his fifth anniversary check-up this spring, he will be considered cured. Clayton, now twenty-three, will graduate from Arkansas State University next spring and plans to study law. My Christmas wish—and prayer—is that readers support children's hospitals, and especially St. Jude's, so that more families can be whole at Christmas.

Editor's Note: C.D. Mitchell's essay about the Christmas tree that became so loaded with symbolic significance that he could not take it down, is poignant and beautifully told. In terms of powerful emotions, *The Tree* tugs at the heart, yet Mitchell never stoops to cheap sentimentality. He tells the story simply, elegantly—and the effect is poetic. In personal terms, Mitchell documents the human struggle to cope with potential loss and the discovery of what is really important. This essay about rituals, routines, and moving forward will stay in the reader's heart because it strikes at the very essence of human frailty.

L.B.P

Personal Essay

The Tree

C. D. Mitchell

The telephone repairmen had no right to talk about my Christmas tree that stood in the family room of my home.

"I've heard of getting an early start on Christmas, but this is ridiculous," Lenny said as he walked into the backyard.

"Hell, Labor Day was last weekend. Do you think he just put it up, or hasn't taken it down?" That was Gus.

"Too lazy to take it down. Look at the dust on it and the bulbs on the floor."

After fixing the lines, they came inside again to make sure I had a dial tone. "That tree was put up by me and my two sons last year," I said. "My youngest son has leukemia. He helped me decorate it."

Lenny and Gus said nothing. The moment of silence was long, and I let it hang. "The tree stays right there," I said.

Gus reached his big hand up and touched the scarlet ribbon that circled the tree. He had a well-trimmed beard and a friendly look and smile that reminded me of Tim Allen's partner on *Tool Time*. "We found your problem. Your dogs most likely chewed on your lines under the house."

"Yep, that's what happened," Lenny said. "That's where the lines separated from the box."

"We stapled the phone lines to the bottom of the joists so it won't happen again." Gus stood calm and patient, still looking at the decorations on the tree.

"I've never had problems with phone lines before. This is the first place I've owned." I stepped to the side as I spoke, bent over, and gathered some of the fallen bulbs from the floor. I found niches on the artificial branches and hung the silver, gold, and crimson ornaments again.

249

"Mr. Mitchell, there won't be any charge for this trip. The lines should have been hung better when they were first installed." Gus patted his tool belt as he spoke.

Gus and Lenny eased toward the door. Lenny stopped. Much younger, Lenny was a tall, heavy man, nearly twice the size of Gus, though Gus was in charge. The back pocket of Lenny's Levis revealed a perfectly round and pale circle from the can of Copenhagen exposed by the threadbare material. "It is a beautiful tree, Mr. Mitchell, and I would never take it down."

I walked through the kitchen to the bar, poured a double shot of Jim Beam in a fruit jar full of ice and slipped back into the den. After I plopped down on the couch, I took a long sip of whiskey. That damned tree. All the ribbon had settled into a mass of overlapping rows on the lowest branches. A dozen ornaments still lay on the floor. Some of them had shattered when they fell. Slivers of the silver tinsel that Clayton loved had fallen to the carpet.

But I didn't know what to do with that tree.

***

Clayton lost twenty-five pounds after he began the chemo and now wears a toboggan hat on his bald head to keep it warm. His naturally lean body looks frightfully thin, and his face is swollen from the steroids he takes daily. Clayton inherited his athletic ability from my family. He accepts that he will not play professional football like my brother, Verl, who signed with the Atlanta Falcons. His desire to play football his last year of high school motivates him now.

The summer before his diagnosis, Clayton built an obstacle course. He ran that obstacle course during the hottest part of the year, trying to develop more strength in his legs so he could stuff a basketball. By September, at age thirteen, he consistently slam-dunked the ball on a ten-foot goal. Then as the fall semester of high school started, he began to experience fatigue. Clayton's struggle to accomplish his goal became even more incredible when the doctors told us in October he had battled leukemia all that time.

Built more like me, my oldest son Clinton resembles a stump, with shoulders nearly as broad as he is tall, towering over his brother by a good foot. The oldest of the three, Candice is a year older than Clinton and six years older than Clayton. After Arkansas Children's Hospital had made their diagnosis and summoned Clayton to Little Rock to share the news, Debbie, my ex-wife and the mother of my three children, called Candice and left repeated messages for her to come to Children's Hospital—to Three Gold. When Candice got off the elevator, she read *Blood Cancer Unit* in front of her, and then she collapsed.

Before my children had been introduced to the words *divorce* and *leukemia*, things were simple. Family events evolved around Santa Claus, the Easter Bunny, and Halloween. The rituals we observed with each season never changed. My children received Easter baskets even after they were too old to hunt the eggs. We always took the children and let them pick out their baskets.

At Halloween we traveled to the fruit stands out on Highway 412 and searched through hundreds of pumpkins scattered over a five-acre field till each child found the best one. Then we'd take the pumpkins home and carve them on the steps of our front porch. Even after we left Fayetteville and no longer had the huge pumpkin patches to search, we still made an event out of going to the store and finding just the right pumpkin.

And every year—even after I divorced their mother—I took the children to find a live tree for Christmas. Candice seemed to enjoy these excursions the most, even after she reached the age when family events were not supposed to be fun. She always made sure we bought the tree that Clayton chose. Clinton really didn't mind.

***

Two months before Clayton's fifteenth birthday in March of 2000, after an unsuccessful bone marrow transplant, the oncologists told us Christmas that year would be the last we shared with Clayton.

251

The visits I made to Arkansas Children's Hospital always reminded me of the seriousness of the situation my son faced. Of course I knew cancer was a killer, but he looked as strong and healthy as he ever had. That made it easy to pretend nothing was wrong. Every time I walked through the halls of Three Gold, I walked past parents, grandparents, brothers and sisters, embracing and weeping over the bad news they had received. As my son's bone marrow transplant and recovery had progressed, I felt guilty walking by the grieving family members. They were family to me also, because we all faced the same demon; we all sought the same miracle. We wanted the Angels of Three Gold to save and restore our children to us.

After the transplant, Clayton came down sick. This lasted for a couple of weeks, so his mother took him to Little Rock to have him checked out. At the time, I was building houses with my father. That day I had gone to work and made it till almost lunch. They call it *mother's intuition*, but I knew something was wrong.

"Dad, I gotta go to Little Rock," I said to my father.

"Go," he said.

"I hate to leave you with this. You know I'm not one to skip a day of work, but I feel it. I need to be there today."

"You don't need an excuse to take a day off. Anytime you do something that puts your children first, son, you'll never be wrong. Now go."

My father had lived by that motto. I had failed miserably.

Three hours later I walked onto the floor of Three Gold and bumped into my children's mother standing in the hall, crying. I never had a chance to say a word.

"I have some bad news I have to tell you."

I leaned back against the wall and bowed my head. I knew what it was; I knew why I felt I had to be there that day.

"He's relapsed again. They say they can't cure him, but they can prolong his life, and maybe science will catch up to him. The decision is his."

The last words she said brought my head upright. "Is he gonna do it?" The chemo and radiation had ravaged his body.

But as long as hope for a long life existed, the devastation was worth the payoff. But now, for the first time, I realized my son had a decision to make, that he had to make on his own.

"He says he's not about to give up."

People passed us in the hall, looking at us occasionally, mostly looking at the floor. One man laid his hand on my back as he passed and said, "Bless him, Jesus." I wanted to chase him down the hall and ask him to pray with me, to pray for me, to pray for my son. But he was on Three Gold. We all prayed for everyone on Three Gold. I wiped the water from my eyes. I didn't want anyone to know we had been given bad news. We had been one of the fortunate families. Our story wouldn't end like this.

"How are Candice and Clinton?"

"It was hard at first, but they're all in there playing *Risk* for now. I'll leave you alone with them for a while if you like."

"That would be fine," I said.

The room Clayton occupied had two chambers. A sliding glass door separated the outer and inner chambers. This was for sterilization purposes when the patients had low resistance due to their treatments. I walked into the outer chamber and began to wash my hands. They saw me. Clinton got up from where he knelt throwing dice at the foot of Clayton's bed, and Clayton rose from where he lay. Candice continued to sit on the far side of the room in the recliner her mother had slept in so many nights.

"Daddy, are you all right?" Clinton asked as he walked around the foot of the bed.

I tried to say something, but I couldn't. I acted like I was busy washing my hands, and then I made a sound like a frog that had been stepped on when I tried to say, "No."

Clayton had sat up now, his feet on the floor with IV lines running in every direction. Clinton continued to stand at the foot of the bed. Candice still hadn't moved.

I eased into the room with them. The weight of my divorce, the nights away from home, the many times I had broken their hearts, the promises I'd made and never kept, the days Clayton had battled for his life while I continued to work, every mistake weighed on my soul as I entered that room.

I had taken for granted that I would have a lifetime to make it up to them. Now I realized those lives I'd taken for granted were fragile, like butterfly wings, and could crumble away before I ever realized it. Kneeling at Clayton's feet, I wrapped my arms around his legs and lay my head in his lap. We reversed the roles we had both become so accustomed to. He ran his fingers through my hair and rubbed my back while I fought for composure. No one spoke.

Clayton hugged me tight. With his head on my shoulder and my body in his weak embrace, he said, "You're forgiven, Dad."

Those words erased years of my failures and gave me a future to correct my mistakes. I got up and began to talk with them. The nurses were taking them to Juanita's that night to eat. Would I come along? Of course I would. Candice walked out into the hall. Clayton went to the nurses' station to be unhooked from his IVs, and Clinton sat behind the door, waiting with me to go to a restaurant where we would all act like nothing had happened at all.

I know rituals have a purpose. They are meant to give familiarity to a season. Observing rituals with my children after divorcing their mother had allowed us to continue as a family. But her absence was always felt. The activities of any holiday can be looked upon as events that bring families together and give us occasion to be thankful for what we have. But family rituals can also remind us of what we stand to lose.

Like we had so many times before, I wanted to cut a tree that Christmas; I wanted to share the experience one more time with my children and go back to a time when they believed the size of the tree determined how many presents they got. But I didn't want the experience tainted by knowing it might be the last time we all went together. I didn't want a videotape of Clayton selecting his last Christmas tree. I didn't want to cut his last tree down. I didn't want to remove the last ornaments he'd hung.

That November I bought an artificial tree at Sears. I wondered why the children acted so funny when I told them about it. Candice even refused to come out and help us decorate it. But Clinton and Clayton helped me put it up. Clayton topped it off with an empty Budweiser can.

Clinton didn't like Clayton's idea for a star. "That's sacrilegious," he said.

"Budweiser's been Dad's Sunday morning communion for years. It has a religious significance," Clayton said as he grinned.

That year Christmas morning dawned on a melancholy house, but we started a new tradition. Our family always took pictures, though we never videotaped any holiday gatherings. That Christmas seven video cameras recorded the event. I felt awkward about the situation. We all wanted to remember that time, to have it permanently recorded.

Clayton did his best to perform for all the cameras pointed at him, trying to give each of his uncles and aunts a special cameo to remember him by. On his Uncle Bill's camera, he gave his Christmas list for next year. On his grandpa's camera, he said he wanted a colt for his sixteenth birthday in May.

"Shine your camera over here, Daddy." After I focused on him, he said, "Graduation's only two years away, and you'd better start saving if you're gonna get me a four-wheel drive. But I'll settle for a Baja like you had if you can't afford a truck."

On his Aunt Donna's camera, he told her daughter Casie he wanted a date with her best friend.

"I know what you want. You'll just get her pregnant," Casie said.

Her mother stopped filming and looked at her. "He can't have any kids, honey. He's had too much chemo. Watch your mouth." The room fell silent.

"See, she's safe with me," Clayton said. Then he laughed, and the moment was over.

I looked around the room for my mother. Down the hall at the far end of the house, a closed door led to the master bedroom. I eased it open. Mom knelt by the side of the bed. Her Bible open in front of her, her kerchief crumpled in her clenched hand, she wept as she prayed.

I closed the door and left her alone.

***

The phone rang. I got up to answer the phone in the kitchen, grabbing the Beam bottle on my way past the counter.

"Dad, when you gonna turn that coon loose on the pups?" Clinton asked.

"Is Clayton all right?" I'd forgotten his appointment that afternoon.

"Clayton's on his way back from the doctor's office. He wants to come out and see the horses."

"I still gotta go see Benny. I'll see you all when you get here."

I bought my hay from Benny Leuker. Benny gave me a discount for hauling off the coons he trapped in his cattle feed, and he had a big boar coon for me to pick up when I came by. I knew my sons would take an hour or more to get there, so I poured whiskey into my glass and returned to the living room where I put one of the videotapes from last Christmas into my video player. I watched our family and thought of how a cautious optimism at Easter had replaced the somber mood at Christmas.

The doctors tried a new protocol for treating Clayton's type of leukemia, and the drugs had placed him in remission again, for the third time. Clayton had celebrated his sixteenth birthday that May with the hope for many more. I bought him a black stud colt for his present. But reality had battered our optimism. The doctors said they could prolong his life, but never cure him. The news of his remission did not mean he would live to be an old man. But five years of remission was considered cured. We counted every week as he continued to take his chemotherapy. Every week I listened for the phone to ring, expecting more bad news. The news—for a change—was all good.

All summer long I had stared at that Christmas tree. As long as I had that tree, Clayton would be there. But that tree began to grow, it seemed, and took on a presence of its own, dominating the room and the house and every conversation I had with anyone who visited me. It no longer stood for an everlasting monument to my son. Its image grew darker over the summer as the dust accumulated on its branches and dulled the sparkling ornaments and silver tinsel that hung from its limbs. The tree reminded me of all my failures as a parent—of how many times I'd taken my children for granted. I began to feel ashamed for my lack of faith in Clayton. He knew why that tree was there—because he wasn't expected to be.

Clayton never said a word when he visited; he just looked at that tree and grinned. Never once did my son entertain the thought that he could lose his battle, and I didn't want to take the tree down. Afraid to lose his tree, afraid I could still lose him, I began to think of it as a jinx. Would he relapse two weeks after I threw the tree away?

***

Clinton and Clayton were waiting when I got back from Benny's. They opened the gate and I drove into the pasture. The horses smelled the bale of Tifton Bermuda and chased the truck as I eased along. Every time he bounced in his cage in the back of the truck, the coon squalled. The hounds heard his cry and set up a ruckus, jumping up on the side of the truck and vying for position with the horses struggling to get at the hay.

The boys took the live trap out of the back of the truck and set it out in the middle of the pasture. The hounds couldn't get to the coon, but it could get to them. Its long narrow snout and small, razor-sharp claws could poke through the narrow bars of the cage. I pushed off the round bale of hay for the horses and listened to the melee. As the dogs pressed their noses against the side of the trap, the old coon took advantage of them, tearing at their noses and shredding their ears. The baying of the hounds became a medley of enraged yelps and frenzied howls of pain mixed with the squalls of the coon. Like yearling colts, the horses took off around the pasture, kicking and snorting.

"Hurry up Dad, this bastard's eatin' the dogs alive," Clayton shouted.

I got out of the truck and came around to where the boys egged the hounds on. The pups jumped at the cage and howled like they had seen the devil himself. The coon squalled and growled and clawed at them through the bars of the trap. I hoped they knew instinctively to trail the animal once we'd set it free. Bandit and Clara had never seen a live coon before. But generations of Night Champions were bred into their pedigrees and I suspected they would figure it out.

"Turn him loose," Clayton shouted at me. He danced around the cage, first on one side with Bandit, then on the other with Clara, calling the hounds by name as he shouted encouragement to each. I hadn't seen him move so deliberately in a long time. He imitated the squall of the coon, pinching his own cheek and emitting a high-pitched squeal that unnerved the ring-tailed animal as it squalled back at him. Bandit lingered too long against the bars and the coon bit him, hanging its teeth in the end of Bandit's nose and tearing open a gash as the hound jerked away in an effort to get loose. Then the trapped animal spun in its cage and shredded one of Clara's ears, and she howled with pain and rage as she pulled away from those needle sharp teeth.

I noticed the slight tremor in Clayton's hands—a side effect of the chemotherapy. But with the cancer still in remission, the chemo would stop for a while.

I managed to get in between the dogs and put my foot on the release lever of the trap. The fur on the coon's back stood on end and made the animal look twice as big as he really was. The front door of the trap sprang open.

For a moment, the coon continued to snarl at the dogs through the cage walls. Then like a gray flash, he sprung from the trap. Instead of running off into the woods with the dogs trailing, he went up the nearest tree, with Clara and Bandit leaping at his tail.

"Who's gonna' shake him out?" I asked the boys.

"I am," Clayton said.

The tree, an elm nearly as tall as the house, stood a short distance from a massive red oak. Its leaves had turned yellow, and many had already fallen. The largest limb was no bigger round than my arm, the trunk no bigger than my leg. Dressed for the occasion, Clinton wore shorts and a sleeveless shirt. He weighed 200 pounds, nearly fifty pounds less than me, but the branches of the elm wouldn't hold him.

With Clinton and me giving him a boost, Clayton pulled himself up the tree. Although tentative at first, he made good progress, disguising stops to catch his breath as opportunities to plot his path. The ascent might have been easier if he'd been dressed differently. Because of his increased sensitivity to sunlight, Clayton wore jeans and a long sleeved shirt.

The coon climbed out onto a smaller branch. Bandit and Clara were Treeing Walkers, and their black, tan, and white bodies stood in perfect form, with their front feet against the tree, their tails straight as rods and swaying like windmills behind them, their eyes skyward as they bawled at the coon above.

"Are ya'll ready?" Clayton shouted down to us. He'd gone as high as he could. His breath came in short quick gulps that made me think he had hyperventilated.

"Give him hell," Clinton shouted.

"Get over on the other side of the tree in case he falls," I said to Clinton.

Clayton began to shake the tree and the coon looked like a trapeze artist. All four paws held onto a branch, and it refused to let go. Spread-eagled and clinging, the animal swayed back and forth as Clayton shook the tree. One paw shook loose and Clinton shouted, "Here he comes," but it managed to regain its grip. In spite of all Clayton's efforts, he couldn't shake him loose, and my son was wearing out a lot faster than the coon.

"I got an idea," I said. I ran to the back of the truck and grabbed the braided lariat we used to catch the horses. I took it back over to the tree and threw it up to Clayton.

"Tie it around that biggest fork, as high as you can reach, then throw the other end down. And get your ass out of that tree."

I got in my truck and backed it up. "Tie the rope to the bumper," I said to Clinton through the split glass in the back windshield.

Clinton fumbled for the other end of the rope. He slapped the back end of the truck to signal he was through. Clayton was struggling to get down from the tree, so Clinton ran over to give him a hand.

I pulled the truck into gear and started to ease forward. The slender trunk of the tree gave easily and bent over as I increased the pressure on the rope. The dogs could see the coon now, as he moved back to get farther up into the tree and away from the hounds. The tree was nearly perpendicular to the ground when I stopped, put the truck into park, and jumped out.

When I shut the truck door, the rope slipped off the ball on the bumper, and the tree slung back. The coon went air-born into the huge oak tree that stood next to the elm.

"He may not have made it," I said as I looked up in the branches of the oak. "He may have gone on off in the woods. See if the dogs can find him."

We tried to get the hounds to pick up the scent of the coon, but they couldn't. We made a wide circle around the tree, going out farther and farther—all the while joking and laughing.

"That coon didn't go high enough to land that far out," I said to Clayton, as he watched Clara pitching about and snuffling, searching desperately for the scent of the coon. Her ear left traces of red on the parched September grass.

The hounds soon lost interest in an animal they could no longer see or smell, and for the first time since Clayton's initial diagnosis, I actually enjoyed his company and forgot about his sickness.

Scared of losing my son, I had expected the inevitable, the unthinkable. I tried so hard to prepare myself for what might happen that I blinded myself to everything going on around me. There was no way to insulate myself from fate. No videotaped footage of a masqueraded Christmas celebration could ever replace the moments we shared that day.

I also realized the significance of rituals, whether holiday rituals or simple day-to-day routines. Even when all has gone wrong, our rituals lend us a sense of normalcy—a feeling that tomorrow will come.

With no cameras, no videotapes, we created memories so vivid I can close my eyes and still smell the horses, the hay. I can feel the course texture of the rope in my hands as I throw it up to my son. I can see the tremor of his hands, the trembling bodies of the hounds as they reared up against the tree, the coon swaying in the wind as he grasped the branches of the elm. I can hear Clara's jack hammer chop, the booming bawl of Bandit. I can taste the salt from the sweat that trickled down my cheeks, the whiskey I sipped earlier in the day.

"I bet that coon thinks he's a duck," Clinton said as he shut the tailgate to my truck.

"He's flying south for the winter." Clayton wandered over to the hay and stood petting his colt. "He never touched down on this property."

I backed the truck up against the tree. They both stood and watched, wondering what I was up to next.

"Which of you is going up the tree to shake that rope loose?"

"Your turn, Daddy," Clayton said.

I hesitated for just a second before I jumped into the back of the truck and went up the tree to get the rope. The first branch I grabbed broke under my weight. I fell to the ground with the boys laughing at me like they'd laughed at the hounds.

"Let's go get the chain saw," I said. "We got too many trees on this place anyways."

I got in the cab of the truck to drive up to the barn, and I watched in the rearview mirror as my boys wrestled in the back.

www.ingramcontent.com/pod-product-compliance
Lightning Source LLC
Chambersburg PA
CBHW030531030726
47495CB00004B/945